Television Families

Is Something Wrong in Suburbia?

LEA's COMMUNICATION SERIES
Jennings Bryant / Dolf Zillmann, General Editors

For a complete list of titles in LEA's Communication Series, please contact Lawrence Erlbaum Associates, Publishers, at www.erlbaum.com

Television Families

Is Something Wrong in Suburbia?

WILLIAM DOUGLAS
University of Houston

LEA

LAWRENCE ERLBAUM ASSOCIATES, PUBLISHERS

2003   Mahwah, New Jersey   London

Lawrence Erlbaum Associates, Inc., Publishers
10 Industrial Avenue
Mahwah, NJ 07430

Cover design by Kathryn Houghtaling Lacey

Library of Congress Cataloging-in-Publication Data

Douglas, William, 1949–
    Television families : is something wrong in suburbia? / William Douglas.
        p.   cm.
    Includes bibliographical references and index.
    ISBN 0–8058–4012–5 (cloth : alk. paper) — ISBN 0–8058–4013–3 (pbk. : alk. paper)
    1. Television and familiy—United States. 2. Television broadcasting—Social
aspects—United States. 3. Suburban life—United States. I. Title.
    HQ520 .D68 2003
    306.4'85—dc21   2002029990

Books published by Lawrence Erlbaum Associates are printed on acid-free paper,
and their bindings are chosen for strength and durability.

Printed in the United States of America
10 9 8 7 6 5 4 3 2 1

Contents

Preface

My daughter, Cara, lived a deprived childhood—a single set of parents, a single pet dog, and a single car in which she occupied the back seat. Even worse, she lived in a home with a single television set which meant, of course, that a great deal of her television viewing was in the company of others—usually her mother, Kate, and/or myself.

It was in this way that I became interested in and, then, fascinated by television families. Each week, families like the Huxtables (*The Cosby Show*), the Keatons (*Family Ties*), and, later, the Conners (*Roseanne*) and Taylors (*Home Improvement*) were welcomed into our living room and, even though they were unlike us in many ways, Kate, Cara, and I immediately recognized them. We were familiar with the relational rules implicit in their family interactions, the distribution of familial rights and responsibilities, the mundane conflict between parents and children, and the routine crises that each family confronted. We understood why television parents talked about their children and worried for their futures. We took for granted the design and decoration of their homes as well as family members' patterned movements through those homes. Indeed, we found the television family experience quite ordinary.

Of course, television families, especially those in domestic comedy, often strike us this way. Although their experience is typically less ambiguous than that of real families, television families habitually enact behaviors and construct relationships that are contextually appropriate and, so, make sense to viewers. What is more, television families, while entertaining, are not simply entertainment. Viewers become invested in particular families and care about the destiny of specific characters. They also extend television family life and relations beyond what is available to them objectively. All one has to do is ask family members or friends about the likelihood that DJ (*Roseanne*) will require psychological counseling or whether the Cleavers (*Leave It to Beaver*) come together each Thanksgiving or whether Marge and Homer Simpson (*The Simpsons*) enjoy a satisfying sex life. Almost always, people respond enthusiastically, as if they know the answer!

It is also intuitively apparent that television families are joined in a coherent history. Even informal comparison of modern families with earlier iterations suggests both stability (e.g., family relations are usually characterized by mutual affection) and change (e.g., family relations have become more hostile across time). Notably, although the evolution of the television family has not been articulated and is not well understood, critics of the contemporary (real) family, from David Popenoe and Susan Faludi to President Bush Sr. and Vice-President Quayle, often invoke television families to illustrate or corroborate arguments about the real family. That is, television families are not only meaningful as fiction, they frequently coexist in cognition with real families, suggesting, first, that television families should be studied within a framework that captures the everyday experience of real families and, second, that examination of the television family experience may yield insight into the experience of real families.

Certainly, inside the classroom, students react both enthusiastically and seriously to the issue of television family life, perhaps because they almost always want to talk about television families and real families in conjunction. Television families like the Ricardos (*I Love Lucy*), Andersons (*Father Knows Best*) and Cleavers (*Leave It to Beaver*) are seen as inherently different from the Bunkers (*All in the Family*), Jeffersons (*The Jeffersons*), and Evans' (*Good Times*), in the same way that real 1950s families are judged dissimilar to American families of the 1970s. Likewise, students not only understand the development of African-American families on television, they map the topography of change in real African-American families by invoking examples such as the Stevens and Jones families of *Amos'n'Andy,* the Jeffersons (*The Jeffersons*), and the Huxtables (*The Cosby Show*).

It appears that the sense of familiarity that Kate, Cara, and I developed about life and relations in television families is not unusual. Nor is the mundane although imprecise reality we saw in those families, nor is the impulse we exhibited to confuse real families with their fictional surrogates. What is unusual, perhaps, is that subsequent study has made me more, rather than less, convinced that the attributions we made and the conversations we shared in our living room those years ago were not only heuristically provocative but also justified.

Chapter 1

The Family and Popular Culture in America

There is, to say the least, considerable disagreement about the state of the American family. While some observers, most notably Popenoe (1988, 1993a, 1993b, 1995, 1996), interpret the structural and demographic changes that have occurred in the family during the past 50 years as evidence of deterioration, others view those changes as the inevitable imposition of more compelling and more enduring social trends. In brief, Popenoe (1988, 1993a, 1993b, 1995, 1996) has argued that such factors as increased divorce rate, decreased fertility rate, and the disappearance of the two-parent family reveal, in an almost commonsense way, the erosion of the American family. In contrast, other observers have argued that the postwar family is obscured by nostalgia but, too, deviated from an established and ongoing trajectory of family change so that its use as a baseline in discussions of family health is misleading and encourages the erroneous conclusion that the family is in decline.

An important part of this debate concerns the ways in which the family is presented on television. Television portrayals are posited variously to influence family cognition and/or family relations and/or to narrate the evolution of the family in postwar America. Television families are presumed to offer implicit lessons about family life and family relations (R. Buck, 1988; Cantor & Cantor, 1992; Greenberg, Hines, Buerkel-Rothfuss, & Atkin, 1980; Lull, 1980; Waters, 1978) that often affect viewers' expectations about the family as well as their own family interactions (Andersen, 1993; Brown, Childers, Bauman, & Koch, 1990; Buerkel-Rothfuss & Mayes, 1981; Gans, 1968; Meadowcroft & Fitzpatrick, 1988; Robinson, Skill, Nussbaum, & Moreland, 1985; Wober & Gunter, 1987). Moreover, although television families are demographically unlike real families (T. Fuller, 1990; Skill & Robinson, 1994), often enjoy unreasonable good fortune (Frazer & Frazer, 1992; Heintz-Knowles, 1995; Jones, 1992; Moore, 1992; Pingree & Thompson, 1990), and involve children who routinely violate standard developmental trajectories (Goedkoop, 1983), they have also been seen to present the family in ways that viewers deem realistic (J. Buck, 1992; Hoffman, 1994; Mayerle, 1991; Rapping, 1994; Spigel, 1992) and in ways that reflect changes in the real American family (J. Buck, 1992; Lewis, 1991; Marc, 1989; Zoglin, 1990). According to this position, families such as the Nelsons, Andersons, and Cleavers have come to represent, for many, the postwar American family (Coontz, 1992; Sheff, 1988) in the same way that families such as the Conners and Taylors have been seen to articulate the modern family experience (Lee, 1995; Mayerle, 1991; Rapping, 1994).

Despite the wide significance of television portrayals, there is considerable disagreement regarding the development and status of the television family. Some critics have argued that comparison of the Nelsons and Cleavers with the Conners and Bundys reveals fundamental deterioration in the television family (J. Buck, 1992; Fields, 1994; Hoffman, 1994). It is not simply that the Conners and Bundys look different, it is that to many they appear less able to function effectively; they are less able to socialize family members appropriately, less able to interact in supportive and nonconflictual ways, less interested in each other, and less able to manage the day-to-day routine of family life. Others, meanwhile, have argued that television continues to present a benign view of the family. Extensive reviews by Lichter, Lichter, Rothman, and Amundson (1988), Cantor (1991), and Moore (1992) have concluded generally that, while television families have become more structurally diverse and gender roles less restrictive, other family features, including the positivity of both spousal and parent–child relations, have remained stable. Likewise, based on analysis of family programming aired in 1991, 1996, and 1999, Bryant and his colleagues (Bryant, Aust, Bryant, & Venugopalan, 2001) not only concluded that no family or individual was clinically disordered but also offered evidence that families had become more cohesive, more adaptable to change, and more effective communicators.

In the broadest sense, the current analysis was designed, on the one hand, to map the development of the television family and assess its current state and, on the other, to provide insight into the tangled relationship between fictional and real family life. In particular, the investigation was intended to evaluate the likelihood that the family on television has become distressed in ways that are seen to characterize the real family experience (e.g., Popenoe, 1988, 1993a, 1993b, 1995, 1996). Preliminarily, however, the inquiry focused on the significance of the television family, the confluence of factors that have elevated the Nelsons, Bunkers, Huxtables, Conners, and others beyond simple entertainment, and the conceptual and methodological difficulties inherent in the study of television families.

VIRTUES OF THE HEARTH:
THE FAMILY IN AMERICA

The significance of popular portrayals of the family and the association between those portrayals and real family life derives, in part, from the significance of the family experience. Even the contemporary family is based on a social model in which the family "raised the food and made most of the clothing and furniture . . . taught children to read, worship their God, and care for each other in sickness and in old age. [The family] was a workplace, a school, a vocational agency, and a place of worship and it carried a heavy burden of responsibility of maintaining social order and stability" (Mintz & Kellogg, 1988, p. 1). Defined in this way, the family was both instrumentally and motivationally significant. On the one hand, the family was responsible for the cultural, vocational, and moral education of its members while, at the same time, it functioned to construct the self-definitions and ambitions of its members; the family was what people were and what they wished to become.

Although the modern family has surrendered an assortment of responsibilities, it continues to be at the center of persons' self-identity. Most obviously, there is a strong mandate for Americans to marry and to produce children; young dating couples are asked when they intend to get married and, once married, when they intend to have children. Women, in particular, have been implicitly and, often, explicitly instructed to define themselves in terms of home and family, and the preferred trajectory, even for the modern American woman, customarily involves marriage and motherhood. Indeed, while more and more women anticipate a career of work outside the home, for many women it is the difficulties that surround the integration of career and family that are the most difficult to reconcile (Buxton, 1998). That is, women have not abandoned their traditional roles as wife and mother; it is their ongoing commitment to the ideology of family and the unwillingness of many husbands to share in family work (see Noller & Fitzpatrick, 1993, for a summary) that produce the tension apparent in Roseanne Conner, Claire Huxtable, Murphy Brown, and a host of other reflections of the modern American woman. Men, too, are encouraged to marry. In the great rush to restore the family during the 1950s, sustained bachelorhood was seen to betray latent homosexuality and/or emotional immaturity, and while James

Bond and Hugh Hefner temporarily invested bachelors with a playboy image in the 1960s, that image, together with the options that went with it, have been swamped by a mixture of sexually transmitted diseases and family values so that men, once again, are motivated to find romance in marriage and personal fulfillment in the family.

For most Americans, the family is fundamental to day-to-day life; family members ask each other for advice, when living apart they visit each other and talk on the telephone, they shop together, they worry about each other, and, when they have reason to celebrate, they often do so with each other. Indeed, the family is such an inherent and expected feature of the American experience that most people simply cannot imagine any alternative. Competing systems, such as open marriage, mate swapping, and the communal family, have never taken root except in the most temporary way. The family, particularly the self-contained family, is empowering so that people are tacitly encouraged to marry and even otherwise marginalized groups, such as lesbian and gay couples, often seek the trappings and status of family.

Perhaps because the family is so compelling, concern for its well-being has been habitual. As Mintz and Kellogg (1988) have observed in their extensive and insightful history of the family, soon after their arrival in the New World, "the colonists feared that their families were disintegrating, that parents were growing ever more irresponsible, and that their children were losing respect for authority" (p. 17). Across the next two centuries, generations of Americans worried about the family for much the same reasons. In general, concern derived from the changing, and less domestic, role of women, which was seen to produce a variety of negative outcomes usually associated with childrearing and the moral integrity of the family, and the necessarily altered role of men, whose independence and authority were seen to have been diminished (Mintz & Kellogg, 1988). Critics of the family pointed, as well, to more visible signals of distress. For example, the changes in the family that occurred around the turn of the 20th century were accompanied by a substantial increase in the rate of divorce, which increased by a factor of 15 between 1870 and 1920, and a significant decline in the birth rate. Family size decreased by 50% during the 19th century, prompting one writer to liken a married women without children to "a soldier who skulks in the trenches when the bugle sounds" (Richards, 1911).

Criticism of the contemporary family has assumed a similar shape. Samuelson (1996), for example, has argued that the "decline of marriage and fatherhood stem from the breakdown of traditional roles in the nuclear family—the man as sole breadwinner, the woman as mother and homemaker. Women can pursue careers and are not confined to the home; they can more easily survive independently. Men feel less essential and are less power-ful; they can more easily rationalize indifference or sexual browsing" (p. 43). Others, including Blankenhorn (1995) and Popenoe (1995), have made simi-lar claims, pointing to the decreased marriage rate and increased divorce rate as evidence that personal achievement has come to take priority over com-mitment to the family. According to these authors, the most specific evidence of this shift, and a causal thread common to marriage and divorce, is the deci-sion of so many women to move into the paid work force. In contrast to their earlier counterparts, especially those of the 1950s, who, when they did work outside the home, were generally motivated by a desire to improve the family's standard of living, contemporary women are more often motivated by per-sonal ambition. That is, women have become more intent on establishing a career and, so, more likely to compromise relational objectives, such as marriage, in favor of professional objectives. At the same time, their financial independence means that women are more able and, it is argued, more willing to dissolve marriages that are unsatisfying.

Critics of the modern family argue further that the reduced commitment to marriage and family produce an array of more specific problems. Both Blankenhorn (1995) and Samuelson (1996) have proposed that family rela-tions have become more conflictual. In addition, Popenoe (1993a) has con-cluded that, compared to the family of the 1950s and early 1960s, the contem-porary family is less able to socialize children effectively, in part because the authority of parents has been reduced, and less able to provide care, affection, and companionship to its members. Finally, there is broad agreement among critics that the effects of these shortcomings are experienced most profoundly by children. Elkind (1995), for example, has argued generally that children are especially vulnerable to the hardships of post-modern family life and has suggested more particularly that their "needs for limit-setting, guidance, and value-modeling are not being met" (p. 28), a position that is consistent in all major respects with that taken by other writers (Blankenhorn, 1995; Popenoe, 1988, 1993a, 1993b, 1995, 1996; Rapping, 1992).

In summary, critics argue that the contemporary family is subverted by an ideology of personal fulfillment. That ideology is posited to infiltrate the family most directly through the altered role of women whose professional aspirations and financial independence are seen as primary contributors to the postponement, delay, and dissolution of marriage. Compared with previ-ous versions, especially the postwar family, the modern family is seen as less able to accomplish outcomes normally expected of families, such as effective conflict management and appropriate socialization of children, and less able to achieve the stability necessary to resist tensions that occur naturally as family relations, such as those between parents and children, change. Additionally, these inadequacies are posited to have particularly negative effects on children.

Several observations should be made about this position. First, it is consistent, at least in general terms, with public opinion. In one recent poll, 62% of respondents expressed general disapproval of the family (Gallup, 1992); in another, only 19% of respondents believed "the family is as strong as ever" (National Family Opinion, Inc., 1994). Likewise, large majorities of people believe that parents' willingness to discipline children has diminished during the past decade (Marks, 1996) and that children are less well cared for now than in the past (Mellman, Lazarus, & Rivlin, 1990; Whitman, Ito, & Kost, 1996). Second, the argument relies on inference rather than observable family life. Formal analyses of the family often center on broad sociological indicators, such as marriage, fertility, and divorce rates, that are presumed to represent either aspects of family cognition, such as commitment to marriage or the priority placed on children, or features of family relationships, such as level of conflict or ability to manage conflict. Likewise, although the basis of public opinion is unclear, it does not seem to be rooted in persons' own family experience. For example, while less than one fifth of the 1,950 participants in the National Family Opinion survey believed the American family was "as strong as ever," 77% described their own family as "loving," 70% described their own family as "supportive," and 67% described their own family as "very close." Hence, while criticism of the modern family is widespread, it does not appear to derive clearly from explicit family dysfunction but, instead, occurs more commonly as a consequence of the ways in which observers interpret broad cultural changes associated with the role of women, the place of children, and the structural diversity of modern families.

THE GREAT LOVE AFFAIR:
TELEVISION AND THE FAMILY

The demise of the family has often been associated with popular culture, in general, and television in particular. When they first visited Muncie, Indiana (or what they labeled Middletown), in the mid 1920s, the Lynds (Lynd & Lynd, 1956) observed that

> Nine motion picture theaters operate from 1 to 11 P.M. seven days a week summer and winter; four of the nine give three different programs a week, the other five having two a week; thus twenty-two different programs with a total of over 300 performances are available to Middletown every week in the year

> . . . About two and three-fourths times the city's entire population attended the nine motion picture theaters during the month of July 1923, the "valley" month of the year, and four and one-half times the total population in the "peak" month of December. (p. 263)

Although the Lynds acknowledged that they could only speculate on the effects of this exposure, they expressed concern both for the sorts of relational lessons available to young couples and the integrity of the family as a whole.

By the time Caplow and his colleagues (Caplow, Bahr, Chadwick, Hill, & Williamson, 1982) examined life in Muncie, moviegoing had been replaced by televiewing, an activity that the researchers concluded was "steeped in mystery" (p. 23). Television, they argued, was one of the "two great streams of influence" (p. 22) in Muncie after 1935 (the other being the federal government). The effect of television was to articulate outside, and competing, ideologies. According to the authors, "change, for Middletown, is something flowing irresistibly from the outside world. Continuity is furnished locally. The outside world continuously proposes new ways of living and thinking" (Caplow et al., 1982, p. 5). Indeed, television content is often seen as threatening either because it validates divisions associated with such attributes as age and gender (Lull, 1980) and, so, contributes to ongoing tensions inside the family, or because it cultivates inappropriate or anti-social behavior, especially in children.

Despite the current debate about television content, the American family has always been infatuated by television. In 1948, fewer than 1 in 200 homes had a television set; by 1956, over half had a set and, by 1962, nine out of ten homes were equipped with television (Andreasen, 1990). Similarly, by 1956, American families were watching more than 5 hours of television each day; by 1971, daily family viewing time exceeded 6 hours and, by 1983, had exceeded 7 hours (Andreasen, 1990). Now, of course, most Americans accept as normal color television, multiple sets in the home, stereo sound, cable, the VCR, DVD, entertainment centers, and more.

Such involvement with television is unique. As Gilder (1992) has observed,

> No one predicted that in a few decades 98 percent of all American households would own a television set, exceeding the level of telephone ownership by five percentage points, and by a far larger margin in the homes of the poor. No one anticipated that the members of an average household would watch the screen some six hours a day, while in poor homes television would become a substitute hearth, glowing constantly day and night. Few people foresaw that television, more than any other force, would provide the unifying images that would define the national experience and consciousness. (p. 22)

In no other culture did television assume such a wide and fundamental place so quickly.

The rapid diffusion of television owes much to the large savings that had accrued during World War II and the culture of consumerism that prevailed in the postwar period, but it is also the case that American families have always simply enjoyed television. This is apparent in the extensive surveys conducted by Steiner (1963) and Bower (1973, 1985). Steiner's (1963) initial analysis revealed that viewers defined television as exciting, important, relaxing, interesting, on everyone's mind, "for me," informative, and lots of fun; in each case, the modal rating was the most positive available. Likewise, when compared to radio, newspapers, and magazines, television was judged the most entertaining, the most likely to create interest in contemporary events, and, together with newspapers, the most important. A majority of respondents also believed that children were advantaged by television; in fact, the primary benefit of television was seen to be educational. Finally, when asked what they did when their set broke down, 47% of respondents reported that they had the set repaired the same day, and 67% indicated they had the set repaired within 2 days; one person admitted that, "When it is out of order I feel like someone is dead" (Steiner, 1963, p. 25), a response similar to those summarized elsewhere (Kubey & Csikszentmihalyi, 1990).

When Bower (1985) conducted his second replication study two decades later, the view of television content in general was less positive. Only 31% of respondents believed that television content was "getting better all the time," and 50% believed it was "getting worse all the time"; in 1960, these ratings had been 49% and 24%, respectively. However, when asked about the quality of the programs *they* watched, the response was quite opposite. Across all levels of education, a substantially higher proportion of persons rated their own television viewing "extremely enjoyable" in 1980 than had done so in 1960; among those with a grade school education, the percentage increased from 49% to 60%, among those with a high school education, from 45% to 55%, and among the college educated, from 37% to 51%.

American families watch a considerable amount of television and, as has always been the case, appear to enjoy what they watch. Television viewing dominates leisure time (Kubey & Csikszentmihalyi, 1990) and occurs at the expense not only of substitute activities, such as listening to the radio, reading books, and going to the movies, but of less closely related activities, such as conversation and sleeping (J. Robinson, 1972; Robinson, Andreyenkov, & Patruchev, 1989). The television set has become a standard part of the American home, and living rooms and bedrooms, in particular, are configured so as to facilitate televiewing (Bower, 1985). As such, televiewing commonly occurs in a context of complex family interaction (Anderson, Lorch, Field, Collins, & Nathan, 1986; Bower, 1973, 1985; Steiner, 1963). Parent–child interaction frequently involves televiewing (Dorr, Kovaric, & Doubleday, 1989; Lemish, 1986; Messaris, 1983; Timmer, Eccles, & O'Brien, 1985), for example, and children use television strategically to enter and promote conversation with adults (Reid & Frazer, 1980a) and to promote play (Reid & Frazer, 1980b). In a broader sense, because television viewing is embedded in the domestic routine, televiewing occurs amid the clutter of everyday family life. Television viewing often competes with other family tasks so that persons' viewing may become distracted (Kubey, 1990; Lindlof, Shatzer, & Wilkinson, 1989). Female family members, in particular, may frequently watch television in an unplanned and opportunistic way (Morley, 1986). On other occasions, however, televiewing is the primary family activity and family members are absorbed (DeGrane, 1991) so that potentially conflicting activities, such as talking, are constrained by the rhythm of television content or prohibited entirely (Brody, Stoneman, & Sanders, 1980; Johnsson-Smaragdi, 1983; Lull, 1980; Maccoby, 1951; Walters & Stone, 1971).

Finally, there is almost universal agreement that television content influences social cognition (Bronfenbrenner, 1970; Brown & Bryant, 1990; Comstock, 1993; Greenberg, 1982; Heintz-Knowles, 1995; Lewis, 1991; Rothschild & Morgan, 1987; Wright, St. Peters, & Huston, 1990). Because content is repetitive and mundane and viewing habitual and extensive, television is posited to act as a "cultural story-teller" (Heintz-Knowles, 1995, p. 1), encouraging viewers to develop expectations that, in significant ways, resemble the social narratives they watch.

THINKING AND TALKING ABOUT THE FAMILY

Popular portrayals, especially those on television, are widely believed to affect the way in which people think about the family (Andreasen, 1990; Fitzpatrick, 1987; Haefner & Comstock, 1990; Harrington & Bielby, 1991; Meadowcroft & Fitzpatrick, 1988; Perse, Pavitt, & Burggraf, 1990; Rothschild & Morgan, 1987). This is not to argue that family cognition relies exclusively on television portrayals, nor that viewers are unable to distinguish between television family life and that of real families. On the one hand, our understanding is affected substantially by our own family experience and, to a lesser extent, by our glimpses of other families in action; on the other, even children appear to construct different schemata for television events and real life events, although such schemata are usually connected so that one informs the other (Fitch, Huston, & Wright, 1993).

There are, however, a number of reasons to suppose that television families influence family cognition. First, public family displays are usually enacted self-consciously and in accord with relatively strict norms of social appropriateness so that they may yield little insight into the private and comparatively unregulated routine of the home. Parents and children walking through shopping malls and young couples in restaurants simply do not act as they do in the privacy of their own homes. Even informed discussion of the family typically relies on observable structural and demographic cues, such as rates of divorce and fertility, to infer hidden aspects of the family, such as the way in which couples define rights and responsibilities or negotiate the tension that is presumed to characterize dual-career families (e.g, Popenoe, 1988, 1993a, 1993b). In contrast, television relies on the routine and the familiar (Spigel, 1992; Taylor, 1989) and, so, allows viewers to infiltrate the day-to-day ritual of family life. Indeed, the versions of the family seen on television may, for many, be in some respects more real and more informative about families in general than are those in their own neighborhoods, cloistered as they are behind closed doors. This position is implied by Rothschild and Morgan (1987), who have observed that the television family, in particular, has "filled the gap left by the virtual disappearance of overt community control over the family and the reduced visibility of family life" (p. 300).

Second, television portrayals are often considered realistic, a condition that enhances the likelihood that viewers will develop beliefs consistent with those of television (Abelman, 1990). Television families usually behave in ways that "make sense" to viewers and are commonly defined as confronting problems and behaving in ways that resonate with viewers. Lewis (1991), for instance, has argued that viewers relate especially well to portrayals, such as those in domestic comedy, in which the characters, events, and relationships are recognizable and, so, treated as authentic. After their examination of life in Muncie, Caplow et al. (1982) arrived at a similar conclusion, positing that televiewing reinforced a traditional view of the family because "television series and commercials portray and idealize a normal family that is indistinguishable from the standard family in Middletown" (p. 30). Viewers may also sometimes be encouraged to treat television family life as real because the off-screen relationships among the players makes the distinction between television family life and real family life ambiguous. As Spigel (1992) has noted, this was the case with some early domestic comedy families, such as the Ricardos and the Nelsons, and has more recently been an aspect of *Roseanne*. In such circumstances, viewers may be substantially less able to locate the boundary between the family-in-play and the family-at-home and assume, instead, considerable leakage between the two. Indeed, some leakage may be fore-grounded, as when Lucille Ball and, so, Lucy Ricardo became pregnant.

Third, television portrayals may influence family cognition because they describe relational circumstances about which viewers have little real-life knowledge. Brown et al. (1990), for example, have suggested that, while a general motive for watching television families is to learn about family inter-action, this motivation may be especially acute in families, such as those headed by a single parent, in which some family members (and, so, some family relationships) are absent. Similar arguments have been made regarding other groups, including the aged (Fitzgerald, 1987), prompting Skolnick (1991) to conclude that, in contemporary society, many people routinely "find themselves in life stages for which cultural scripts have not yet been written; family members face one another in relationships for which tradition pro-vides little guidance" (p. 164). To the extent that this is the case, television con-tent may play a significant role in shaping the beliefs that viewers develop about real family life, especially when television families are seen to act in ways that appear appropriate and/or effective (Comstock, 1993). It is worth noting that this line of reasoning is congruent with an assumption implicit in the debate about television and public policy. For instance, many adults consis-tently express concern about the way in which television portrays sexual relations (Barnes, 1995; Jensen, 1995; Yankelovich Partners Inc., 1995). Un-derlying that concern surely is the assumption that many children, with no actual experience of sexual intimacy, will develop sexual attitudes and behave sexually in ways that mimic popular portrayals. Similar concerns often sur-round the presentation of minority family life. The organized opposition to *Amos'n'Andy*, for example, was surely based on the logic not only that the show presented African Americans in a disparaging way but also that the pres-entation would cultivate or reinforce stereotypic and negative attitudes toward African Americans in (White) viewers who otherwise had little or no contact with the African American community.

Finally, there is evidence that, at least in a narrow sense, television content influences viewers' expectations of family life and family relations. Compared to their light viewing counterparts, for example, heavy viewers of soap operas develop substantially less positive expectations of marriage across a range of indicators, including the likelihood of divorce and extramarital affairs as well as the probable relational effects of a partner's prolonged absence (Buerkel-Rothfuss & Mayes, 1981; Wober & Gunter, 1987). Similarly, exposure to por-nographic material is associated in males with comparatively negative images of females and increased distrust of marital partners (Zillmann & Bryant,

1988), again suggesting that heavy viewers and light or nonviewers of particular types of programming construct dissimilar family schema.

In the most general sense, television portrayals are seen to affect cognition because together they form a public record of the family and, as such, provide a consensual reality to viewers, a shared way of thinking about and interpreting family life and family relations. Fictional families such as the Cleavers, Bunkers, Huxtables, and Conners have been invoked routinely in the debate about social and family policy, implying that such families represent, for many, something more than fictional characters engaged in fictional relationships. During the 1992 Presidential campaign, for example, George Bush repeatedly urged American families to be "a lot more like the Waltons and a lot less like the Simpsons." As Mr. Bush's remarks demonstrate, the lexicon of popular families is attributionally rich. While the lexicon may carry information about surface characteristics, such as family structure, it includes, as well, information about more elusive issues, such as those that involve family relations, family objectives, and family ideologies. When he offered the Waltons as a family model, for example, George Bush was not advocating that couples produce large numbers of children and live in rural poverty nor that Americans reject the traditional nuclear family structure portrayed by the Simpsons. Instead, like a host of other fictional families, the Simpsons and the Waltons capture in the most vivid way the detail of family life and, so, allow immediate and coherent comparison of everything from parenting styles and parent–child relations to family sex roles and family cohesiveness.

Television families may also affect cognition because they contribute to persons' sense of change in family life and family relations. Not only are viewers able to recall and compare television presentations across time, but many earlier versions of the family remain available in more complete form through syndication, especially since the introduction and adoption of cable. Again, this aspect of television portrayals, as a public history of the family, is implicit in Mr. Bush's admonition. Minimally, his comparison of the Waltons and the Simpsons implies a landscape of change in the television family although, significantly, that landscape remains unmapped. Nonetheless, the sentiment is clear that the television family has changed, and more specifically has deteriorated, across time. Notably, however, Mr. Bush was not talking about television families but, instead, was arguing that, *like* television families, *real* families have become less functional.

This "double decay hypothesis" is of considerable importance, because it uses fictional families to describe the projected developmental trajectory of real families; that is, the remarks assume that changes posited to have occurred in real family life and in real family relations can be expressed meaningfully through a lexicon that relies on television families. However, the hypothesis goes further and acknowledges, in the most explicit way, the widespread belief that there is some conjunction between television families and real families. Later in the 1992 presidential campaign, this presumed conjunction was presented in its strongest form when Vice President Quayle argued that Murphy Brown's actions were encouraging similar outcomes in a segment of the female viewing audience. While this represents an extreme, although not solitary, view, linkage between television and real families is seen to occur because, at the very least, television families narrate the development of real families; that is, television families reflect the changes that have occurred in real families (Buck, 1992; Lewis, 1991; Marc, 1989; Zoglin, 1990). This implies, on the one hand, that examination of the family on television may enhance our understanding of life and relations in real families and, on the other, that the television family has evolved in ways that mimic development of the real American family.

There are clearly limitations to this argument, and they should be recognized. In the first place, the congruence between television families and real families is necessarily inexact. In particular, the distribution of family structure on television is skewed and departs substantially from reality. Skill and Robinson (1994) examined the demographic characteristics of television families during the period 1950–1989 and concluded that there was minimal convergence between fictional families and real families. Likewise, Fuller (1990) compared television and real family configuration for the years 1960, 1970, 1980, and 1987 and noted that households headed by a married couple were consistently underrepresented on television, whereas those headed by a lone male were consistently overrepresented.

Similar arguments can be made regarding the depiction of family life. Both Newcomb (1974) and Cantor (1991) have argued that television families adhere to traditional values, such as hard work and responsibility, regardless of their social or economic circumstances, and Larson (1993) has concluded that television presentations exaggerate the amount of interaction between family members. Other researchers, meanwhile, have observed that television presents an incomplete view of family life. In particular, it has been argued that television presents families in isolation; that is, television portrayals exclude political and economic issues, such as those that surround poverty, homelessness, and drug use, which contextualize and potentially disrupt life and relations in real families (Cantor, 1991; Frazer & Frazer, 1992; Heintz-Knowles, 1995).

Television portrayals have been criticized, as well, because they are seen to rely on stereotypic formulations. According to this position, television versions of American society historically have been biased in terms of ethnicity, gender, and class such that a White, male, middle-class voice has been especially strong. Sweeper (1984), for instance, concluded that Black males were presented as more hostile, self-centered, unreliable, vain, and pompous than White males and that Black females were presented as more obese than their White counterparts. More recently, Cummings (1988) has argued that Black characters have traditionally been portrayed in ways that perpetuate stereotypic beliefs; women have been presented as the "Black matriarch, the castrating Black female, the domineering, overpowering Black woman" (p. 76), while African-American men have been portrayed as "classic minstrel types" (p. 76). Other researchers have presented similar arguments regarding gender and class, proposing, on the one hand, that television fails to take up issues such as the feminization of poverty (Moore, 1992) while habitually portraying females as subservient to males (Frazer & Frazer, 1992; Harrington & Bielby, 1991; Mellancamp, 1986) and, on the other, that working-class fathers, in particular, are consistently presented as oafish and inept (Andreasen, 1990; Cantor, 1991; Glennon & Butsch, 1982).

While these arguments appear to limit severely the heuristic value of television families, it should be remembered, first, that viewers select strategically among available programming and, so, may well seek out families that look and behave like their own. Morley (1986), in fact, has reported that viewers are often especially attracted to characters with whom they can identify and situations similar to their own, suggesting that viewers may indeed work to maximize the resemblance between real families and those they watch on television. It should be noted, too, that, while recurrent use of stereotypic formulations represents a significant consideration when trying to map the landscape that connects the family in television and the family in reality, it does not undermine the contention that television portrayals affect the way in which people think and talk about the family. Indeed, the fear of marginalized groups has often been that such presentations *do* influence viewer cognition. Finally, although structural dissimilarity and surface relational incongruence are critical to assessment of television's objective reality, such features may be incidental to viewers' understanding of television family life. Instead, viewers' attention may be directed to more salient episodic themes, such as family interaction or the sort of problems that television families face and the way in which they solve those problems, which are generally seen to mimic real families (Berkman, 1993; Haralovich, 1989; Lewis, 1991; McCrohan, 1987). And, because they are relationally rich, these themes may be more critical to understanding family life and family relations.

SEEING THE FAMILY THROUGH PLAY

To assert that television presentations influence family cognition does not explain the influence process. The position taken in the current analysis is that fictional portrayals can inform viewers about family life and family relations in at least two ways. First, they include action and conversation that is strategic; it is included knowingly and is designed to entertain but often contributes, as well, to the achievement of plot goals. For example, when Roseanne and Dan Conner (*Roseanne*) argue after Dan has lost his job, the event functions as a context for humor but, too, is associated with and, in fact, may be seen as the cause of subsequent action: the family's inability to pay bills, Roseanne seeking employment outside the home, and so on. Indeed, the event may be designed to contribute to some even broader and intended message concerning, for example, the state of the modern working-class family. At the same time, however, such action is embedded in a broader and less critical familial landscape. When, during the argument, we see Roseanne Conner move from the kitchen to the bedroom, her action is meaningful. That is, we understand that she is empowered to move from the kitchen to the bedroom whereas other characters, visitors to the house, even extended family members and children, may not move freely about the house. Neither this action nor the abundance of co-occurring events (Dan taking a beer from the refrigerator, the children going upstairs to their bedrooms or watching television in the living room, and so on) is likely to have been designed to entertain or contribute to plot outcomes in anything more than the most tangential way. Likewise, when Laura Petrie (*The Dick Van Dyke Show*) serves cookies, first to Gerry, the neighbor, then to Rob, her husband, then to Millie, Gerry's wife, and then to herself, and achieves the move from Gerry to Rob only by turning 180° away from Millie, the action is not part of the plot and, again, is unlikely to have been constructed strategically. Instead, such sequences reflect something about the assumed nature of wives and husbands, parents and children, family and neighbors and, to the extent that participants and viewers share the assumption, require no explanation.

This "taken-for-granted" component of domestic action is also likely to be relationally rich. Both Newcomb (1974) and Leibman (1995), for example, have pointed to the significance of place in domestic relations. According to these authors, power accrues, in part, from the context in which characters are generally situated; hence, males, who are commonly situated in the living room, a place of relaxation, are defined as more powerful than females, who are more commonly situated in the kitchen, a place of work.

Moreover, it is not simply that the living room is masculine space and the kitchen feminine space, it is that action is influenced by this association, regardless of which family members are involved. Newcomb (1974) argued this explicitly, suggesting that, "whenever personal problems are taken to the kitchen, they are soon to be defined or solved in the softer, more 'feminine' manner" (p. 45).

The demand for congruence between domestic place, familial role, and domestic action not only specifies the relationship between family members but also silently influences the construction of domestic episodes, *as it does in real families.* Neither viewers nor participants, for example, expect that female family members will prepare food in the living room or that male family members will iron clothes in the children's bedroom or that spouses will sit casually on the stairs and argue. In contrast, both viewers and participants are likely to accept as normal sequences in which female family members prepare food or iron clothes in the kitchen or spouses talk in raised voices and move erratically from room to room during conflict.

Because strategic action and the taken-for-granted are integrated seamlessly, study of the family in domestic comedy should be holistic. This means, first, that analyses should attend to the ordinary as well as to action that, for one reason or another, is more salient. Verbal conflict, physical aggression, or sexual intimacy, for example, are generally more conspicuous than co-occurring sequence features that deal with dress, domestic duties, or parts of the house considered "out-of-bounds" to particular family members. When, in *Father Knows Best,* Kathy, the younger daughter, complains to her sister, Betty, their conversation is especially prominent, in part because it contributes to subsequent action. However, a variety of surrounding features, also available to the viewer, provide additional insight into family life and family relations: throughout the scene, Betty dusts the living room (this is apparently a routine chore since Kathy does not remark on the event); Kathy has no domestic duties and is "at play" when she enters and when she leaves the room; both sisters are well-groomed, Betty is wearing a shirt and jeans while Kathy is wearing a dress; the living room, in which the sequence occurs, is richly decorated although empty on this Saturday morning (the father, Jim Anderson, has just passed through, picking up some papers that he requires to "get some work done"); and so on. Life in the Anderson home is comfortable and orderly; the family places a priority on work and distributes rights and responsibilities by gender such that males assume the role of provider and females assume the role of homemaker; children, however, appear to have few duties, suggesting that the family defines childhood as a distinct developmental stage that involves a unique set of role requirements.

Notably, the sequence features that contextualize the sisters' talk do not relate directly to the conversation; that is, the features are not simply visual amplification of verbal performance. Rather, the features allow for an independent, although consistent, set of inferences that provides a familial infrastructure within which the conversation occurs. What is more, while the sisters' conversation is a unique event, the surrounding features are recurrent, encouraging viewers to construct a view of the Andersons that includes elements that endure across episodes. As such, examination of the television family should involve strategies that are sensitive to the presentational implications of both foreground and background features (Goffman, 1974).

Likewise, study of the television family should be expansive. To the extent that there is some conjunction between television portrayals and real family experience, those portrayals should yield insight into a wide range of family attributes. In their exhaustive reviews of family theory, Fitzpatrick and Badzinski (1985, 1994) distinguish between factors associated with the distribution of *family power and affect,* such as the rights and responsibilities of family members, family rules, support structure, and communication structure; factors associated with *family performance,* such as problem solving, child socializing, and management of tension; and factors associated with *family satisfaction and stability,* such as marital and parental satisfaction and family solidarity. Additionally, based on her extensive review of domestic comedy, Cantor (1991) has concluded that television presents the family as "the chief haven from worldly cares" and encourages the view that "it is through the family that the American Dream becomes a reality" (p. 215), suggesting that television portrayals explicate a general *family ideology* that details those principles fundamental to family life and, in doing so, instructs viewers about the place and significance of the family.

Clearly, such routine complexity is not knowingly addressed in each television portrayal. As suggested already, much content may be taken for granted and reflect uncritical assumptions about family life, whereas other, perhaps major, aspects of the family are strategically included or excluded from particular presentations as a function of their plot relevance. However, examination of the television family, and the impressions that viewers develop, is probably most usefully conducted in a framework that captures viewers' familial experience.

Finally, study of the television family, particularly as it relates to family cognition, should focus on the meanings that viewers construct. Certainly, the interpretation of television content is not uniform across viewers (Liebes & Katz, 1990; Schramm, Lyle, & Parker, 1961). Even within a restricted context, such as domestic comedy, the meanings that viewers derive from television presentations are personal. In the first place, domestic comedy presents multiple visions of the American family so that its content varies both within and across time (Douglas & Olson, 1995, 1996). Also, while television content is presumed to limit the sorts of interpretations that viewers construct (Morley & Silverstone, 1990; Taylor, 1989), those interpretations are a function, too, of a host of viewer and context attributes, such as the extent to which the viewer knows people like those portrayed (Livingstone, 1990), on the one hand, and the sorts of behaviors exhibited by coviewers (Linz & Donnerstein, 1989), on the other. Nonetheless, because of the repetitive use of common conventions, television content is posited to induce some level of consensus in viewers' interpretations (Gilder, 1992; Hawkins & Daly, 1988). For example, popular portrayals have traditionally relied on families that involve a mother, father, and dependent children who share the same home. In those families, parents typically are allowed to enter a young child's room without permission and routinely offer instruction and advice to children. Recurrent exposure to such conventions, particularly when they are consistent with real family experience (Rothschild & Morgan, 1987), is presumed to encourage congruent expectations across viewers. Taylor (1989), for instance, has argued that, through its conventions, television "suggests that certain visions of family life are normal and others deviant, strange, or (by exclusion) nonexistent" (p. 19). This view is similar to that expressed by Butsch (1992), who has proposed that television's "pervasive and persistent images crystalize as cultural types and form the mainstream culture, the context within which exceptions, alternative and oppositional images, may appear and to which they must refer" (p. 388).

DOMESTIC COMEDY AND THE STUDY
OF TELEVISION FAMILIES

The bulk of television family research has studied the family in domestic comedy. This is often defended on the basis that domestic comedy not only relies on the family as a vehicle for the narrative (Cantor, 1991; Marc, 1989; Mitz, 1980) but portrays domestic circumstances that are familiar to its audience (Goedkoop, 1983; Lewis, 1991; Newcomb, 1974). In contrast to potentially compelling but, nonetheless, uncommon events such as the kidnapping of a child or the murder of a family member that often form the substance of television drama, and unlike soap operas, in which characters are often linked by associations of family although the relationships are irregular and the circumstances fantastic (Livingstone & Liebes, 1995; Pingree & Thompson, 1990), domestic comedy "celebrates the ordinary" (Taylor, 1989, p. 19), it deals in those routine events that comprise the day-to-day of family life: sibling conflict, birthday parties, school report cards, paying bills.

Such mundane realism may be rooted in the inherent nature of home, family, and domestic entertainment. In her examination of television and family during the postwar period, Spigel (1992) demonstrates that domestic entertainment has traditionally provided a commentary on the family and concludes that, "like the play within a play structure of the parlor theatrical, family comedies presented an intensely self-referential world where the distinction between fiction and reality was constantly thrown into question" (p. 163). A similar position has been taken by Marc (1989), who has described domestic comedy as "the living room within the living room, the mirror of family life, the barometer of the normal thing" (p. 127).

However, while there is little doubt that many domestic comedies are considerably more than frivolous amusement, it would be naïve to assume that all domestic comedies are reflective of the American family. In his discussion of *I Love Lucy,* Jones (1992) reasons that "to have had such a huge impact . . . and to have stayed so popular in rerun for forty years, it had to have communicated very strongly with the American family experience" (p. 69). Similar arguments have been presented elsewhere about domestic comedy in general (Douglas & Olson, 1995, 1996; Friend, 1993) and imply the usefulness of distinguishing between those portrayals that resonate with the audience, and which might be studied as a portal to the real American family, and those that do not. Such a distinction can be made in a variety of ways but one method, implied by Jones (1992) and used explicitly by Douglas (1996) and Douglas and Olson (1995, 1996), is to examine only those television families that have achieved extended and wide visibility. Such a method usually involves the use of ratings data (Stavitsky, 2000) and would favor families like the Ricardos (*I Love Lucy*), Bunkers (*All in the Family*), and Huxtables (*The Bill Cosby Show*), which remained broadly popular for a sustained period of time, over families like the Bronsons (*Meet Milly*), Bogerts (*Doc*), and Russells (*My Sister Sam*), which failed to become fixed in the public mind. Unfortunately, studies of television families, even those in domestic comedy, sometimes lack any such rationale so that television families are studied for a mixture of reasons that may rely on their appeal to a limited audience, their momentary popularity, or their simple availability.

An associated issue concerns the status of television work groups, like those presented in *M.A.S.H., The Mary Tyler Moore Show,* and *Cheers,* which not only have often achieved wide visibility but have sometimes been treated as surrogate families (Andreasen, 1990; Marc, 1989; Mitz, 1980; Taylor, 1989). Such an expanded view of family contrasts with more conventional approaches (e.g., Thomas & Callahan, 1982), largely because it does not restrict family to situations in which people are genetically or legally related. Instead, the determination of what is and is not a family relies on the related claims that work groups function like families, that they provide members the same resources, and that work groups possess a similar role structure to families, so that some members generally fulfill the role of parent, for example, and others are more often placed in the child role.

However, although work groups perform some family functions, they clearly violate other, important, family norms. For example, while television work groups often provide support to each other, at least some of the group members are usually linked sexually, and their sexual displays are made explicit to other "family" members so that the relationships are inconsistent with a normative family model. This is the case in *M.A.S.H.*, where Frank Burns and later Hawkeye Pierce become sexually involved with Margaret Hoolihan, and in *Cheers*, where Sam Malone's sexual exploits with a variety of partners are celebrated. Work groups are also governed by an often rigid organizational structure that obviates the negotiation of roles, increasingly common in modern families (Fitzpatrick & Badzinski, 1985, 1994). Again, in both *M.A.S.H.* and *Cheers*, rank and function are fixed as are the distinctive rights and responsibilities of doctor and patient and saloon employee and customer.

Television work groups may make statements that refer to the family, but these are generally made obliquely and have not been the focus of research; the family relationships that emerge through the conversations and reading and writing of letters in *M.A.S.H.* and Norm Peterson's relationship with his absent wife in *Cheers* are examples. The appearance and popularity of such presentations may also, in more general terms, function as an inverse measure of the perceived performance and integrity of the conventional family; that is, audiences may be more predisposed to search out television portrayals that feature work groups when they conclude that the conventional family is failing to meet either its members' or their own relational needs adequately. However, work groups appear to differ in critical ways from families, suggesting that their dynamics should be studied under the interpersonal rubric of friendship or within an organizational framework such as that used to examine superior–subordinate relations.

CONCLUSIONS AND IMPLICATIONS

Televiewing is a habitual and often shared activity in which real families routinely find themselves absorbed by life and relations in fictional families.

Although some television families are blatantly unrealistic, others, especially those of domestic comedy, are frequently seen to behave in ways that somehow confirm the family experience of many viewers. Indeed, in the debate that surrounds the American family, both popular and informed opinion have sometimes suggested not only that the real family is in decline but that such decline is reflected in, if not encouraged by, fictional presentations, particularly those on television.

Despite broad intuitive appeal, there is no clear map of the television family's development so that statements about the status of the popular family are necessarily speculative. There is simply little empirical sense of the extent to which evolution of the television family is characterized, on the one hand, by erosion of traditional family roles, reduction of parental authority, increased conflict, less successful socialization of children, and/or less parental care, affection, and companionship or, on the other, by altered demographics but relatively stable and supportive family relations.

To the extent that these issues are to be addressed, that is, to the extent that the television family's development is to be mapped and the performance of television families assessed, two observations should be made. First, a great deal of information about family life and family relations is likely to be available in the taken-for-granted aspects of television portrayals, emphasizing that the investigative focus should not be exclusive to salient episodic features, such as conflict and sexual expression, which are usually constructed as part of the narrative foreground but which, for the most part, shift from show to show. Second, any analysis of the television family should adopt a framework that reflects viewers' family experience; that is, the analysis should be sensitive to issues associated with family power and affect, family performance, family satisfaction and stability, and family ideology.

The significance of the television family derives, in part, from the importance of the family in America and, in part, from the popular and ubiquitous nature of television. Fundamental to the current analysis is the family model that emerged, on and off the television screen, in postwar America. Not only was this the first iteration of the television family, and, as such, essential as a baseline in assessing the development and performance of subsequent television families, but critics often invoke the real 1950s family as the benchmark against which to evaluate life and relations in the contemporary family. What is more, of course, both Skolnick (1991) and Coontz (1992) have argued that these two versions of the family have become confused, that observers imagine the postwar family largely as it existed on television and, because of the disparity between fictional and actual experiences, mistakenly conclude that the American family is in decline.

This accusation is important not only because it points to the tangled relationship between the world of television and the world of the living room but also because it implies that, when examined objectively, these worlds are quite dissimilar, one provides no insight into the other, and, more specifically, the postwar family was both anomalous and misrepresented by television families such as the Nelsons, Andersons, and Cleavers. The next chapters deal with each of these issues: the evolution of the American family, the extent to which popular portrayals are independent of real family life, and the relationship between the real and television postwar family experience.

Chapter 2

Coming Together and Coming Apart: The Development of the American Family

There is little doubt that, when contemporary Americans judge the relative state of the modern family, many reflect on the American family of the 1950s. It is also the case that such a comparison often leads to the conclusion that the family is in decline. Critics of the modern family point to a variety of changes that have occurred in the family during the past 50 years that they see as evidence of decline. These include delayed marriage, decreased fertility rate, increased divorce rate, the disappearance of the two-parent family, and the increased number of children for whom after-school parental care is absent. In contrast, observers such as Skolnick (1991) and Coontz (1992) argue that the family model that emerged in the 1950s is remembered inaccurately and, anyway, violated established and ongoing revision of the family so that its use as a baseline in discussions of family health is misleading and, more specifically, fosters the erroneous conclusion of decay. Notably, both Skolnick (1991) and Coontz (1992) point to popular culture, and in particular television, as the source of misleading images of the American family of that period.

This debate is significant, first, because it suggests the usefulness of placing the postwar family into a broader analytical framework—a framework that emphasizes the family experience and the extent to which that experience has changed across time. In turn, emphasis on family experience implies that, as much as possible, analyses should focus on family life and family relations rather than family structure. While much has been made of family structure and while structural changes may be associated with important changes inside the family, they may also reflect transient and incidental sociological shifts, such as the elevated but short-lived divorce rate at the end of World

War II, or they may be absent even though family dynamics have changed dramatically, as may have occurred in the 1950s family, which retained a traditional appearance even though the role of fathers in day-to-day family life was undergoing radical alteration (Faludi, 1999; Popenoe, 1996). At the same time, there exists an implicit mandate for longitudinal analysis. Only by tracing the development of the family across time can one assess the extent to which the postwar family was aberrant and, as such, an inappropriate model against which to compare the contemporary family's performance.

The debate also points to the potentially defining role of television families. Again, because television portrayals emerged from a history of family entertainment, it is important to examine not only the immediate surround but also the popular relational images that evolved into postwar television families such as the Nelsons, Andersons, and Cleavers. Vaudeville, comics, and radio had established a tradition of characters and family episodes that were already familiar to audiences and influenced the domestic narratives that populated evening television during the 1950s. Hence, investigation of those earlier family-related images is likely not only to yield insight into the conversion of the family onto television but to provide, as well, a preliminary test of the proposed conjunction between the experience of real families and that of their fictionalized surrogates.

The next three chapters take up these issues, looking, first, at the evolution of the family prior to World War II. This analysis pays particular attention to the development of the family during the 20th century and incorporates both studies of Middletown (Muncie, Indiana) conducted by the Lynds (Lynd & Lynd, 1937, 1956) in 1924 and, again, in 1935. Study of the family in popular culture investigates the cultivation of stock characters and contexts and the sociology of family explicated by vaudeville, comics, and radio. Finally, the postwar family is examined. That analysis includes detailed appraisal of Gans' (1967) study of Levittown III (Willingboro, New Jersey) and is conducted in conjunction with examination of the 1950s television family.

DEVELOPMENT OF THE FAMILY:
I. REVOLUTION AND ORDER

The early colonial family stood at the center of persons' experience, defining both the day-to-day routine of family interaction and the more general principles of community government. Because of the universal range of family responsibility, the division between family and community was indistinct, an indistinctness that emerged in the architecture and furnishings of homes that distinguished minimally between familial and communal space and, internally, between work and leisure, adult and child, and female and male space (Mintz & Kellogg, 1988). For early colonists, marriage was more often based on economic considerations than mutual love so that spousal relations were rarely designed to provide emotional fulfillment, sexual satisfaction, and companionship. Instead, priority was more normally placed on outcomes associated with production, on the one hand, and childbirth, on the other. Parent–child relations, too, were unsentimental (May, 1995). While parents were not unaffectionate, a high infant mortality rate coupled with a resource-based view of children discouraged deep attachments. Finally, like the communities into which they merged and the scriptural model they sought to mimic, "Godly" families were intensely patriarchal. Authority resided with the husband-father, who guided the family through strict application of Christian principles.

By the late 1920s, the family had changed in a variety of ways. At the root of those changes were the increasingly wide separation of public and private space and the altered cultural view of women. It was not simply that the family became divided from the community, although that was significant and soon became manifest even in the architecture of the home (Mintz & Kellogg, 1988), it was that the family divested itself of many functions, especially those associated with production, so that domestic space came to be seen as "a site of comfort and rejuvenation" (Spigel, 1992, p. 12) while public space became associated with work and hardship. Moreover, the division of public and private space became conjoined to gender such that males dominated the public, work-space and females the private, domestic space of the home.

This ideology was articulated explicitly by many writers, including Beecher and Stowe (1869), who proposed that the home should be "a harbor of comfort and peace" (p. 466) in which the mother "is habitually gentle, sympathizing, forbearing, and cheerful" (p. 212). In contrast, they argued that to "man is appointed the out-door labor—to till the earth, dig the mines, toil in the foundries, traverse the ocean, transport merchandise, labor in manufactories, construct houses, conduct civil, municipal, and state affairs, and all the heavy work, which, most of the day, excludes him from the comforts of a home" (p. 19). That is, consistent with the gender-based division of domestic and public space, the "father undergoes toil and self-denial to provide a home, and then the mother becomes a self-sacrificing laborer to train its inmates" (p. 18). While the husband-father dominated the civic world, outside the home, and while the natural domain of the wife-mother was the domestic world of the family, the husband-father retained ultimate authority, even in the home. According to Beecher and Stowe, in marriage "it is man who is the head and chief magistrate . . . when differences arise, the husband has the deciding control, and the wife is to obey" (p. 203). Nonetheless, the level of authority granted to husband-fathers in early colonial families represented a high water mark and, although rights and responsibilities remained strictly divided on the basis of gender, across time families came to function in increasingly democratic ways, congruent with broader affective changes in the family that influenced both spousal and parent–child relations.

Most fundamentally, by the late 1920s it was generally accepted that marriage should be based on mutual love and affection rather than economic considerations, as had earlier been the case. One of the attributes of the democratic family that emerged toward the end of the 18th century was an increased emphasis on companionship and mutual affection (Mintz & Kellogg, 1988). Across the course of the 19th century, this standard took root and became sexualized in the companionate family model that arose during the early part of the 20th century so that, by the eve of the Depression, the preferred model of spousal relationships was one based on mutual love and designed to provide sexual and emotional fulfillment to both partners.

Likewise, the family evolved to become more child-centered. As the cooperative economic model of colonial family life gave way to increasingly higher levels of task specialization, infants were less likely to be defined in economic terms, at least among the urban middle-class, so that childhood emerged as an acknowledged and separate developmental phase (Aries, 1962) characterized by extended dependence, on the part of the child, and abiding love, on the part of the parents. The parent–child relationship was stabilized, too, by the reduced death rate in childbirth and infancy. In New England, during the 17th century, infant mortality had been as high as one in three and, in the Chesapeake colonies, two thirds of all children lost one parent before their 18th birthday while one third of all children lost both parents by that time (Mintz & Kellogg, 1988). In contrast, by the turn of the 20th century, 79% of children reached the age of 15 and the probability of at least one parent dying before a child's 15th birthday had been reduced to less than one in four (Uhlenberg, 1980). As a result of these factors, the average number of children per family declined by 50% during the 19th century (May, 1995), to an average of a little more than four children per mother (Uhlenberg, 1989), and in those smaller families, parent–child relations placed increased emphasis on enduring mutual affection and emotional interdependence.

Such changes in the family meant, first, that, unlike the early colonial design, family and community stood in opposition; home and family articulated a value structure based on harmony and comfort while community promoted competition and hardship. This, in turn, had two consequences; first, it elevated the notion of family and, second, because the division of space was associated with gender, it established a potentially conflictual relationship between males and females. As Mintz and Kellogg (1988) have observed, by the middle part of the 19th century, "the family vacation had appeared, as did a series of new family oriented celebrations, such as the birthday party, Christmas, and Thanksgiving. The birthday cake, the Christmas tree, Christmas presents, Christmas caroling, and the Thanksgiving turkey were all manifestations of the reorientation of daily life around the family" (p. 48). The new priority placed on home and family necessarily invested the role of wife-mother with a substantial significance. Beecher and Stowe (1869), for example, argued that "no statesman, at the head of a nation's affairs, had more frequent calls for wisdom, firmness, tact, discrimination, prudence, and versatility of talent, than such a woman" (p. 221). In a limited sense, the importance of the wife-mother, yoked as it was to the centrality of the home and family, contributed to the steady erosion of the husband-father's authority that characterized the family's development. In a more general sense, it produced a tension between gender, space, and power that Beecher and Stowe (1869) sought to resolve directly by explicitly allocating ultimate authority, even inside the home, to the husband-father. Although that formula endured for some time, the tension that had been created remained ongoing and was fundamental to the subsequent development of family life and family relations.

While the construct of family had been elevated across time, the family had also, in some sense, been reduced. Compared to its early colonial counterpart, the family of the early 20th century had substantially fewer obligations; the family was no longer expected to produce its own food or manufacture its own clothing and furniture or educate its children or care for its aged. The most immediate effect of this reduction was to raise the importance of the functions that remained; childrearing, cleaning the home, cooking, providing for the family's economic well-being. What is more, those functions that remained became divided and, once more, coalesced around gender to produce what may be termed the "Tarzan" and "Jane" principles. These principles indicated the domains in which males and females should, and should not, become expert. According to the "Tarzan principle," men were expected to provide for the family's physical and economic security and participate in childrearing, although this participation should be limited to relatively high-order managerial functions such as those associated with family discipline and major family purchases; men were expected not to become involved in cleaning the home, preparing meals, caring for children, and the day-to-day aspects of the family budget. As Beecher and Stowe (1869) observed, "few things are in worse taste than for a man needlessly to busy himself in women's work" (p. 229). The "Jane principle," meanwhile, articulated a quite opposite set of expectations. In marriage, women were encouraged to dedicate themselves to child care in its most general sense, meal preparation, and care and decoration of the home; married women were not expected to pursue, or even possess, professional ambition. This is apparent in Beecher and Stowe's (1869) manual that comprises 38 chapters and deals with topics ranging from preferred family structure to proper ventilation of the home to effective child care to nutritious cooking to methods of interior decoration to the care of domestic animals but does not include any discussion of women outside the home.

Despite its explicit restrictions, the ideology that prevailed by the late 1920s represented a relatively "feminized" view of family life and family relations. It was not simply that women were no longer "associated with deviousness, sexual voraciousness, emotional inconstancy, and physical and intellectual inferiority," an image of womanhood that had prevailed well into the 18th century (Mintz & Kellogg, 1988, p. 55), nor that women had achieved a divine place in the home; it was that family life and family relations had become increasingly constructed around traditionally feminine values such as beauty, moderation, comfort, courtesy, selflessness, and sensitivity. Parents, both mothers *and* fathers, were encouraged to socialize children through example and praise rather than command and discipline (Beecher & Stowe, 1869; Calhoun, 1945); women became more sexually active (Kinsey, 1953), and sexuality and emotionality became linked so that marriage was redefined to involve expectations of sexual and emotional fulfillment for both partners (Mintz & Kellogg, 1988); and the notion of the ideal home expanded to include comfort and beauty as well as utilitarianism, a traditionally male virtue (Beecher & Stowe, 1869). It is important to note that, while such changes centered on the nature and place of women, they affected the family in a much broader way. Both spousal and parent–child relations became more egalitarian and more emotionally charged, and family life was increasingly expected to serve a therapeutic function.

The observation should be made that the family models discussed here, and in other analyses, applied almost exclusively to the middle class. At the most basic level, working-class families—and this included just about all minority families—did not exhibit the critical separation of public and private space. Working-class mothers, for example, had long performed paid work inside the home in the form of laundry, dress-making, and so on, substantially limiting the extent to which they could reasonably treat the home as a site of comfort and rejuvenation. Such a definition was made even less likely by frequent unemployment and low wages, which denied working-class families many of the emerging domestic technologies available to the middle class. Indeed, it has been estimated that, as late as the turn of the 20th century, two tasks—cleaning and meal preparation—consumed 6 hours of each working-class family day (Mintz & Kellogg, 1988). Frequent unemployment and low wages also undermined the link between space and gender, another salient feature of the middle-class family model. Exposed to such routine hardships, working-class families often adopted a cooperative economic model in which mothers and children, as well as fathers, entered the paid work force. Clearly, too, medical science and contraception were least effective and least available at the low end of the socio-economic ladder so that the changes in life expectancy and family size that had contributed so significantly to relational revision in middle-class families were substantially less likely to occur among members of working-class families.

Hence, the middle-class model of family life and family relations is significant not because it described the evolving experience of all, or even most, American families; rather, the model is important because it was one to which others aspired and against which others were judged. Working-class life, including working-class family life, appeared to hold few benefits; economic uncertainty, illness, scarcity, and hardship. In contrast, middle-class families were surrounded by evidence of their advantage; extended formal education, prestigious occupations, automobiles, and leisure, all of which advocated the family model on which it was constructed. Moreover, families that deviated from this model were judged inadequate. Families in which husband-fathers could not provide for their family, that is families in which the husband-father violated the "Tarzan principle," were judged negatively, as were working-class wife-mothers who were compelled to work outside the home, thereby violating the "Jane principle." In each case, the departure from middle-class standards was seen to imply inability to sustain and care for the family and, even more fundamentally, inadequacy of family form and family ideology.

Case Study:
I. Middletown, 1924

When the Lynds chose to examine life in Middletown (Muncie, Indiana), they did so because Muncie displayed a high level of demographic congruence with the nation as a whole. What is more, because the researchers used a variety of methods and investigated day-to-day life in Muncie in such extensive detail, their analyses (Lynd & Lynd, 1937, 1956) are not simply informative about life and relations in Muncie but offer a rich and more general insight into the American family in the mid-1920s and 1930s. Indeed, after reviewing their second report (Lynd & Lynd, 1937), Burke (1973) concluded that a reader

would more often have a sense of being reminded than informed. The Lynds'
initial study (Lynd & Lynd, 1956), conducted in 1924 and 1925, provides
substantial confirmation of the evolution of family life and family relations
suggested in the present inquiry. Most generally, Middletowners believed in
marriage and family. The Lynds identified the family, "consisting usually of
father, mother, and their unmarried children" (p. 110), as "Middletown's most
'sacred' institution" (p. 102). By 1925, fewer than one in four males over the
age of 15 was unmarried, and the proportion among females was even lower.
Although Middletowners considered romantic love the "only valid basis for
marriage" (p. 114), emphasizing the local priority of mutual affection, business-class mothers advocated, as well, the appropriateness of establishing relationships with "the 'right' people" (p. 115). Hence, daughters were encouraged
to seek out a man with "the ability to provide a good living" (p. 116). Sons,
meanwhile, were motivated to find a woman able "not only to 'make a home'
for her husband and children, but to set them in a secure social position"
(p. 116). Further, because they were believed to contribute to social expertise,
"good looks and dress for a woman" (p. 116) were also considered important,
although intelligence was not regarded as a virtue. This ideology is reflected
in a young business man's contention to a group of high school seniors that,
"The thing girls get from high school is the ability to know how to choose a
'real one' from a 'near one.' When a girl gets around 18 or so I begin to expect
her to get married" (p. 117).

The people of Muncie also appear to have endorsed Beecher and Stowe's
(1869) axiom that women had a natural place in the home and the corollary,
that they had no place in the professional world. In 1925, 80% of Middletown's total workforce was male. As the investigators observed, "a healthy
male, whether married or unmarried, loses caste sharply by not engaging
with the rest of the group in the traditional male activity of getting a living"
(Lynd & Lynd, 1956, p. 25). In contrast, business-class women had almost no
legitimate presence in the paid work force and, again, the rules that governed their participation are reminiscent of those articulated by Beecher and
Stowe (1869) a half-century earlier, which permitted only unmarried or
widowed women to work for pay. Responding to one of the many surveys
distributed by the Lynds, 89% of 446 high school girls indicated their inten-
tion to work after graduation. Among the daughters of business-class parents, however, this potential for paid work either led through the narrow
breach that confined them to public school teaching and, in most cases,
spinsterhood (80% of Middletown's teachers were unmarried women) or was
abandoned as a necessary condition of marriage. Paid employment among
business-class women was not only rare in Middletown (only 1 out of 40

professional women interviewed by the Lynds had worked for pay during the previous 5 years) but was actively discouraged, both by other business-class wives, who were likely to impose punitive social penalties on their working counterparts, and by a pointed and prohibitive local ideology that maintained that working-women "displace men and lower wages, and that they neglect their children or avoid the responsibility of child-bearing, while through their free and easy association with men . . . they encourage divorce" (pp. 26–27).

The sentiment of gender-based difference and division continued into the family, where it was expressed in ways consistent with the "Jane" and "Tarzan" principles. Although family size had decreased in Muncie, as elsewhere, child-bearing remained a "moral obligation" (Lynd & Lynd, 1956, p. 131) in the community and childrearing the exclusive and essential responsibility of the mother. Indeed, the researchers noted that, "many Middletown mothers, particularly among the business class, are devoting a part of their increasing leisure to their children" (p. 146). Likewise, when the authors examined wives' other primary domestic responsibility, housework, they reported a strict separation based on gender, at least among middle-class families. Specifically, they observed that "even in families of the business class the manual activities of the wife in making a home are being more and more replaced by goods and services produced or performed by other agencies in return for a money price, thus throwing even greater emphasis upon the money-getting activities of the husband" (p. 168). Despite the increasing availability of such labor-saving devices as irons, vacuum cleaners, toasters, washing machines, and heaters, however, most business-class wives comprised a "large group who by careful management fit everything somehow into the morning and an afternoon hour or two and contrive to keep many afternoons and evenings relatively free for children, social life, and civic activities" (p. 169).

Notably, such a system restricted the male's role to that of provider and, in middle-class families, extended that narrow responsibility to include the purchase of domestic goods and services increasingly viewed as necessary to a wife's successful maintenance of the home. In turn, like all Middletown women, those of the business-class sought to "reduce their hours spent in housework" (Lynd & Lynd, 1956, p. 168). In this they were abetted by a new generation of domestic gadgetry, although they remained dependent on their husbands to endorse its usefulness and provide for its purchase. As the burden of housework eased, many of these women seem to have devoted at least some part of the saved time to their children, thereby elevating the familial and emotional significance of parent–child relations, in general, and mother–child relations, in particular.

Indeed, when the Lynds examined parent–child relations, they found evidence that, consistent with the broader model of family life, families had become increasingly child-centered and the relationship between parents and children had become more egalitarian. Not only were some mothers dedicating potential leisure time to interact with and care for their children but, when high school students were asked to identify the most desirable attributes in a mother and father, they indicated that the second most important characteristic in a mother, next to being a good cook and housewife, and the most important in a father was willingness to spend time with her/his children. That is, children expected parents to pay attention to them and, while such a demand is congruent with the mother's domestic identity, it is not an inherent feature of the "Tarzan principle" and suggests that the principle was being revised, perhaps by mutual consent, so that fathers, too, were defined to some extent in domestic terms. Parent–child relations had also become less severe. Although the Lynds (1956) observed that child care was seen necessarily to involve discipline and obedience, they also reported that a "more democratic system of relationships with frank exchange of ideas is growing up in many homes" (p. 144). Business-class mothers, for example, rated "independence" and "frankness" as important as "strict obedience" in raising children, and business-class fathers, although considered less central than mothers in childrearing, were expected to respect their children's opinions.

The Lynds' investigation revealed, as well, some evidence that children and parents were growing apart. The automobile, which had become "an accepted essential of normal living" (1956, p. 253) and had been credited with bringing families closer together, was seen to divide the family, allowing children to function independent of their parents. Most straightforwardly, the automobile was believed to encourage children to spend more time with each other than in the company of their parents, as had previously been the case. Indeed, 55% of boys and 44% of girls reported spending fewer than four evenings per week with their parents and almost one in five boys reported that they spent zero evenings per week with their parents. More threatening was the automobile's assumed facilitating role in the increased sexual activity of young adults. Not only were couples dating earlier and spending more time together but "petting parties" had become common—88% of boys and 78% of girls interviewed indicated that they had participated in such an event—and the automobile was believed, quite literally, to be the vehicle of that sexuality. As the authors observed with some gravity, "of thirty girls brought before the juvenile court in the twelve months preceding September 1, 1924, charged with 'sex crimes,' for whom the place where the offence occurred was given in the records, nineteen were listed as having committed the offence in an automobile" (p. 258).

In Muncie, the fissure that separated females and males extended beyond family responsibilities. While marriage was commonly based on mutual love, the Lynds noted that ongoing social involvement between spouses was not considered necessary. Instead, married couples "frequently either gravitate apart into separate groups to talk men's talk and women's talk, or the men do most of the talking and the women largely listen" (p. 118). Such division reflected and was, perhaps, an outcome of a broader belief that females and males were simply different. According to the researchers, "Middletown husbands, when talking frankly among themselves, are likely to speak of women as creatures purer and morally better than men but as relatively impractical, emotional, unstable, easily hurt, and largely incapable of facing facts or doing hard thinking" (p. 117). Women, too, appear to have subscribed to this ideology. Not only were wives who sought public companionship with their husbands frequently ostracized by their peers but one women's club had the motto, "Men are God's trees; women are his flowers," while another had the motto, "True womanliness is the greatest charm of women" (p. 118).

As suggested already, the gender-based division of space and function was likely to be more uncertain in working-class families, and this appears to have been the case in Muncie. While working-class men and women may have endorsed the "Tarzan" and "Jane" principles, the economic crush under which they typically lived frequently rendered those principles meaningless as relational maps. As the Lynds observed, "The husband must 'support' his family ... but recurrent 'hard times' make support of their families impossible for many workers; the wife must make a home for her husband and care for her children, but she is increasingly spending her days in gainful employment outside the home" (p. 129). Likewise, ongoing economic hardship coupled with the relative scarcity of either proper medical care or contraception often desexualized working-class marriages: "Husband and wife must cleave together in the sex relation, but fear of pregnancy frequently makes this relation a dread one for both of them" (p. 129).

Not surprisingly, the Lynds (Lynd & Lynd, 1956) found working-class marriages to be quite dreary, reporting that "not infrequently husband and wife meet each other at the end of a day's work too tired or inert to play or go anywhere together; many of them have few if any close friends ... such conversation as there is may be of a bickering sort, or may lapse into apathetic silence" (pp. 119–120). Increasingly, such marriages ended in divorce, an outcome the Lynds attributed to the necessary financial independence of working-class wife-mothers. Notably, however, while they may have considered working-class families especially distressed, the researchers concluded that families in general were often characterized by relatively low levels of satisfaction, noting that "there are some homes in Middletown among both working and business class families which one cannot enter without being aware of a constant undercurrent of sheer delight, of fresh, spontaneous interest between husband and wife. But such homes stand out by reason of their relative rarity" (p. 130). Even in middle-class marriages, the relationship between wife and husband often appears intentionally opaque. Indeed, this seems to have been the community norm, permeating the guidance offered to young couples. For example, a minister is quoted as saying that, "I always tell my young men when they marry ... that they must get over any habit of thinking that they must be frank and tell everything they know to their wives" (p. 120), while newspaper columnist Dorothy Dix advised, "'Let well enough alone' is a fine matrimonial slogan. . . . What we don't know doesn't hurt us in domestic life, and the wise do not try to find out too much" (p. 120).

In Muncie, then, the Lynds found evidence that, by the mid-1920s, there existed a deep and widespread commitment to marriage and family. Marriage was to be based on mutual love although, among the middle-class, there remained the constraint that sons and daughters select partners able to fill the roles of nurturer/caregiver and provider, respectively. Despite the mandate of romantic and reciprocal love, and while marriages could be satisfying, that was not necessary—nor, it appears, was it common. Rights and responsibilities in the family remained divided as a function of gender and the emotional gulf between spouses was reinforced by a community belief system that held men and women to be inherently different and suited to dissimilar tasks, a social system that advocated gender-specific interpersonal networks, and a system of marriage that devalued openness between spouses. In contrast, there is substantial evidence that, despite increased independence among adolescents in particular, Middletown families had become more child-centered. Business-class mothers were devoting more time to playing with and caring for their children and even business-class fathers were expected to administer the family based on a relatively egalitarian set of principles.

DEVELOPMENT OF THE FAMILY:
II. TRAUMA AND RESILIENCE

In 1929, 3% of the population was unemployed; in 1930, the unemployment rate climbed to almost 9%; by 1931, it had reached 16%; and, in 1932, it rose to nearly 24% (U.S. Bureau of the Census, 1960). During the same period, labor income fell by over 40%, manufacturing wages fell by 60%, and farm income fell by more than 55%. Between 1929 and 1932, more than 100,000 businesses failed and, during the 3 years ending in 1931, 4,305 banks with deposits of more than $2.75 billion failed (Blum et al., 1968). During 1932, more than one in four households lacked even a single wage earner (U.S. Bureau of the Census, 1960).

As Blum and his colleagues have suggested, "liquidation carried a frightful burden of suffering. Thousands of middle-class families, their incomes dwindling, sometimes entirely gone, lost next their savings, then their insurance, then, unable to pay their mortgages, their very homes . . . The times were even harder on laboring men and their families. The lost job, the fruitless search for work, the shoes worn through, and the clothes worn thin, the furniture and trinkets pawned, the menu stripped of meat and then of adequate nutrition, no rent, no joy, no hope; and finally the despair of breadlines—these visited every city, leaving in their path sullen men, weeping women, and hungry children. So, too, on the farm—vanished incomes, foreclosures, tenancy, migrancy, and with them, as in the cities, the death of self-respect" (Blum et al., 1968, p. 664).

The Depression traumatized the American family. Most directly, fewer couples married and fewer had children; between 1928 and 1932, the marriage rate fell by almost 20% and the birth rate by more than 13% (U.S. Bureau of the Census, 1960). How life and relations changed inside families is less clear, although the middle-class model that advocated a system of divided responsibilities, relational commitment, and mutual affection also relied on economic prosperity and, so, is likely to have become less compelling. As the Lynds (Lynd & Lynd, 1956) had observed in Muncie, the model did not flourish under economic hardship, and there is no reason to suppose that it did so during the Depression. In particular, the "Tarzan principle" must often have become unrealistic as large numbers of husband-fathers lost their jobs and/or savings and, so, became unable to provide for their families' economic and physical well-being. Likewise, the "Jane principle," which instructed women to define themselves in the context of home and family, lacks authority when Tarzan is unable to provide. In fact, the traditional family model may be most vulnerable under trauma. The mother's lack of expertise outside the home, which may be guarded jealously, as was the case among Middletown's business-class, has been characterized as "a bad way to organize a family's survival" (Newman, 1988, p. 119) in that it reduces substantially a family's ability to generate the resources necessary to maintain itself. In a more general sense, the misery of deep and prolonged economic hardship must surely have weakened the sexual intimacy of marriage and eroded even further spouses' relational satisfaction.

By the end of the decade, however, there appears to have been renewed commitment to the prior model. While almost 30% of women were employed outside the home and while the proportion of married women employed outside the home had risen marginally, "public praise was reserved for self-supporting single women, or for frugal and resourceful homemakers whose domestic endeavors helped their families through the crisis" (May, 1988, p. 50). Indeed, 82% of respondents to a 1936 Gallup poll, including 75% of the women polled, believed that wives of employed husbands should not work outside the home (Gallup, 1936). The sentiment seems to have developed, even among working-class families, that it was acceptable for a married woman to work outside the home only if her earnings were an important, although secondary, contribution to the family's standard of living (Lynd & Lynd, 1937; May, 1988). Certainly, the Depression had not produced anything approaching parity among female and male income levels. In 1939, the median income of White females was 60% that of their male counterparts; among non-Whites, the median female income was little more than half that of males (U.S. Bureau of the Census, 1960). Nor had the Depression appeared to alter significantly women's comparative income potential. In 1928, compared to women, 1.55 times as many men received Bachelor's degrees, 1.66 times as many received Master's degrees, and 6.33 times as many received doctorates; by 1940, these ratios were 1.43, 1.61, and 6.67, respectively (U.S. Bureau of the Census, 1960). Similarly, while the number of women employed outside the home increased between 1930 and 1940, the proportion of women in high skilled and high status positions decreased. By 1940, a comparatively larger proportion of women were employed in clerical positions, in sales, in service, and as factory workers; in contrast, relatively smaller proportions of women held professional and technical positions (U.S. Bureau of the Census, 1960). That is, despite the trauma of the Depression that had propelled women into the workplace and threatened the integrity of the "Tarzan" and "Jane" principles, there is substantial evidence that disparity between females and males increased and commitment to a divergent family model increased, although by the close of the 1930s the traditional family appears, again, to have been advocated by a large section of the public.

Case Study:
II. Middletown, 1935

When the Lynds revisited Middletown (Lynd & Lynd, 1937), the effects of the Depression on the family were apparent. Although some families reported a sense of increased closeness, perhaps a function of increased time spent together, the researchers noted that, even "in the less exposed homes, behind the brave, solid front that local canons of respectable competence require a family to present to its neighbors, difficult problems were being faced in augmented numbers: mortgage foreclosures, the postponement of having children, the shattering of plans for financial security, the crumbling of affection under the hard hand of disappointment and worry, the decision not to send children to college, and the answering low drumbeat of a frustrated younger generation" (p. 145).

As elsewhere, the marriage rate in Middletown dropped dramatically during the Depression. In 1930, the marriage rate was 8.1 per 1,000 total population, a decline of 27% from 1929; by 1932, the rate had fallen to 7.0 per 1,000 total population, a decline of 37%. Even in 1935, when the overall marriage rate recovered to 10.6 per 1,000 total population, the researchers reported an enduring fear of marriage among the young, especially among those of middle-income families. Such fear is captured by the response of a college graduate, employed as a store clerk, who remarked, "Hell! What's the use of my even thinking of getting married, let alone tying myself up in an engagement. I'm stuck! There's just no future for our generation, and there's nothing we can do about it. I don't expect to marry" (p. 151). Marriage rates might have fallen further had it not been for the attenuating effect of two groups. First, the authors speculate that some number of desperate couples were motivated to marry, despite widespread poverty, by a relief system that placed priority on those with dependents. Second, there was a felt increase in the number of secret marriages between high school students. The researchers attributed these clandestine marriages to "the growing restlessness of the younger generation . . . the relaxation of discipline and the lessened contact with their children by harried working-class parents . . . the tendency of more reckless couples to plunge ahead in quest of the one thing two people can achieve together even in the face of a blind future—personal intimacy . . . (and) the growing belief among many children of high-school age that marriage need not be final since divorce is no longer a serious disgrace" (p. 152). Such reasoning implies, in the most straightforward way, that Middletown's familial ideology had been revised to incorporate increased acceptance of divorce and, in more subtle ways, to accommodate looser family relations and a wider divergence between parents and children as well as more relaxed standards associated with sexual intimacy prior to marriage. Inherent in this position, as will become apparent, was the claim that the changing role of women had altered fundamentally Middletowners' sense of family. The divorce rate had, in fact, increased after the Lynds' initial exploration of Middletown, when the divorce rate was 5.0 per 1,000 total population; in 1928, the rate reached 5.4 per 1,000 total population. However, the rate declined steadily across the next 5 years, reaching a low of 3.1 per 1,000 total population in 1933, and, despite increases in 1934 and 1935, stood at 4.8 per 1,000 total population when the Lynds returned in 1935. Of course, the reality of divorce, at least during the Depression, is obscured to some extent by the silent dissolution of marriage effected by a partner's disappearance, either in search of work or in escape from an intolerable family situation. Perhaps more informative of family life during the Depression is the Lynds' analysis of 90 divorce cases handled by an unidentified law firm between January, 1931, and September, 1935. While the authors concluded that persons offered four primary reasons for divorce (temperamental differences, the husband's loss of employment, infidelity, and mutual loss of attraction), the interrelatedness of such issues is illustrated through a collection of case summaries, two of which are presented here. Case 5 involved "Husband and wife middle-aged. Married about twenty years. Three children. Husband out of work most of depression, though willing to work. She grew irritable and quarrelsome and made life unbearable. He sought other female company" (p. 159). Likewise, case 57 involved a couple "In mid-twenties. Married about three years. One child. Husband got out of work and wife went to work in a factory. She lost attraction for him. They became very bitter toward each other" (p. 160). These cases, and others, suggest a complex family experience in which economic hardship introduced emotional distress into the marriage and, so, distorted and damaged family life and family relations irreparably. However, while it is impossible to reach any demonstrably valid conclusion as to the public view of divorce that evolved and held sway in the wake of the Depression, the divorce rate data do not seem to provide evidence that the community had altered its position dramatically since the Lynds' first visit. Not only was Middletown's divorce rate lower in 1935 than it had been prior to the Depression but, when discussing the "Middletown spirit," the authors argue that such beliefs as "the family is a sacred institution" (p. 410), "the monogamous family is the outcome of evolution from lower forms of life and is the final, divinely ordained form" (p. 410), and "it is pleasant and desirable to 'do things as a family'" (p. 411) dominated and guided the community.

Consistent with the more general trend, the Lynds observed that increased numbers of Middletown women had entered the workplace since 1925 and contended that, in so doing, the women were "incidentally changing significantly the pattern of 'marriage,' 'family life,' 'wife,' and 'mother' in Middletown" (p. 181). That is, rather like critics of the modern family, the Lynds argued that the role of women was changing such that increased emphasis was being placed on personal goals, which were achieved through paid work, and less emphasis was being placed on community goals, which were achieved through involvement in the family. Additionally, the researchers argued that women's increased presence in the paid workforce produced negative outcomes such as weaker family ties, increased emotional distance between parents and children, increased acceptance of pre-marital sex, and decreased satisfaction in marriage.

Despite the intuitive appeal of this position, thorough examination of the Lynds' analyses provides little evidence of radical change between 1925 and 1935. First, while it is the case that, between 1920 and 1930, the number of women in the paid workforce increased by 15.7%, that increase occurred almost exclusively in two low-skill, low-status fields in which women traditionally sought employment, clerical work and the service industry. During the 1920s, the number of women employed in clerical positions increased 31% while the number of women employed in the service industry increased 61%. Second, it is also the case that many working-class women had come to anticipate life-long employment outside the home. However, during the same period, the number of men in the paid workforce increased by 19.2% so that, in 1930, women constituted 20.6% of the paid workforce, a slightly *smaller* proportion than in 1920, when they represented 21.1%.

Nor did the largest contingent of employed women, married working-class women, fare well by the end of the Depression. In 1920, women between the ages of 25 years and 44 years comprised almost 39% of all women employed outside the home; by 1930, the share had risen to more than 45%. Further expansion probably occurred during the early years of the Depression when women, because of their "tolerance ... of a wage below male wages, and their greater disinclination to unionization" (p. 56), were replacing men in the Middletown labor market. However, as the Depression eased, there developed a widespread practice of offering employment first to males (preference was given to older males with families), then to unmarried females, and finally to married females, a policy made more viable by the willingness of males to work for much less than they had a few years earlier, thereby reducing significantly the disparity between "women's wages" and "men's wages." Even in 1930, 86% of Middletown's families included a wife/mother who was employed neither full-time nor part-time and it appears that, by 1935, an even larger number of the town's working-class women were living in accord with a traditional, gender-based ideology.

Among the middle-class, commitment to a traditional ideology appears to have been even stronger. Even though, when reflecting on their first visit, the Lynds concluded that "the things a man is and does have remained fairly clearly and comfortably fixed" (p. 178), whereas a "woman's place has been less exclusively in the home" (p. 178), the balance of evidence suggests otherwise. Most fundamentally, as the researchers acknowledged, "One of the most strongly rooted of Middletown's values is that concerning the goodness of a wife's being a homemaker rather than a toiler in the rough outside world of men" (p. 181). The same sentiment emerges from examination of the "Middletown spirit," which, according to the authors, maintained that "men should behave like men, and women like women" (p. 410), "most women cannot be expected to understand public problems as well as men" (p. 410), and, most pointedly, "a married woman's place is first of all in the home, and any other activities should be secondary to 'making a good home for her husband and children'" (p. 410).

During the decade since the Lynds' initial examination, Middletown's business class had come to accept, to some degree, the prospect of young women seeking paid employment, at least prior to marriage. As the authors observed, "There is more indulgent tolerance of a business girl's working between school and marriage" (p. 182). However, as the Lynds quickly acknowledged, "when she marries 'all that foolishness stops'" (p. 182). A similar philosophy seems to have been applied to higher education. Females had long constituted the majority of high-school graduates in Middletown; between 1925 and 1935, 52% of all high-school graduates were female. Females had also traditionally formed a slight minority of college admissions; between 1929 and 1931, for instance, 48% of students entering college were female. However, between 1932 and 1934, that trend was reversed; in 1932, almost 61% of college freshmen were female, in 1933, 55% were female, and in 1934, 60% were female. While this might appear to signal reversal or, even, abandonment of previous policies that favored young males, the Lynds attributed the pattern, first, to the fact that business-class women's employment, often as a teacher, was typically dependent on a college education but, second, "that going to college means to a girl, more than to a boy, an enhanced opportunity to find a mate" (p. 212). That is, among Middletown's business class, paid employment and higher education for young women were usually temporary and could even serve a matrimonial function.

Among the adult community, the divide was even less yielding. First, Middletowners, as a whole, continued to subscribe to a philosophy that maintained both that "men and women do different things" *and* "are different kinds of people" (pp. 176–177). That is, not only was it supposed that men "get the living" while women "look after affairs within the household" (p. 176) but also that these dissimilar responsibilities were consistent with, and arose from, the dissimilar nature of men, who were seen as logical and reasonable but, "at home needing coddling and reassurance" (p. 177), and women, who were seen as intuitive and emotional. What is more, the Lynds reported that, according to local standards, a woman "should not be too intelligent, too witty, too aggressive and independent, too critical, or too different . . . She should not want a career, and should not compete with men, but rather back them up" (p. 421). Indeed, as the researchers observed, "the cultural pattern dinned into Middletown's girls and women on every hand has no uncertainty as to their different and secondary role, and shows no appreciable change since 1925. The women's pages in both local papers carry syndicated articles telling them: 'Women the weaker sex? Yes, and we're glad of it!,' 'The wise wife takes a minor role and gives her husband the lead' . . . an editorial in 1932 observed '. . . They take their views of life as a hand-me-down from men and model their demands on life by those of men'" (p. 180). It is little wonder that, according to the Lynds, "most married women of the business class in Middletown, particularly those in their thirties and older, desire no gainful activity and regard themselves as fortunate in being limited to their orthodox pattern of home and social life" (p. 185).

However, while family life and family relations continued to be governed by an ideology of gender division and female domesticity, some aspects of the family experience do appear to have become less robust by 1935. While the birth rate, which declined only 16% during the Depression, proved more resilient than the marriage rate, which declined by 41%, large families were rare. Likewise, women, especially business-class women, no longer were required to dedicate vast amounts of time to housekeeping. Relieved, to some extent, of these burdens and offered the illusion, at least, of increased academic and professional opportunity, some business-class women began to redefine themselves, "to find a socially and personally self-justifying role" (p. 282). Many, of course, reinvested time in child care, believing that more attention and additional interaction would produce a better child and testify to a better mother. Others developed "'study' clubs with their programs of reading 'good' books and discussing 'broadening' topics" (p. 283), all of which the Lynds felt were "earnestly pursued rather than reflecting the spontaneity of acute personal interests" (p. 283). At the same time, however, some women appear to have felt impulses similar to those of a later generation. Anticipating Friedan (1963) a quarter of a century later, the Lynds (Lynd & Lynd, 1937) wrote that, "Woman's traditional great dependence upon man has been less acceptable and more irksome. . . . Not only has the alternative path of independence, career, and power beckoned harder, but the traditional world of the affections has become more demanding as the franker modern world has emphasized more openly extreme femininity, including less passivity, more positive allurement, and a richly toned sexual response" (p. 178).

CONCLUSIONS AND IMPLICATIONS

In summary, prior to 1940 the American family developed in coherent and relatively consistent ways. The colonial model of family life and family relations, which had been based in part on economic considerations and in part on scriptural doctrine, had given way to a therapeutic and secular model in which home and family were defined in opposition to the harsh disorder of the public workplace. As such, mutual love became the accepted basis for marriage and, once married, couples were encouraged to construct and maintain enduring and relatively supportive relationships. In reality, many marriages appear to have been characterized by mutual opacity and low levels of satisfaction. Additionally, of course, social activity was often gender-based, encouraging spouses to maintain essentially separate public lives.

At the same time, rights and responsibilities of males and females became increasingly divergent. Although husband-fathers retained final authority in family affairs, their familial power had steadily diminished so that they were defined more and more by their duty to provide. Wives-mothers, meanwhile, had come to assume a separate and fundamentally domestic role. Such domesticity was seen to be consistent with both females' physical structure, which facilitated childbearing, and their emotional and innocent psychology, which precluded higher-order responsibilities but allowed them to perform familial duties, especially those associated with child care. At the same time, evidence suggests the emergence of a more feminized family model and a stronger female voice, even if that voice was frequently rather muted in practice. Families had become both more home-centered and more child-centered. Mother–child relations had become more enduring and more intimate while, more generally, typically female values such as beauty, courtesy, and sensitivity had been incorporated into family life. In summary, while males' rights and responsibilities inside the family seem to have evolved along a steady trajectory marked by erosion of authority, increased relational involvement, and narrowed focus on the ability to provide, the role of women appears to have become considerably more ambiguous, promising companionship in marriage, personal fulfillment, and public ambition, even if, in the end, it remained largely filled with domestic routine.

The division between family and community not only became reflected in the oppositional sex roles of females and males but also privatized the family experience. Family episodes were more commonly enacted outside of the public gaze so that the detail of family life and family relations became obscured. However, vaudeville, comics, radio, and very soon, television continued to articulate the family experience, sometimes in stereotype, sometimes in caricature, but sometimes in self-reflective ways that audiences deemed realistic.

Chapter 3

From Vaudeville to Radio:
The Family in Popular Culture

A case can probably be made that the family is an inherent feature of both public and private entertainment. Even a cursory examination of publicly performed plays reveals a long list in which the family and/or family relationships played a significant part, including Shakespeare's *King Lear, The Taming of the Shrew,* and *Henry IV* (parts I and II). Similarly, in the Victorian home, where entertainment was routinely created and enacted by family members, performances often depicted family life and family relations in self-reflexive and self-conscious ways (Spigel, 1992).

The American television family, while it may share some conventions with early literary families, is more clearly rooted in the family-related acts that dominated vaudeville during the late 19th century. Vaudeville eschewed the ethnic humor prevalent in concert saloons and variety theaters and emphasized the family experience instead, so that, by 1870, performers began to portray "the adventures and cares of true-to-life characters in their own homes . . . with humor, sympathy and loving detail" (Staples, 1984, p. 44). This tradition was continued both in comics and on radio and, subsequently, on television. As Smith (1983, p. 35) observed, "Many early radio programs came from vaudeville . . . and many early television programs came from radio." Likewise, comic strips adopted many of vaudeville's conventions, including stock characters, like the overbearing mother-in-law, and stock sequences, like courtship. These would become incorporated into radio and television through a variety of characters and families, including the Bumsteads (*Blondie*), the Gumps, L'il Abner, and Tillie the Toiler.

THE FAMILY IN VAUDEVILLE

Although not the first form of public entertainment in America, vaudeville is a natural point at which to begin examination of the family in American popular culture. Vaudeville emerged in opposition to the concert saloon and variety theater, both of which catered to male-only audiences so that the context and content of performances were predictably unsophisticated. A common vehicle for amusement in these blue-collar venues was the blackface minstrel show which, as Kibler (1999, p. 8) has observed, "appealed to average Americans, primarily working-class men, by attacking women's rights, ridiculing the temperance movement, and making fun of a wide variety of intellectuals, experts, and authority figures." Additionally, of course, the minstrel tradition was explicitly racist and attended to issues of family only through a collection of unsympathetic and essentially unconnected characters, including the "mammy," "zip coon," and the "pickaninny," each of which is examined more extensively in subsequent chapters.

Critically, vaudeville sought to attract women into its audience so that, in contrast, theaters were made to appear homelike and safe, and performance content was altered to include male–female interaction and the presentation of family issues. The introduction of male–female interaction was significant, first, because the sequences, at least initially, were often enacted by married couples, such as Fred and Annie McAvoy, Dan and Josie Morris, and Harry Watson and Lizzie Sherman, insinuating into acts an implicit sense of real family. Notably, Ozzie and Harriet Nelson, Lucille Ball and Desi Arnaz, and others would infuse the same ambiguity between real and fictional family life into early television. Male–female interaction was important, too, because it altered fundamentally the content of public entertainment. "Immigrant" sketches, which, for the most part, focused on the social aspirations of Irish- and German-Americans, were replaced by sketches constructed around romantic and domestic themes. Not only did this reflect "the influence of the most important new audience in vaudeville, middle-class women, whose lives were male- and home-centered" (Staples, 1984, p. 113), it also compelled performers to develop narratives that demonstrated a sensitivity to relationships and the emotions inherent in those relationships.

Following the popularity of an assortment of sketches dealing with domestic or parlor issues, the agenda of vaudeville became dominated by courtship. Significantly, these sketches rarely dealt with relationship initiation, relationship development, or partners' emergent love for each other but, instead, tended to concentrate on the difficulties of courtship. Sketches such as "Flirting in the Street," "Flirtation Under Difficulties," and "The Bashful Lover" portrayed a variety of difficulties, including those of meeting, those associated with social or parental disapproval, and those deriving from a partner's personality trait(s). It has been suggested that this narrow and repetitive focus "reflected the real-life anxieties of both parents and youths about modern courtship" and that sketches "depicting novel courtship patterns—flirting, courtship over the tennis net, automobile eloping, defiance of betrothal—also had the effect of teaching audiences about the new facts of life" (Staples, 1984, pp. 106–107). That is, because dating no longer led inevitably to marriage and because of the potential conflict between the old rule, parental selection, and the new rule, personal choice, and because of the urban dislocation between parents and children, persons were uncertain about how to achieve relational goals associated with marriage and parenthood. Vaudeville, it is argued, both reflected that uncertainty and offered possible solutions. Such sequences not only reassured audiences but, in a larger sense, signified that, like television, vaudeville may not simply have entertained but may have performed a socializing function, as well.

While dating continued to be a popular subject, and was the most common topic when mixed-sex couples began to perform stand-up conversational routines during the early part of the 20th century, there developed a broader interest in the family and domesticity. In particular, audience interest expanded to include family unrest, especially between husbands and wives. A review of the most frequently performed sketches during the early 1880s reveals such titles as "Trouble in the Family," "The Marriage Saved," "Domestic Difficulties," "Marriage, a Failure," and "A Matrimonial Dual," each of which point explicitly to spousal conflict. Indeed, in the 10 seasons between 1895–1896 and 1904–1905, at least 20% of approximately 550 mixed-sex couples performed routines that dealt with problems of courtship and/or marriage, whereas fewer than 9% of 190 teams had done so during the period 1882–1883 to 1887–1888 (Staples, 1984).

It is worth noting that the increase (and increased interest) in sketches dealing with marital unhappiness coincided with elevated public concern about the state of the real family. Like their modern-day counterparts, 19th-century Americans were alarmed by a variety of issues, including the divorce and birth rates. Between 1870 and 1920, the number of divorces granted in the United States increased by a factor of 15 and, in 1889, the country reported the highest divorce rate in the world (Mintz & Kellogg, 1988). At the same time, family size continued the decline that had been manifest across the 19th century. The most acute reduction in birth rates was among the urban middle class, where children were rarely defined as an economic investment and where medical science had been most effective in reducing the rate of death during childbirth and infancy. This, together with the elevated birth rate among the poor and the high level of immigration, contributed substantially to the growth of the Eugenics Movement (May, 1995) that, in part, encouraged middle-class women to increase their commitment to motherhood.

Persons worried, too, about the changing role of women, which, like today, was often seen to have a negative effect on the family. Not only were women becoming more educated and more often involved in the paid workforce, they were altering their appearance and becoming more sexualized. Between 1890 and 1910, the level of college enrollment among women tripled, while at the same time women's participation in the paid work force doubled (Filene, 1976). Young women of the period also rejected their mothers' conservative dress and restricted sexuality and adopted, instead, the "flapper" style together with a considerably liberated sense of their own sexuality. The latter is suggested by studies that indicate a precipitous decline in the rate of virginity among women at marriage, declining from 90% of women born before 1890, to 74% of women born between 1890 and 1899, to 51% of women born between 1900 and 1909 (Terman & Miles, 1936).

All of this seemed, to some, to demonstrate decay in the American family, a position that may have been narrated and reinforced by many vaudeville performers. Certainly, audiences showed a broad interest in family issues, and the popularity of such playlets as "A Happy Pair," "In Clover," and "A Quiet Evening at Home" indicates that audiences and vaudeville retained a taste for the contented family. However, there is no doubt that portrayals of spousal conflict and marital unhappiness were widely embraced and may have reflected on the real family experience in the same way that courtship routines have been seen to mimic the new reality of dating (Staples, 1984).

As vaudeville developed, performers and audiences negotiated a sociology as well as a catalog of stock characters and sequences. As Beuick (1984) observed, vaudeville audiences nightly learned that "marriage is an unfortunate institution to which the majority of us resign ourselves; women are fashion-crazy, spend money heedlessly and believe that their husbands are fools; . . . mothers are the finest people in the world . . . next to grandmothers; fathers are unfortunate persons upon whom fall most of life's woes; marital infidelity is widespread . . . the main thing to do is get all the money you can and keep your mother-in-law as far off as possible" (pp. 329–330). Audiences became familiar, too, with the "old maid"—defined by her ugliness, lack of femininity, aggressiveness, and desperation to "get a man" and featured in such acts as "The Old Maid and the Horsecar," "The Disappointed Old Maid," and "The Old Maid and the Fortune Teller"—and the "bumbling working-class father"—defined by his poor social skills, lack of education, and general incompetence and featured in such presentations as "Mag Haggerty's Father" and "Mag Haggerty's Father's Daughter" (Kibler, 1999). There were others, as well, including the "dumbbell" and "dumb Dora," both of which tended to converge into the same petite and attractive but intellectually vacuous stereotype, the spendthrift wife, often presented in conjunction with the dishonest salesman, the reformer wife, and the shrew.

Finally, there evolved a set of standard interaction sequences. In his discussion of male–female comedy teams in vaudeville, Staples (1984) discusses three of these, each of which depicts a woman's relational demise. In the first, a reformer wife, that is, a wife intent upon achieving some great public good, is taught in one of a variety of ways the harsh lesson that time spent away from home and family places the family in jeopardy so that, at the end of the narrative, she is penitent and mindful of her domestic imperative. In the second, a working wife is chased back into the home when confronted by her professional incompetence. In the last, a shrewish wife, to her private relief and pleasure, is silenced and dominated by her previously brow-beaten husband. Staples (1984) described one such act in the following way: "In Gibson and Cornelli's 'The Honeymoon,' for example, the team plays newly-weds at Niagara Falls, where the bride has taken her uncurbed temper, and her dog to cuddle instead of the groom. At the end, he turns on his wife and informs her he means to dominate. Terrified, she gives in; when she tearfully asks who told him to act this way, he says, 'Your father' . . . When the curtain came down, William Gibson reappeared and expressed his hope that 'every married man will profit by his illustration of masculine dominance'" (p. 183).

These conventions are significant, in part, because they represent an early contribution to the public lexicon of marriage and family and provide insight into the complex relationship between the real family experience and its fictional counterpart. Clearly, some of the characters, once familiar, have become less salient. The ice man and, to a lesser extent, the traveling salesman, for example, no longer are commonly presented as the cause of marital unhappiness, infidelity, and divorce. Likewise, while fictional husbands may continue to exhibit a variety of shortcomings, the drunken husband has become irrelevant as the foil to a reforming wife. In contrast, characters such as the bumbling working-class father, the dumb blonde, and the old maid remain a vital part of popular culture as does much of vaudeville's family sociology.

Analysis of vaudeville suggests that its popular portrayals of the family may have performed a mixture of functions, functions that are remindful of those associated with television. Most apparently, they entertained an extensive and relatively heterogeneous audience. Customers expected to be amused and were, and although some people were excluded, either as a matter of theater policy or personal choice, vaudeville audiences were considerably more varied than those who attended the concert saloon and variety theater (Beuick, 1984). Second, despite the large and mixed audiences, performers soon came to rely on a limited set of conventions. These conventions not only included the prototypic members of the popular family but also placed them in domestic conjunction, so that they were endowed with rights and responsibilities. Finally, family interactions were expressed as coherent narratives; that is, the sequences were recognizable segments of family life that involved appropriate role-related displays and meaningful relational outcomes. In this way, vaudeville articulated a necessarily partial but, nonetheless, comparatively complex family ideology that functioned to elevate some roles, like the dominating husband, and diminish others, like the shrewish wife; it encouraged some displays, like dominance in men, and discouraged others, like intrusiveness in women. In this way, vaudeville performed a socializing function, one that may have been especially strong in contexts of audience uncertainty, such as courtship and the changing family roles of women and men.

THE FAMILY IN COMICS AND ON RADIO

While the popularity of vaudeville waned, its conventions were adopted both in comics and on radio. Even early comic strips, such as those created by Howarth, focused on the problems of courtship, including problems deriving from oppositional parents. In "Love Will Find a Way," for example, Howarth depicted the conflict between a young couple's love for each other and the desire of the woman's father that they remain apart. In this strip, and in comics generally, as in vaudeville, mutual love routinely prevailed over competing parental ambitions.

At least preliminarily, some stock vaudevillian characters and contexts were not a part of comic-strip narratives. The reforming wife and the dumb blonde, for instance, lost their prior prominence, as did interaction sequences involving these characters. At the same time, comic strips added to the family lexicon. Most notably, the character of the mischievous child was invented and popularized through strips such as Busch's "Max und Moritz" and Outcault's "Hogan's Alley." Whereas early iterations appeared irregularly and aimed the child's waywardness at a variety of local residents and storekeepers, "The Katzenjammer Kids," first published in December 1897, not only institutionalized the character of the mischievous child but, with the incorporation of Mamma Katzenjammer into the strip, contextualized him within the family. Indeed, Mamma was commonly the target of Hans and Fritz's disobedience so that the strip evolved to tell a story that was implicitly familial. The same framework surrounded "Buster Brown," which first appeared in May 1902 and featured a mischievous, middle-class boy whose practical jokes often involved family members and often backfired, prompting weekly remorse but no change in behavior.

In time, comic strips began to articulate a larger narrative and, in so doing, reinvented the world of home and family, so common in vaudeville. Although adventure strips appealed to male readers, they held little interest for the increasing number of young women in the paid workforce. This audience, it was believed, sought stories that provided "reassurance that the trivial tasks comprising day-to-day existence have cumulative meaning and that the milestone events of courtship and marriage . . . are meaningful experiences reflecting the purposeful nature of the universe" (O'Sullivan, 1990, p. 58). That is, like vaudeville theater owners, newspaper publishers appear, first, to have been motivated by a desire to enlarge their comic-strip audience to include women readers and, second, to have arrived at the same conclusion as to how that should be achieved. Originally called "girl" strips, the domestic strip dealt with "courtship, marriage, childbirth, and child-rearing" (O'Sullivan, 1990, p. 58) and did so by using a set of conventions reminiscent of vaudeville.

An early example of the domestic strip was "Bringing up Father," first published in 1913. Because the strip narrated the experiences of a newly successful, although socially awkward Irish immigrant, and his socially ambitious wife, a model long popular in vaudeville but now essentially abandoned, it can be considered somewhat anachronistic. However, like later versions of the domestic strip, "Bringing up Father" was deeply domestic, portraying the mundanity of family life and family relations in the most detailed way.

Perhaps the leading example of the domestic strip was "Blondie," first published in September, 1930, which narrated the courtship and marriage of Blondie Boopadoop and Dagwood Bumstead and, after the addition of their children, Alexander and Cookie, family life in the Bumstead home. The strip, which is discussed extensively later, was syndicated in more than 1,800 newspapers (Young & Marschall, 1981), a level of popularity often attributed to its familial detail. For example, Waugh (1947) observed that the Bumsteads "have a thousand quarrels and triumphs along strictly normal lines" (p. 103), a sentiment echoed by Perry and Aldridge (1971), who concluded that the Bumsteads offer readers "a very familiar and readily identifiable situation"

(p. 107). D. Young and Marschall (1981) have been even more explicit, assert-ing that, "Even if the reader doesn't know it, it's there . . . he senses it. When Dagwood leaves for work, he kisses Blondie; or he kisses the children before they go to bed; or he's leading Blondie down the hallway holding her arm; or helping her into her coat. He does, and she does, all the loving, caring things a couple in love would do for one another. Even if you don't pick it up, it's always there" (p. 140).

The structural convention of *Blondie* is one that would become both famil-iar and compelling; that is, provider-father, caregiver-mother, and dependent children. Just as familiar is a large part of the strip's sociology, which teaches that children should be loved and nurtured, wives should be beautiful if not especially intelligent, fathers should retain ultimate authority in the home but, otherwise, be involved minimally in family relations, husbands are domestically inept, and, above all, marriage is a female institution, it reveals naturally a woman's strengths and a man's weaknesses. Repeatedly, the once uneducated and often socially inappropriate Blondie demonstrates her ap-parently innate familial and domestic competence, caring for Dagwood and the children, preparing meals, and retaining order in the home; Dagwood, meanwhile, is transformed by marriage from a dapper and much desired bachelor into a domestic incompetent, bewildered by both Blondie and the children, unable to resolve the simplest problem, and unable to regulate his own life without Blondie's constant supervision. Harvey (1990), for example, has argued that Blondie "became a model of wifely patience and tolerance, the principal stabilizing element of the family" (p. 38) while Gorer (1964) has asserted that "the family would constantly risk disintegration and disaster, if it were not for Blondie" (p. 49).

Like vaudeville, comic strips gave relatively little space to elaboration of the African-American narrative and, as is discussed later, relied on stereotypic images in the stories that were told. In a larger sense, comic-strip families, characters, and events invited readers to imagine and enter an America that was predominantly White and middle-class and an America in which a high value was placed on consumption (Gordon, 1998). Families like the Bum-steads owned their homes and lived in White, suburban neighborhoods with White friends and neighbors, surrounded by an increasing array of domestic gadgets. In addition, the Bumsteads, in particular, anticipated a postwar fam-ily model both in appearance and ideology, thereby modernizing the family lexicon established by vaudeville.

While the comic-strip tradition continued to grow, its conventions mi-grated to radio through a mixture of strips, including *Blondie, Bringing up Father, The Gumps, Archie Andrews,* and *L'il Abner.* Vaudeville, too, affected radio, despite its declining popularity, in part because they shared a performance element absent from comic strips and, in part, because of the prolonged and influential radio presence of Gracie Allen and George Burns but, most especially, because, like vaudeville, women constituted a significant part of the radio audience and, as such, influenced program content in predictable ways.

The advent of radio initiated an explosion of shows dealing with family life and family relations. As Smith (1983) has observed, "During the day, those at home and even on certain kinds of jobs could go about their chores while listening to the trials, tribulations, and celebrations of such 'soap operas' . . . as 'Ma Perkins,' 'Backstage Wife,' and 'Stella Dallas'" (p. 12) while "during the dinner hour, young and old alike were entertained by 'Amos and Andy,' 'Lum and Abner,' and 'One Man's Family,' as well as others" (p. 13) and "Later, most of the family would enjoy such comedy-variety shows as those of . . . George Burns and Gracie Allen" (p. 13). Some shows were adaptations of popular family comic strips so that the Bumsteads, Gumps, and others extended their conventions and sociology to radio. Radio also reinvented the ethnic family. Some of these, like *Abie's Irish Rose,* were based on successful Broadway plays but most were created for radio. *The Amos'n'Andy Show, Beulah, The Goldbergs, Life With Luigi,* and others often attracted huge audiences and introduced listeners to an America quite different from that articulated in most contemporary comic strips. This America was strongly ethnic, often non-White, almost universally urban, and typically struggling at the fringes of the middle-class. Finally, radio drew upon the vaudeville tradition. This connection relied, in part, on the "dumbbell" archetype, a character made familiar by Burns and Allen in their vaudeville act and defined by her scatterbrained nature, physical attractiveness, petite build, and blonde hair. This figure became a stock part of radio, and later television, not only because of Gracie Allen but also through such characters as Jane Ace (*Easy Aces* and *Mr. Ace and Jane*), Joan Davis (*The Joan Davis Show*), Liz Cooper (*My Favorite Husband*), and Lucille Ricardo (*I Love Lucy*).

Besides the scatterbrained wife, radio's standard family lexicon included the mischievous child, inherited from the comic pages, and its close relative, the meddlesome teenager, the meddlesome woman, the argumentative husband and wife, the incompetent and/or bewildered husband, and the henpecked husband and controlling wife. These stock figures were captured by characters such as Baby Snooks (*The Baby Snooks Show*) and Henry Aldrich (*The Aldrich Family*), Billie Burke (*The Billie Burke Show*) and Dora Featherstone (*The Gay Mrs. Featherstone*), the Bickersons (*The Bickersons*), Dagwood Bumstead (*Blondie*) and Chester A. Riley (*The Life of Riley*), and Jiggs and Maggie (*Bringing up Father*) and Mortimer and Agatha Meek (*Meet the Meeks*), respectively. Radio also relied on a small set of stock African-American characters, although, like vaudeville and the comics, these were narrowly cast and negatively defined, a problem discussed more extensively later.

Perhaps because many radio programs pursued the same middle-class family audience as vaudeville, radio tended to adopt the stock contexts of vaudeville, courtship and day-to-day family life. Those who had controlled vaudeville, particularly B. F. Keith, had reasoned that, because such contexts placed natural emphasis on relationships, interaction, and displays of emotion, they would have special appeal to women, thereby enlarging theater audiences as women, accompanied by husbands or boyfriends, became regular patrons. A similar logic appears to have prevailed in regard to early radio. For the most part, women comprised the daytime audience and, while men may have different interests and prefer different kinds of programming, women were also a large and influential part of the evening and nighttime audience. Certainly, the stream of soap operas, situation comedies, and comedy-variety shows suggests a keen sensitivity to women listeners.

Radio's version of courtship often reflected a familiar sociology. In *The Alan Young Show, The Eddie Bracken Show,* and *The Mel Blanc Show,* for example, young couples, motivated by their love for each other, sought to overcome the objections and opposition of the young woman's father. In several instances, including *The Alan Young Show* and *The Eddie Bracken Show,* this struggle is made more difficult by the young man's failures and/or inability to avoid trouble. Although it had not yet appeared in either comics or radio, this persona would develop a more malevolent parallel, the "bad boy," whose failure and attraction derived not from ineptitude but from knowing and hostile disregard for adult rules and objectives.

Radio also featured the young, married couple, enjoying the mundane intimacy and managing the novel problems of early marriage. Programs such as *The Honeymooners* and *The Munros* and, later, *My Good Wife, The First Hundred Years,* and *Young Love* each presented a young husband and wife, clearly in love with each other but, in one way or another, just as clearly wrestling with the unaccustomed responsibilities of adulthood. In *The Munros,* for example, the new wife, Margaret, finds housework more strenuous and more challenging than anticipated, while in *Young Love* two college students attempt to keep their prohibited marriage secret from the school's administration.

Finally, radio fixed on the routine of everyday family life. Indeed, between 1929, when *The Goldbergs* and *Mr. and Mrs.* were first broadcast, and 1957, when *The Couple Next Door* first aired, more than 50 separate portrayals of mature married life appeared on the radio. Families such as the Goldbergs (*The Goldbergs*), Nelsons (*The Adventures of Ozzie and Harriet*), Andersons

(*Father Knows Best*), Aldriches (*The Aldrich Family*), Bumsteads (*Blondie*), Ricardos (*I Love Lucy*), Rileys (*The Life of Riley*) and the Brown, Jones, and Stevens families from *Amos'n'Andy*, all of whom migrated to television, came to dominate radio. This mass of families was Black as well as White, rural and urban as well as suburban, ethnic as well as non-ethnic, poor as well as rich, and childless as well as with children, although, across time, the White, middle-class, suburban family with dependent children emerged as the archetype.

In summary, radio's family lexicon was relatively complex. Conventions, dealing with both character and context, were often inherited from vaudeville and comics but adapted to the serial nature of radio. Most obviously, in contrast to most previous efforts that had offered "slice-of-life" glimpses, radio's family narrative involved extended visions of courtship, marriage, and parenthood. Likewise, the radio family was relatively diverse. Although, by the mid-1950s, most radio families were White and decidedly middle-class, competing versions of the family were available.

DEVELOPMENT OF THE POPULAR FAMILY:
THE BUMSTEADS

There are several reasons to suppose that *Blondie* is a potentially rich public record of the American family experience. First, the familial adventures of the Bumsteads were extremely popular. Not only did Blondie and Dagwood appear as comic-strip characters, syndicated in more than 1,800 newspapers (Young & Marschall, 1981), but the couple, together with their children, were the subject of 28 movies, a radio series, and two television series, as well as a host of comic books and children's readers. Second, the comic-strip version, in particular, is often seen to reflect the routine of real families. Harvey (1990), for example, has characterized the Bumsteads as "ordinary folks" (p. 38) while Young and Marschall (1981) have suggested, more broadly, that *Blondie* became "America's reflection of itself" (p. 29). Even more explicitly, Waugh (1947) argued that, "When the boys came home and married, there were millions more Blondies and Dagwoods to experiment with the fascinations and frustrations of life in a cottage built for two or more. These are days when the young husband is apt to roll up his sleeves and help with the dishes, which is exactly what Dagwood would do, or at least what Blondie would expect him to do. This pair reflects the lives of a large group of people at the present time" (p. 105). Others have made similar arguments (McLuhan, 1951; O'Sullivan, 1990; Perry & Aldridge, 1971; Robinson & White, 1963), reinforcing the conclusion that *Blondie* captures the commonplace detail of family life and family relations and that, indeed, "readers can see beneath the humor and recognize their own patterns of behavior being acted out" (Berger, 1973, p. 109). Third, while *Blondie* offers a necessarily incomplete model of family life, it is relatively rich in what it may tell us about how and why people marry and the ways in which people are changed by marriage. In contrast to other depictions, which provide only glimpses of a family's development, *Blondie* introduces us to the Bumsteads long before they are married and, so, may offer considerable insight into the nature of courtship and the connectedness of courtship and marriage.

When *Blondie* was first published in September, 1930, the comic strip narrated the social experiences of Blondie Boopadoop, a young employee of the Bumstead Locomotive Works, a company owned by Dagwood Bumstead's father, J. Bolling Bumstead. After an interrupted courtship—one opposed by Dagwood's parents—Blondie and Dagwood were married in February, 1933, in what Young and Marschall (1981) described as "easily the most notable marriage in America" (p. 24) that year. Because he had been disinherited as a result of his "bad" marriage, Dagwood pursued an independent career, the details of which have remained obscure although it is clear that Dagwood has achieved only limited success. Nonetheless, the Bumsteads became parents, first in April, 1934, with the birth of their son, Alexander, and again in April, 1941, when their daughter, Cookie, was born, and continued to live on Dagwood's income until Blondie established her own business in 1991.

Examination of the comic strip during the period 1930 to 1940 reveals numerous points of contact between the Bumsteads and the families of Middletown (Lynd & Lynd, 1937, 1956). Like real couples, Blondie and Dagwood articulate the view that marriage must be based on mutual love. For instance, in a 1931 strip, Dagwood promises, "I'll weave a magic carpet out of moonbeams and strands of stardust and we'll ride away thru [sic] pink clouds to the land of love dreams," and, in a 1932 strip, admits to Blondie, "I've never loved anyone but you, my darling." Likewise, Blondie's love for Dagwood is made apparent both through nonverbal affiliative behaviors, such as direct gaze and touch, which she enacts routinely, and through explicit verbal disclosures that she makes to Dagwood and others. Indeed, it is Blondie who declares, "I love Dagwood and he loves me." It is also the case that the comic strip endorses mutual love as the basis for marriage because it rejects other possible criteria, particularly those associated with wealth and status. Not only does Dagwood relinquish his family's fortune for Blondie but he repeatedly tells Irma, a more status-appropriate partner selected by his parents, that he cannot marry her because he does not love her. In a 1932 strip, Blondie, too, laments, "poor

Dagwood—married to a girl he doesn't love just to further the social ambitions of his selfish parents." That is, the Blondie and Dagwood narrative commonly conjoins marriage and mutual love and disassociates marriage from other, competing motivations. When Dagwood rejects Irma and, at the same time, loses his inheritance, he validates that configuration and embraces the prevalent ideology of contemporary Middletowners that mutual, romantic love is the "only valid basis for marriage" (Lynd & Lynd, 1956, p. 114).

When the Lynds (1937, 1956) explored Middletowners' gender-related attitudes, they observed that young, unmarried females were expected to be physically attractive, socially adept, illogical, and emotional. Inside marriage, the "Jane principle" mandated much the same attributes but placed new emphasis on a female's ability to nurture young children, and her husband, and establish a quiet, comfortable home. In contrast, while males were expected to spend time with their children, their primary role was to provide for the family's well-being. Hence, young males were expected to cultivate skills and abilities that would prepare them to assume such a responsibility, an ethic that placed value on such qualities as intelligence, common sense, industry, independence, and problem solving. The role of husband-father was defined largely by the ability to provide, although it was also expected that the married male would meet the emotional and sexual needs of his wife and the emergent needs of his children.

Analysis yields substantial evidence that Blondie and Dagwood communicate essentially these sets of attributes. As young adults, Blondie is the attractive but simple-minded woman desirable because of her looks and charming innocence while Dagwood is the affluent, cosmopolitan man pursued because of his wealth and family name. When she first appeared, for example, Waugh (1947) described Blondie as "all dewy and fresh; cute as the devil with nice calves, nice everything, bouncing into the heart of America with long, lovely legs and bold as brass" (pp. 101–102) and, more recently, O'Sullivan (1990) pointed to Blondie's "alluring independence and sexuality" (p. 57). Indeed, even the most cursory examination of the comic strip encourages the conclusion that Blondie—especially the pre-marital version—was intended to be seen as physically attractive. Just as clear, however, is Blondie's limited intelligence. In a 1930 strip, for instance, Blondie is shown in conversation with Dagwood and his father. She is sitting on the father's desk, playing with her hair, and trying to remember which college she attended. She first guesses that it was Yale, but then suggests that "it was near Yale—we used to go over there to the dances and things." Soon, she explains that she "didn't go to college for very long—it was just a short time—a term or so" and, eventually, remembers, "I didn't go to college at all—I just sent for an application blank." While this may represent an extreme example and while Blondie's illogic is often a device for humor and, so, presented in caricature, it is also the case that she is habitually depicted as relatively uneducated, naive, and without personal ambition beyond a suitable marriage. That is, she is portrayed in ways that are consistent with Middletown's revised ideology of domesticity (Lynd & Lynd, 1937). Dagwood, too, conforms to the Middletown model of desirability. At the outset, he is presented as the dapper and outgoing heir to a railroad fortune and, even when disinherited, retains his "eligible bachelor" status by working diligently to provide for himself, and for Blondie, independent of his family. Moreover, Dagwood enjoys the esteem of his peers, as is evidenced by a 1931 strip in which Blondie reports that Dagwood's roommate has described him as "the brightest, finest, most clean-cut boy" in the college.

Previous analyses of the Bumsteads have paid minimal attention to their courtship and have focused, instead, on Blondie and Dagwood as wife and husband. In general, those analyses have evaluated Blondie's performance as wife-mother positively; that is, they have concluded that Blondie is presented in ways that are congruent with a female's familial role. Harvey (1990), for example, has argued that, although Blondie "does have her weak moments when she falls under the spell of a new hat or dress, and at times, in discussions with her husband, her logic can take on a distinctly scatterbrained quality," she "became a model of wifely patience and tolerance, the principal stabilizing element of the family" (p. 38). Indeed, there is little doubt that, as Mrs. Bumstead, Blondie would have been recognized and applauded by contemporary Middletown audiences: she became a mother and nurtured and cared for her children; she supported Dagwood in all that he attempted and provided him a clean and comfortable home; she retained her physical attractiveness and her social expertise; she had no aspirations beyond the home and family; and, too, she exhibited the frail logic and vanity presumed to be characteristic of women.

In contrast, prior investigations have been substantially critical of Dagwood's inability to fulfill the role of husband-father. Berger (1973), for instance, has suggested that "Dagwood Bumstead represents an important archetype in the American psyche—the irrelevant male" (p. 103), and McLuhan (1951) has proposed that *Blondie* narrates "the sufferings, the morose stupidities, and the indignities" (p. 68) of the husband-father. Even more sympathetic analyses are consistently critical of Dagwood's poor role performance. Becker (1959), for example, argued that the comic-strip promotes the view "that the American husband and father is at least bumbling and more often downright incompetent, but that his instincts are good" (p. 182) and, more recently, Harvey (1990) concluded that the strip presents the husband-father as "good-intentioned and faithful, but otherwise lazy and fairly inept" (p. 38).

While Dagwood's shortcomings are evident, so, too, is his ability to provide for his family, a requirement that, in 1940, substantially defined the adult male's familial role. The Bumsteads live in relative comfort and gradually accumulate both personal and domestic signs of achievement; they wear well-tailored clothes, they provide their children with an assortment of toys as well as separate space in the home, they eat regularly and well, they decorate their home in contemporary ways, and so on. That is, Dagwood's portrayal is fundamentally congruent with the husband-father culture of Middletown described by the Lynds (1937, 1956). This is not to say that Dagwood adheres precisely to the "Tarzan principle." His limited and uneven professional success, like his inability to repair various household appliances and his occasional reluctance to investigate "bumps in the night," erode the goodness-of-fit between Dagwood and the ideal husband-father. Nonetheless, it must surely be presumed that Middletown was full of such imperfect Tarzans, further suggesting that *Blondie* narrates a set of family experiences familiar to its readers and, so, may function as a public family history.

To the extent that *Blondie* is, in part, a record of the construction and development of the family, the strip implies that courtship is romantic, involving, and at times volatile. Blondie and Dagwood are routinely presented together and apart from others; they are often shown holding each other and are invariably animated in each other's company; they are attentive toward one another; they frequently express their mutual affection in ways that are unambiguous; and they sometimes act impulsively. While these attributes are recurrent, they are exemplified in three strips. In the first, which was published in 1931, the couple is shown walking arm-in-arm by themselves as Blondie, gazing directly at a smiling Dagwood, discloses that she has heard he is "the brightest, finest, most clean-cut boy in college" and is "awfully proud" to be engaged to him. The second, published in 1932, shows the couple at a party; in the first panel, Blondie tells another guest that she believes herself "not good enough" for Dagwood; this apparently is overheard by Dagwood, implying some level of monitoring on his part, because he appears in the second panel and, with his arm around Blondie, proclaims, "That's nonsense Mrs. Vanderviller, she's the most perfect little angel in the world—I'm the one that's not good enough for her;" in the final panel, the couple is presented hand-in-hand as Blondie announces that neither of them is good enough for the other. Later, in that series of strips, the couple is presented alone on a couch; Dagwood has his arm around Blondie who has her head on his shoulder and her upper body turned toward him as he announces that the "obstacles between us seem unsurmountable [sic] but don't worry, dear, our love is strong enough to see us thru [sic]." Finally, in another strip published in 1932, Dagwood is compelled by his parents to telephone Irma, Blondie's roommate and their choice as a partner for Dagwood; Blondie takes the call and, when she discovers that it is from Dagwood, impulsively collects up Irma and throws her into a bathtub full of water. In summary, both through conversational content and nonverbal affiliative cues, such as direct gaze, smiling, physical distance, and touch, courtship is consistently portrayed as involving mutual affection, attentiveness, and emotionality.

According to *Blondie*, courtship also involves family members other than the dating couple. Although the narrative ultimately rejects the economic and status considerations of Dagwood's parents, their involvement and concerns are otherwise presented as legitimate. For example, in a 1932 strip, the couple is shown waiting passively for the extended Bumstead family and the Bumstead family attorneys to decide the conditions under which the courtship can occur. Although the specific generalizability of these circumstances to real dating couples of the period is clearly limited, the event does suggest the appropriateness of parental involvement and is part of a more general relational theme in which Dagwood and Blondie repeatedly yield to priorities that are determined by Dagwood's parents, even when it means they cannot remain together. Moreover, while the involvement of Blondie's mother is much less obtrusive, she, too, offers relational advice that the daughter accepts without objection. That is, neither Dagwood nor Blondie provide any evidence that parents were expected to remain outside of courtship; indeed, all evidence suggests that the normative parental role was at the center of the emergent relationship.

Third, *Blondie* presents a model of courtship-as-test. In particular, courtship is shown to involve tests of a couple's love for each other, of a male's ability to provide, and of a female's fidelity. The most salient test of Blondie and Dagwood's mutual affection is provided by Dagwood's parents. As discussed already, this challenge not only implies that parents may have represented an obstacle in courtship fairly frequently but also suggests potential tension between mutual love, on the one hand, and status and wealth, on the other, that, in the comic-strip as in Middletown (Lynd & Lynd, 1937, 1956), is resolved so as to place priority on a relational or family ideology rather than one of personal achievement. *Blondie* also portrays courtship as a test of a male's capacity to provide. At the outset, Dagwood is heir to an enormous family fortune so that his ability to provide is taken for granted and, in fact, contributes to his attractiveness, as is evidenced in a series of strips published in 1932, in which he is taken on a cruise and pursued by several females whose common motive is to "grab a nice slice of those Bumstead millions." When Dagwood is threatened with disinheritance, however, that ability, together with the attendant desirability, is called into question. Dagwood's response is to seek out work for himself; that is, he confirms the "Tarzan principle," which mandates the ability to provide but involves, too, a virility requirement that is satisfied, in part, by achieving independence. This is captured in a 1932 strip in which Dagwood asserts to his father, "I can get along by myself . . . I'm happy for the first time in my life—independent—and as soon as I get a little better job, Blondie and I will be married." Finally, examination of Blondie and Dagwood's dating relationship promotes the conclusion that courtship tests a female's fidelity. Blondie's loyalty is tried repeatedly; it is tried by the opposition of Dagwood's parents, by the threat and, then, the reality of Dagwood's disinheritance, by Dagwood's relationships with other partners, two of which almost end in marriage, and by her own romantic involvement with others. In each instance, Blondie acts in ways that confirm her devotion to Dagwood, suggesting that contemporary females demonstrated their marital desirability (and their desire to marry) through a reactive and relatively passive system in which they were required simply to remain faithful, both emotionally and physically. Notably, these "virtues" do not appear to be tied directly to the "Jane principle" as it became manifest in marriage. That is, while *Blondie* often portrays courtship as a period during which males rehearsed their familial role as provider, the narrative offers no evidence that courtship anticipated or tested a female's ability to produce and nurture children, cook and clean, and so on.

One potential explanation for this disjunction is that these abilities were presumed innate so that brides were expected to emerge naturally and without training into their domestic family roles. Such an interpretation is consistent with the metamorphosis that occurs at the marriage of Blondie and Dagwood. In the marriage strip, the couple is shown kneeling solemnly at the altar of a grand church; they, like the large array of guests, are impeccably dressed and a minister, with choirboys behind him, has just concluded the ceremony. In the next and final panel, the couple is presented outside of the church; Dagwood has a gleeful smile and sweat is flying from him as he pulls Blondie across the scene; Blondie, now Mrs. Bumstead, is shown asking, "You'll help me with the dishes, won't you, darling?"; and Dagwood replies, "Yeh, but we'll worry about the dishes after we get back from our honeymoon."

The implications of this strip appear obvious and inescapable. First, males define marriage as a gateway to sexual intimacy. Second, female sexuality, an important aspect of a female's physical attractiveness and, so, significant in the process of mate selection, is rarely actualized; in courtship, it is denied and, in marriage, it is domesticated and emerges largely in conjunction with childbirth. Hence, third, females are reluctant sexual partners. Fourth, spouses engage in an exchange in which females contribute sexual intimacy and males contribute domestic support.

More generally, *Blondie* promotes a view of marriage as an arrangement that reveals a female's strengths and a male's weaknesses. Notably, in marriage, Blondie retains her beauty, charm, and devotion to Dagwood; that is, she retains the qualities that made her desirable in courtship. Additionally, she becomes invested with the ability to produce and care for her children, and Dagwood, and the ability to run a home; that is, the ability to provide "a harbor of comfort and peace" (Beecher & Stowe, 1869, p. 466). This point has been made by Gorer (1964), who described Blondie as "a self-possessed, good-looking, neatly dressed middle-class woman" (p. 48) and argued that "the family would constantly risk disintegration and disaster, if it were not for Blondie" (p. 49). In contrast, while Dagwood is always able to provide for the family and, so, meets the core requirement of the "Tarzan principle," he quickly develops into a comic-like figure, unable to ready himself for work, capable only of performing that work at a mediocre level, unable to understand Blondie or, subsequently, the children, unable to perform even routine tasks in care of the children, and often subordinate to Blondie. This is reflected in a 1934 strip in which Dagwood is presented in conversation with two male neighbors; the men, including Dagwood, belong to the "husband's back fence club" whose slogan is "you can't win;" the neighbors have arranged to go fishing the next day and invite Dagwood, who explains, "I'll have to see if it's okay with my wife . . . I haven't gone any place without her yet;" in the second panel, Dagwood is shown leaning out of a window, telling the other men, "She wants to know more of the details;" in the third panel, the neighbors are shown waiting in silence; and in the final panel, Blondie leans out of the window and asks, "If it's so respectable, why aren't the wives invited?" Likewise, in a later strip, when Dagwood is forced to work late because of a mistake he has made in a contract, his boss explains to a secretary that, "He's a married man. The punishment comes when he gets home and tries to explain to his wife why he's an hour late for supper."

Sequences of this sort prompted McLuhan (1951) to describe the married version of Dagwood as "weakly dependent" (p. 68) and Berger (1973) to call him a "castrated family man" (p. 105). While these verdicts may be extreme, it is certainly the case that analysis of Blondie and Dagwood's marriage yields the impression that marriage is a natural state for females and one that, at best, offers an awkward fit for males. This is recognized by Dagwood, who remarks to Blondie in a 1954 strip, "I think that marriage is a wonderful institution. It teaches a man to be thrifty, patient, persevering, understanding, punctual . . . and many other things he wouldn't need if he stayed single." In *Blondie*, the "Tarzan principle" appears to have expanded to involve a variety of domestic duties that males perform inconsistently and with difficulty. Because of Dagwood's undistinguished career, it is unclear whether his relatively diminished relational power derives directly from his domestic inadequacies, or from some linear combination of his performance in the workplace and his performance inside the family, or from his domestic performance only because he performs with marginal effectiveness in the workplace; that is, it is unclear whether *Blondie* implies a broad ideological shift, away from the workplace and toward the family, or suggests that the "Tarzan principle" becomes enlarged to include a substantial family component only when males perform below some threshold achievement level in the public workplace. The Lynds' (Lynd & Lynd, 1937) second analysis of Middletown offers some support for the latter position. In that investigation, the researchers observed that success in business excused, or even encouraged, shortcomings and excesses in other domains, including the family. In *Blondie,* this is made manifest in the character of J. C. Dithers, Dagwood's boss, who retains considerable family power despite frequently behaving in ways that imply low commitment to family. For example, in a 1950 strip, Dithers is shown entertaining clients; the men go from club to club, dining, drinking, smoking, and gazing at chorus-girls; at three in the morning, they appear, singing, at Dagwood's door; Dagwood is compelled to prepare coffee and sandwiches and, when the group leaves in the early morning, he is told by Dithers, "I'm going to stay home and sleep all day, Dagwood . . . Here's the key . . . you open the office for me and be sure to get there on time." In a later series, Dithers discloses to both Dagwood and a sales clerk that Dagwood looks better in a negligee than does Mrs. Dithers and, in a second strip, Mrs. Dithers tells Blondie, "Julius says I should lose some weight. And I think he's right. Last night I sat on his lap and sprained both ankles." That is, although Julius Dithers violates what may be considered a normative family model, that is a model articulated by other married couples in the comic-strip, both he and Cora Dithers act to confirm his relational status, potentially because of the comparatively high status he has achieved in the workplace.

Blondie also cultivates the view that, like courtship, marriage involves mutual love although, in contrast to the passion and unpredictability of courtship, marriage emphasizes responsibility and responsibilities. Although Berger (1973) has described Dagwood as a cuckold and has speculated that he "is probably inadequate in the bedroom" (p. 104), there is little reason to suppose this is the case. Although the displays become muted, Blondie and

Dagwood continue to show affection toward each other; they kiss each other, they share the same bed, they talk openly to each other, they resolve conflict effectively, and so on. Nonetheless, their interactions are increasingly uninvolving and, in broad terms, *Blondie* presents a marital trajectory in which duty, routine, and family come to replace ardor, spontaneity, and the couple. Blondie, in particular, is rarely portrayed independent of her family and/or home; indeed, in a 1944 strip, when Dagwood reports that he has dreamed about Blondie cooking dinner, she replies, "I can't get out of the kitchen even in his dreams." Dagwood, too, is frequently seen performing tasks in support of the family; he works for pay, he investigates the "bumps in the night," he answers questions about homework, and he helps maintain the home. Two other strips, one that appeared in 1934 and the other in 1945, reflect the changed nature of Blondie and Dagwood's affection. In the first, Dagwood arrives home and asks, "Where's the baby? How's he feeling? Did his rash go away? Does that new milk agree with him?"; in the penultimate panel, Blondie is shown standing angrily in the doorway, listening to Dagwood's stream of inquiries about the baby; and, in the final panel, has turned away, snapping, "I'm all right, too!" In the other, Dagwood is again shown arriving home; this time he kisses Blondie, who asks, "Do you call that peck a kiss? Why don't husbands make love like actors in the movies?"

Blondie comments, as well, on the relationship between parents and children. First, Alexander's birth, 14 months after Blondie and Dagwood are married, implies that children are a natural and encouraged product of marriage. Second, the birth of both Alexander and Cookie are welcomed and celebrated, by Blondie and Dagwood and their neighbors and friends, suggesting that parent–child relations are loving. This conclusion is reinforced by Blondie and Dagwood who, as parents, inquire routinely about the children's health, go to them when they wake in the night, answer their questions, buy them toys, and initiate play with the children. Third, preliminary parent–child relations appear primarily a function of mother–infant interaction. It is Blondie who nurtures and cares for the children and, indeed, even when he is asked to become involved, Dagwood, the husband-father, generally proves unable. Fourth, children appear to produce tension in spousal relations. In early childhood, this seems to occur because of the extent to which young children crowd and disrupt a mother's day-to-day family experience. Blondie is frequently seen trying to perform household tasks while engaged in childcare and, in a 1934 strip, remarks to a friend about her son, Alexander, "He requires my attention 24 hours of the day . . . I've been trying to think what I did with all my time before the baby came." This level of task involvement is often juxtaposed with panels in which Blondie behaves in ways that imply frustration or anger toward Dagwood, suggesting some causal conjunction between the mother–infant relationship and the relationship between mother and father. In a 1935 strip, for example, Blondie is shown preparing a meal while Alexander is whirling across the kitchen floor with a toy; Blondie asks, "Please don't make so much noise . . . Mama is trying out a new French recipe for meat-sauce for daddy's dinner and I want it to be perfect"; subsequently, Blondie is shown serving dinner to Dagwood, who places ketchup on his plate; in the final panel, Dagwood is inquiring to a locked bedroom-door, "Why are you mad? Why did you run off like that? What the dickens is the matter?" In a second strip, published in the same year, Dagwood is shown tasting meatballs in the kitchen while Blondie implores Alexander, "will you *please* get away from those jars? How can I get supper?"; Dagwood continues to eat from the pan of meatballs while Blondie pursues Alexander; in the final two panels, Blondie is shown, first, shouting at Alexander after he has pulled the table-cloth and a bottle to the floor and, finally, to have locked both Dagwood and Alexander out of the kitchen. In both strips, spousal conflict appears to derive from tension in the relationship between mother and infant, promoting the view that, although children may be loved and loving, they may produce increased hardship for a mother and reduced marital satisfaction for both spouses, especially the wife. Finally, analysis of *Blondie* suggests that parent–child relations are generally democratic; the children are unafraid to approach their parents, as Alexander does when he asks that they call him Alexander rather than Baby Dumpling; the children quite frequently negotiate such things as their diet; and they often cooperate with their parents in problem-solving, as Alexander does when he and Dagwood regulate the flow of visitors to Blondie after she has given birth to Cookie. Likewise, discipline typically relies on verbal instruction. Notably, in those rare instances in which punishment is physical it is administered by Dagwood and may involve Alexander or Cookie; that is, *Blondie* yields the impression that fathers impose physical punishment and that both male and female children may be punished in this way. Nonetheless, the children are generally well behaved and the parents tolerant so that discipline is, more frequently, unobtrusive and tends to take the form of instruction and encouragement.

There are two other aspects of *Blondie* that are worth observing. First, the narrative suggests that couples marry when they are young. Although there is some ambiguity regarding the age of both Dagwood and Blondie, we do learn, in a 1932 strip, that Dagwood is 19 and, given her early disclosure about her college career as well as her appearance, it must be assumed that Blondie is approximately the same age. Second, examination of the Bumstead marriage, including the period prior to 1940, provides the clear impression that young couples established their homes in White, middle-class, suburban neighborhoods and that they and their neighbors were close friends. Minorities are not seen in the strip and, certainly, are not residents of the out-of-town community in which the Bumsteads and their friends live. Instead of developing ongoing relationships with family members, parents, cousins, aunts, and uncles, the Bumsteads are "best friends" with their next door neighbors, Tootsie and Herb Woodley. More broadly, Blondie and Dagwood are known and, for the most part, liked by a wide range of persons in the community; neighbors, shop owners, bank employees, the mail man, and a host of repairmen and door-to-door salesmen.

CONCLUSIONS AND IMPLICATIONS

Examination of the family in vaudeville, comic strips, and radio sheds insight into the evolution of the popular family, the significant influence of women on that evolution, and the tangled relationship between the fictional family experience and the experience of real families. Additionally, the analysis provides intuitive understanding of the conjunction between extant popular depictions of the family and subsequent portrayals of the family on television.

Vaudeville, because it sought to attract middle-class women into its audience, presented domestic/family narratives to fit the assumed preferences of female customers. This tradition leaked into comic strips, radio, and, eventually, television through an assortment of stock characters and stock situations. The tradition persisted, too, through an accumulating sociology of marriage and family, a sociology that explicated desirable and undesirable gender attributes and narrated the rules governing family relations and family life. It is worth noting that gender-appropriate behavior, in particular, was articulated through a series of stock characters. The "old maid," for example, because she was the butt of the joke, advocated physical attractiveness, femininity, and passivity in contrast to her own ugliness, lack of femininity, and aggressiveness, all of which combined to make her unattractive to men, a profound failure for a woman. However, such portrayals may have been more deeply misogynous in that even female characters who exhibited desirable attributes, such as the dumb blonde/dumb Dora figure who was physically attractive and not especially intelligent, were also commonly the butt of jokes.

Fictional families often revealed the ideology and experience of real family life. The Bumsteads and others expressed, in a more holistic way than did stock figures, a relational philosophy that would have been familiar to readers: marriage was based on true love; women were expected to be physically attractive, sexually unblemished (although capable of conceiving), and relatively uneducated; women were also expected to be emotional, enthusiastically adept caregivers to both their children and their husband, and committed to establishing a tranquil and restorative family home; the defining role of the father was as provider; although fathers remained "head of the family," their familial power varied as a function of their income and, so, their ability to provide; and marriage was child-centered.

All of this would have been easily recognizable to Middletowners. Their own families were guided by a community code that assumed a fundamental difference between men and women and, as such, emphasized a gender-based division of rights and responsibilities. Especially among Middletown's middle class, women appear to have accepted their domestic/familial status and men, too, sought to fulfill the provider mandate. At the same time, children seem to have become a more central feature of the family. Mothers spent increasing time with their children and fathers, too, were expected to be attentive. Further, childhood had been extended and the duties of children reduced. All of this reflected closely the family experience of the Bumsteads and other salient fictional families of the period.

Chapter 4

Love and Marriage,
Horse and Carriage:
The Family in Postwar America

A recurrent argument in family research is that the experience of war fundamentally altered the family in America so much that the family model that emerged at the end of World War II departed radically from prior iterations and must be considered anomalous. Mintz and Kellogg (1988), for example, argued that "the pattern of life characteristic of the fifties differed dramatically from any that has been observed earlier in our history or since" (p. 178). The same position has been taken by others, including May (1988), Skolnick (1991), and Coontz (1992), who have attributed negative evaluations of the contemporary family, in part, to the use of the postwar family as a benchmark. In broad terms, these authors contend that the wartime migration of women into the paid workforce produced confusion about male and female sex roles, particularly as those roles related to public (work) and private (home and family) space. In order to reduce that confusion and reestablish the family, the government (supported by the popular media) embarked on a policy of social construction, articulating policies that systematically favored the traditional family and, as such, chased women back into the home and resurrected the role of provider husband-father. In support of this position, authors point to such things as the G.I. Bill, which linked higher education and loan programs to military participation and, so, provided the bulk of those services to males (Hartmann, 1982; May, 1988), popular images of the family that presented women in sexualized but domestic ways (Honey, 1984; Kozol, 1994; Westbrook, 1990) and so encouraged the "notion that motherhood was the ultimate fulfillment of female sexuality" (May, 1988, p. 140), and a cultural ideology that emphasized a woman's need for husband and children (Friedan, 1963) and so defined women in the narrow context of the family.

According to this position, the traditional family model, involving the provider husband-father, the subservient, nurturer wife-mother, and the dependent children, was never viable, not only because it was an artificial construction but because it violated reality. Mintz and Kellogg (1988), for instance, concluded that, because the enlarged wartime involvement of women in the paid workforce included substantial numbers of married women, the "middle-class taboo against a working wife or mother had been irrevocably repealed" (p. 161). As such, any effort to confine women to home and family was doomed to failure, as was any broader effort to define the family in a way that incorporated such confinement. Likewise, Skolnick (1991) has attributed the social and familial upheavals of the late 1960s to the disjunction between family ideology and lived family experience of the 1950s. Specifically, this author has argued that it "was precisely because the family gender and sexual patterns of the 1950s were so at odds with twentieth century realities that the revolt against them was so fierce, and their unraveling so traumatic" (Skolnick, 1991, pp. 76–77).

Critics point, as well, to the role of the media—and most especially television—in this process. Coontz (1992), Jones (1992), and Skolnick (1991) have each argued that contemporary dissatisfaction with the family occurs, in part, because persons rely on postwar television portrayals when they think about real families of the period. According to these authors, not only were those portrayals consistently constructed around a traditional family model but they significantly distorted family life and family relations so that the postwar family is often falsely remembered in ways that associate a specific and invariant family structure with a wide range of unrealistically positive outcomes, including high relational satisfaction, family stability, and individual and family achievement.

While these arguments have wide appeal, however, it is not at all clear that the dominant postwar family model violated an ongoing pattern of revision and, so, should be considered aberrant nor that television portrayals systematically misrepresented the family experience. Certainly, the federal government enacted policies that implicitly favored some family configurations over others and encouraged families to act in specific ways (move to the suburbs, buy their homes, and so on) and, certainly, popular presentations tended to promote the same family narrative. This does not demonstrate, however, that the postwar model of family life and family relations was either anomalous or that it ran contrary to public ambition. Indeed, that position appears to ignore both prewar (public) sentiments about the family, when amended versions of the "Tarzan" and "Jane" principles seem to have been widely advocated, and the quintessentially "Tarzan and Jane" nature of the family in war. What is more, contemporary audiences routinely judged television portrayals to be realistic, suggesting, as well, that the contact between real family life and fictional family narratives may have been comparatively robust.

INTO THE DARKNESS: THE FAMILY IN WAR

On the eve of World War II, the public appeared relatively committed to a traditional family model. By the mid-1930s, both national and local (Lynd & Lynd, 1937) analyses indicated that a large majority of people, including a large proportion of women, supported the notion that wives of employed husbands should enter the paid workforce only as a last priority. Despite the muted ambivalence of some, middle-class women, in particular, appear to have accepted a family ideology in which female domesticity was fundamental. In Middletown, homemaking remained "women's chief occupation" (Lynd & Lynd, 1937, p. 180) supplemented by a "competitive social life and the brief experiences of childbirth" (Lynd & Lynd, 1937, p. 64). Indeed, even teaching in the public school system was considered "queer or unnecessary" (Lynd & Lynd, 1937, p. 184). By the end of the decade, men were not only more likely to be part of the paid workforce, they were more likely to attend and graduate from college, more likely to pursue professional careers, and more likely to hold positions of authority, even in female-dominated occupations such as elementary school teaching. Inside the home, men continued as titular family head but their power was diminished. As a consequence of a mixture of factors, including the increased emphasis on the male's ability to provide and the new wave of domestic gadgetry that seemed to reduce the drudgery of housekeeping, women were becoming more central to family relations, especially those involving children, and more commonly responsible for the day-to-day running of the home.

Fictional families often promoted a similar ideology. As previously shown, the period's most popular fictional family, the Bumsteads (*Blondie*), not only reflected a traditional family structure but the family members, Dagwood, Blondie, Alexander, and Cookie, were habitually portrayed in ways that mimicked and endorsed the roles of provider-husband, nurturer/caregiver-wife, and dependent children, respectively. Dagwood was presented, first, as the dapper and outgoing heir to a railroad fortune so that his potential ability to provide was apparent. However, even when disinherited, Dagwood worked diligently to achieve independence and, although his accomplishments were modest, he always managed to provide effectively for the comfort and welfare of his family; the Bumsteads lived in safety and relative comfort and gradually accumulated both personal and domestic signs of achievement, they wore well-tailored clothes, the children were provided an assortment of toys as well as separate space in the home, the family ate regularly and well, they decorated their home in contemporary ways, and so on. That is, despite a variety of shortcomings (Becker, 1959; Berger, 1973; Harvey, 1990; McLuhan, 1951), Dagwood appears to have adhered in the most fundamental way with the husband-father culture of Middletown. Likewise, Blondie conformed to the Middletown model of desirability. Most obviously, she was intended to appear physically attractive. Waugh (1947), for instance, has described Blondie as "all dewy and fresh; cute as the devil with nice calves, nice everything, bouncing into the heart of America with long, lovely legs and as bold as brass" (pp. 101–102) and similar observations have been made by others, including Gorer (1964) and O'Sullivan (1990). At the same time, the narrative exposed Blondie as both relatively uneducated and illogical and without personal ambition beyond a suitable marriage, all of which is likely to have been familiar to readers. In Middletown, marriage at a relatively young age was normal, especially among women for whom marriage and family took priority over self and education. Indeed, the "Middletown spirit" maintained that "a married woman's place is first of all in the home" (Lynd & Lynd, 1937, p. 410) and argued that "a woman who does not want children is 'unnatural'" (Lynd & Lynd, 1937, p. 410). Again, the Bumsteads articulated a similar imperative. Not only was Alexander, their son, born a little more than a year after Blondie and Dagwood were married but, after her marriage, Blondie was almost always presented in conjunction with her family and generally either engaged in some domestic task, such as cooking, cleaning, or caring for Alexander in a variety of ways, or thinking and/or worrying about those responsibilities.

Hence, on the eve of war, the "Tarzan" and "Jane" model appears not only to have governed relations in real families, such as those in Muncie, but also to have extended into popular fictional families, such as the Bumsteads. What is more, as war approached, the public acted in ways that confirmed their commitment to a traditional family model. First, they married. Between 1939 and 1942 the marriage rate increased by 26.7% (U.S. Bureau of the Census, 1960). Second, they had children. During the same period the birth rate increased by 18.1% (U.S. Bureau of the Census, 1960). Third, husbands left home to provide for the physical well-being of their families. Between 1939 and 1942 the number of military personnel on active duty, almost all of whom were male, increased from a little over 334,000 to almost 4 million and, by war's end, had reached in excess of 12 million (U.S. Bureau of the Census, 1960).

At the same time, women entered the paid workforce in unprecedented numbers. Between 1940 and 1945, the percentage of women employed outside the home increased from 27.9% to 35.9%, placing an additional 5 million women in clerical, service, and other industries. This incursion has been interpreted as rejection of an ideology of domesticity, one that invalidated or, at least, contradicted the traditional family model (Mintz & Kellogg, 1988; Skolnick, 1991). It can be argued, however, that expanded representation of women in the wartime workplace was "Jane's" natural role in "Tarzan's" absence. Both "Jane" and "Tarzan" principles are likely to include exemptions that stipulate altered sets of rights and responsibilities under specific conditions. Even Beecher and Stowe (1869), writing in the 19th century about a family model in which males were substantially more dominant, recognized that unmarried women were not subject to the same role restrictions as their married counterparts; they could own property, run a business, and so on. It seems reasonable to suppose, too, that sex role requirements may change during crisis; when a partner is sick, when a partner is unemployed, and, of course, when a partner is away at war. Under such circumstances, women may be encouraged into the public workplace for any of several reasons—to increase their own earnings temporarily, to compensate for the lost earnings of a husband, father, or brother, to fulfill a patriotic need—with no expectation that their involvement will be permanent.

Notably, the raised wartime employment rates among women were not uniform across age and marital categories. Substantially larger increases occurred among 14- to 19-year-olds, where there was an increase of over 16%, and 45- to 64-year-olds, where there was an increase of almost 10%, than among 20- to 24-year-olds, where the employment rate increased by less than 5% (U.S. Bureau of the Census, 1960). That is, the overall increase in female employment derived primarily from higher levels of employment among young, unmarried women and older women without dependent children. Moreover, the image of "Rosie the riveter" was exceptional and transient (May, 1988) in that most newly employed women found their way into low-skilled positions, such as those in the service and clerical industries. Nor does examination of college graduation rates yield any evidence that women were becoming more intent on entering the paid workforce in skilled and/or professional positions. Between 1940 and 1946, the number of baccalaureates awarded to female students increased by only 0.7% (U.S. Bureau of the Census, 1960), suggesting further that paid employment was, for many women, a wartime expedient rather than a revision of the prevailing family ideology. It is worth observing that, viewed in this way, postwar marriage and birth rates imply not an artificial reconstruction but a celebration of family, which seems much more reasonable given the separation and hardships of war.

While there is considerable evidence of persons' work and marital status during the war, there is minimal record of family life and family relations. There is, however, a fairly extensive interpersonal literature that suggests that the relational consequences of long-term separation are generally negative. In their review, Knapp and Vangelisti (1992) indicate that the effects include "decreased physical and psychological stimulation; awkward and infrequent receiving and giving of favors; curtailed or indirect information exchange on all topics (especially the relationship); and experiences and activities performed without the intimate, which eventually causes misalignment of previously synchronized attitudes and behaviors" (pp. 296–297). In more general terms, these effects suggest increased uncertainty and, so, reduced ability to predict a partner's cognitions and actions (Berger & Calabrese, 1975), reduced intimacy, reduced involvement, reduced trust, and increased unilateral decision making. Such outcomes are also associated with relational dissolution (Berger & Bradac, 1982) and, at the very least, imply diminished cohesiveness in families that experienced extended spousal separation. It is likely, too, that such families were often characterized by decreased parental authority, especially among absentee fathers who were necessarily unable to sustain their day-to-day relational involvement and influence.

In summary, while government programs encouraged families to conform to a particular structure and empowered males in unique ways, and while popular portrayals of the family tended to reflect those biases, there is also considerable reason to suppose that the war experience did little to weaken persons' ongoing commitment to a traditional family ideology. Not only did large majorities of people approve of such an ideology immediately prior to war but the very nature of war appears consistent with a family model in which rights and responsibilities are divided on the basis of gender. This is not to suggest that family life and family relations were unaffected. Long-term spousal separation and the widespread involvement of women in the paid workforce, in particular, altered both family operations and family relationships, sometimes dramatically. However, those changes appear, for the most part, not to have been deep-rooted and, instead, to have reflected persons' temporary inability to actualize a preferred and traditional family ideology rather than abandonment or fundamental revision of that ideology.

INTO THE LIGHT: THE POSTWAR FAMILY

It has become customary to discuss the postwar family in terms that emphasize female domesticity and, at the same time, imply that the associated roles of wife and mother were both uniquely narrow and reluctantly enacted. Breines (1992), for instance, has argued that "the 1950s were politically and culturally conservative, particularly regarding gender and family issues" (p. 11) so that "getting married and becoming a mother were the only genuinely valued activities for a woman" (p. 50). In support of this position, Breines points to the postwar increases in marriage and fertility rates and to the substantial college drop-out rate among women. Likewise, Skolnick (1991) proposed that the postwar family was characterized by reemergence of the Victorian "cult of domesticity" that involved polarized and strict sex roles together with reverence for hearth and home. Like Brienes (1992), Skolnick (1991) focused on the conjunction between gender and academic achievement, noting that, compared to their fathers, three times as many men who "came of age" during the period graduated from college while the proportion of women obtaining college degrees barely equaled that of the previous generation. Similar arguments have been made by May (1988), who suggested that, according to postwar ideology, "strong families required . . . traditional gender roles in marriage" (p. 99) and, more recently, has argued that the "ideal of cold-war womanhood was the glamorous and sexy wife and mother" (May, 1995, p. 135). Inside the family, this system is seen to have invested males with special power and, as such, to have marginalized females even further. Mintz and Kellogg (1988), for example, have concluded that, while the prevalent model presented marriage as a partnership, "partnership did not mean equality. A wife's primary role was to serve as her husband's ego massager, sounding board—and housekeeper" (p. 186). May (1988) took the same position, claiming that "postwar Americans believed wholeheartedly that men should rule the roost" (p. 88).

Perhaps the most significant explication of this position is Friedan's (1963). Not only has Friedan's analysis so clearly influenced both public sentiment and subsequent inquiry, it also posits a causal rationale for the nature of the postwar family, in general, and the familial role of women, in particular. Like later critics, Friedan proposed that "Fulfillment as a woman had only one definition for American women after 1949—the housewife-mother" (p. 44). According to Friedan, such a view transformed motherhood from an option to a mandate, first, because there became "no other way for a woman to be a heroine" (p. 45), and, more broadly, because it generated expectations that involved "the high school girl going steady, the college girl in love, the suburban housewife with an up-and-coming husband and a station wagon full of children" (p. 34). That is, the role of women not only was essentially domestic and defined, in the most fundamental way, by motherhood but was articulated by a more elaborate relational code that relegated women to a dependent and, so, subservient status. Indeed, Friedan argued that "The end of the road is togetherness, where the woman has no independent self to hide even in guilt; she exists only for and through her husband and children" (p. 47), a state that the author concluded was both emotionally corrosive and relationally unsatisfying. In support of this position, Friedan (1963) cited the example of an "upper-income development" of 28 families. Among the 28 wives in the community, only 1 worked professionally, 16 were in analysis or analytical therapy, 18 were taking tranquilizers, "several" had attempted suicide, and 12 were engaged in extramarital affairs "in fact or in fantasy" (p. 235).

According to Friedan, the narrow role of women was not a function of a separate and freely developed self-identity; indeed, Friedan hypothesized that "an American woman no longer has a private image to tell who she is, or can be, or wants to be" (1963, p. 72), but, instead, derived from the "expectations of feminine fulfillment that are fed to women by magazines, television, movies, and books . . . and by parents, teachers, and counselors who accept the feminine mystique" (p. 77). This argument is significant not only because it posits a causal framework, at least in general terms, but also because it places popular portrayals of the family in that framework, encouraging the conclusion that fictional families like the Andersons (*Father Knows Best*), Nelsons (*The Adventures of Ozzie and Harriet*), Cleavers (*Leave It to Beaver*), and Ricardos (*I Love Lucy*) may have incorporated a family ideology familiar to postwar audiences. Additionally, of course, Friedan's analysis, like others, presumes that the postwar family model was neither natural nor desired but, instead, was a strategic variation of an ancient system imposed on an unwilling (female) public.

In general, then, the prevalent view of the postwar family is constructed around two propositions: first, spousal rights and responsibilities were strictly divided on the basis of gender such that males assumed a strong provider role and retained authority in the family while females were relegated to a domestic and subservient role in service of the family; second, inasmuch as "reproduction became a national obsession" (May, 1995, p. 18), the role and expectations of women collected narrowly around their anticipated motherhood. Critics argue that such a model violated ongoing trends and point to a variety of indices, most especially postwar marriage and birth rates as well as women's' reduced involvement in the paid workforce and their reduced levels of academic achievement during the period, as evidence both of the model and of its lack of precedent. Finally, popular portrayals, including those on television, are posited to have expressed and encouraged this artificial family system.

Despite the fairly wide acceptance of this position, there is reason to suppose that the terrain of postwar family life and family relations was more uneven. Certainly, the family was the centerpiece of postwar social reconstruction. Propelled by a mixture of motivations—but, most obviously, by their own, often suspended, relational needs—a rush of couples married and became parents immediately following the war. Compared to 1945, the marriage rate a year later increased by 42.8% and the birth rate by 18.1% (U.S. Bureau of the Census, 1960). What is more, the birth rate increased by 10.4% the following year (U.S. Bureau of the Census, 1960) and remained elevated throughout the 1950s. Even at its peak, in 1947, however, the birth rate was only comparable to that of 1925, the most recent birth rate that can be considered "normal," that is, unaffected by the relational trauma of the Great Depression and World War II that severely suppressed the rate at which couples married and/or became parents. Likewise, the marriage rate, which spiked dramatically in 1946, fell in the next year by 11.5% (U.S. Bureau of the Census, 1960) and continued to decline so that, by the end of the decade, it had returned to the 1945 level. Indeed, by 1952 the marriage rate had decreased to prewar levels (U.S. Bureau of the Census, 1960). Notably, the pattern of divorce followed a similar trajectory. In 1946, the divorce rate increased 22.8% over the previous year but decreased by 23.0% in 1947 and by 1950 had stabilized at around 10 per 1,000 married females (U.S. Bureau of the Census, 1960). That is, first, it is as reasonable to conclude that the birth rates in the two decades *prior* to the postwar period were anomalous as to conclude the opposite and, second, there appears to have been a great deal of relational maneuvering immediately subsequent to the war but that maneuvering, in the form of both marriage and divorce, rapidly returned to lower and more ordinary levels.

Examination of patterns of employment and educational achievement also provides a less clearly defined impression of the postwar family than is usually proposed. As is often stressed, women dropped out of the paid workforce in substantial numbers at the end of World War II. Compared to 1945, when 35.9% of adult women worked outside the home, the rate in 1946 fell 13.4% so, at the end of that year, only 31.1% of adult women were employed (U.S. Bureau of the Census, 1960). However, that rate immediately stabilized and by 1956 the proportion of women in the paid workforce was, again, at wartime levels. In fact, even including 1946, postwar employment among women always far exceeded the prewar high water mark.

It is worth noting that the profile of women employed outside the home changed in the postwar period. Between 1945 and 1956, the proportion of 14- to 19-year-old women in the paid workforce declined by 8.0%, and the proportion of 20- to 24-year-olds by 7.7%; in contrast, the proportion of 25- to 44-year-old women in the paid workforce remained essentially unchanged, while the proportion of 45- to 64-year-olds increased by 9.1% and the proportion of women over 64 years old by 1.3% (U.S. Bureau of the Census, 1960). That is, first, there is no support for the notion that middle-class, married women filled the postwar workforce (Mintz & Kellogg, 1988) but, more generally, women employed outside the home in 1956 were older than their wartime counterparts. Nor was this change unique to women. During the same period, the proportion of 14- to 19-year-old men in the paid workforce declined by 13.3%, and the proportion of 20- to 24-year-olds by 4.8% (U.S. Bureau of the Census, 1960). That is, the paid workforce as a whole, both female and male, became relatively older.

One possible explanation for these effects, and one that is consistent with customary observations about the postwar family, is that young males remained outside of the paid workforce because they entered higher education in unprecedented numbers while young females were removed from the workforce, and driven into the home, by their role as wife-mother. However, while it is true that, between 1948 and 1956, the number of baccalaureates awarded to males increased by 12.9%, the number of Master's degrees by 36.1%, and the number of doctorates by 129.8% (U.S. Bureau of the Census, 1960), it is also the case that very similar increases occurred among females. In the same period, the number of baccalaureates awarded to females increased by 15.7%, the number of Master's degrees by 47.3%, and the number of doctorates by 79.5% (U.S. Bureau of the Census, 1960).

This is not to suggest that opportunities outside of the home were not gender-biased nor that large numbers of women did not perform an exclusively familial and domestic role. In 1956, as in 1948, for example, approximately two out of every three degrees awarded were to male students and the discrepancy was even more extreme among doctoral candidates. In 1948, 64.8% of baccalaureates, 68.2% of Master's degrees, and 87.6% of doctoral degrees were awarded to males; in 1956, those proportions had changed minimally and were 64.2%, 66.4%, and 90.1%, respectively (U.S. Bureau of the Census, 1960). Additionally, the public response to Friedan's (1963) claims suggests that some significant number of women developed educational and professional ambitions that were not fulfilled because more compelling cultural expectations assigned them a narrower role inside the family. Nonetheless, the data do argue that discussion of the postwar family frequently exaggerates the extent to which family life and family relations, especially as they involved females, were defined by a renewed and artificial domestic imperative. In fact, it can be argued that, when the socially traumatizing effects of the Great

Depression and World War II are controlled, the postwar family was governed by an ideology that derived directly from an established and evolving system of family values. Further, the changes that occurred in that ideology can be viewed as consistent with a more expansive and ongoing pattern of change in the American family, a pattern characterized by diminished separation of adult sex roles so that spouses were comparatively more likely to share domestic responsibilities, decreased parental authority, especially among fathers, so that parent–child relations became relatively egalitarian, and increased levels of education, among both women and men, so that spouses were more likely than earlier generations to develop similar interests and share the same social network.

Two features of postwar family life, however, are indisputable. First, families were increasingly separated as a function of age, ethnicity, and class so that young, White, middle-class families were more and more commonly situated in the suburbs while older, and/or minority, and/or working-class families remained, for the most part, urbanized. Single-family housing starts, which had returned to prewar levels in 1946, increased by more than 25% in 1947 and by an additional 45.3% in 1950 (over 1949) when more than 1.15 million units were started (U.S. Bureau of the Census, 1960). Because almost all of the construction occurred as part of large-scale suburban development, that population expanded rapidly. Between 1950 and 1970, the suburban population more than doubled, increasing from 36 million to 74 million, an increase that accounted for over 80% of the national population growth (Jones, 1992; May, 1988). What is more, as Gans (1967) noted, those who moved to the suburbs were "primarily young families who came to . . . raise their children" (p. 22). Gans could have added that most of the young families were White. Minority families were routinely marginalized by a mixture of government policy, which denied them access to new communities in the most explicit way; economic factors, which denied them the ability to purchase housing even when provided the opportunity; and social factors, which denied them the sort of friendship and support that new residents find essential. Even in 1958, when families sought to move into the new William Levitt community of Willingboro, New Jersey, "salesmen refused to sell to Negroes and assured whites . . . that the community would be as lily-white as other Levittowns" (Gans, 1967, p. 14).

The postwar family was also prosperous. Propelled by war bond savings in excess of $185 billion (Py-Lieberman, 2002), not only did an unprecedented number of families buy new homes, the majority for the first time, they also installed into those homes all the trappings of the modern family. As Jones (1992) observed, "No one, it seemed, dragged old furniture and appliances from the city apartment to the new 'ranch house.' Besides, there were so many astounding laborsaving devices rolling off the assembly lines. Everything was bought new and at remarkably low prices: refrigerators, deep freezes, barbecues, washer-dryers, butterfly chairs, massive cars, and, of course, televisions" (p. 89). Between 1946 and 1955, retail sales of both nondurable goods and general merchandise increased dramatically (56.0% and 36.5%, respectively), but these increases were dwarfed by the increase in retail sales of durable goods (142.9%). During this period, sales of furniture increased by 87.3%, sales of household appliances by 150.0%, sales of building materials by 100.7%, and sales of hardware by 48.7% (U.S. Bureau of the Census, 1960). That is, prosperity was expressed and enjoyed in the context of the family.

Case Study: Levittown III

Perhaps the most extensive examination of the postwar suburban family is Gans' (1967) analysis of Levittown III (Willingboro). His investigation focuses on the 3,000 families who moved into Willingboro between October, 1958, when the community opened, and June, 1960. While the builder, William Levitt, had intended to exclude "marginal buyers and the socially undesirable or emotionally disturbed" (pp. 13–14), Gans concluded that the families that purchased homes in Willingboro were, in all major respects, like those who had purchased homes in Levitt's earlier developments, in Long Island and Pennsylvania.

In the most general sense, the first residents of Willingboro were "primarily young families who came to the new community to raise their children" (p. 22). Almost 80% of male residents were less than 40 years old, and 44% were between 30 and 40 years of age. Additionally, 84% of the families included at least one child, although almost a third included three or more children. While such homogeneity was not considered unusual and, according to Gans, contributed to the generally high level of sociability among Willingboro residents, it also seems to have promoted the relative social isolation of older residents who often reported that, since moving to the suburbs, they had experienced increased boredom and loneliness.

According to Gans (1967), the initial wave of homebuyers resembled a much broader population in other ways. First, for more than half of the families, the house that they bought in Willingboro was their first home purchase and, for another third it was their second. That is, the early residents reflected the more general move from renting to home ownership that characterized the postwar period. Second, like other new communities, the families of Willingboro were ethnically homogeneous; only 6% of residents were foreign-born and fewer than 1% were African-American. While Levitt voluntarily desegregated Willingboro in early 1960, he did so in the most strategic way, minimizing the number of Black homeowners, and only when confronted with the prospect of court-mandated action. Third, the families reflected a relatively low level of "intergenerational rootedness" (p. 198). Of those families that Gans was able to classify, 57% were defined as "settlers," families who intended to stay permanently in Willingboro, while 43% were defined as either "transients," families who anticipated additional, often work-related, moves, or "mobiles," families who hoped to move into more expensive homes in the future. Gans reasoned that such a mix was common to all new communities in that "intergenerational rootedness is seldom found today in any suburban or urban community—or, for that matter, in most small towns— for it requires the kind of economic stability (and even stagnancy) characteristic only of depressed areas of the country" (Gans, 1967, p. 198).

Gans identified three family types in Willingboro; working class, lower middle-class, which accounted for approximately three fourths of Willingboro families, and upper middle-class. While Gans' labels imply divisions based exclusively on socio-economic status, category membership was a function of a more extensive set of relational attributes that reflected commitment to dissimilar family ideologies. For example, sex roles became less separate across groups such that working-class families were "sexually segregated" (1967, p. 25), whereas upper middle-class families "shed almost all sexual segregation" (p. 30). This meant that, in working-class families, spouses "exchange love and affection, but they have separate family roles and engage in little of the companionship found in the middle-class. The husband is the breadwinner and enforcer of child discipline; the wife is the housekeeper and rears the children" (p. 25). Working-class spouses also appeared to conduct essentially independent lives outside the home in that adult social networks were similarly gender exclusive. In contrast, wives and husbands in upper middle-class families frequently shared both family rights and responsibilities, including those involved in childrearing, and leisure interests. Moreover, many adult females in such families were not only college educated but had developed professional ambitions they sought to pursue in addition to those associated with marriage and parenthood.

Parent–child relations also varied systematically across family types. In working-class families, such relations were "adult-centered" (Gans, 1967, p. 26); that is, children were expected to adhere to a wide variety of parental rules and were punished, often physically, when they did not. Although working-class parents advocated academic achievement, they were necessarily unable to offer themselves as models so that realistic aspirations generally extended no further than high school graduation, especially for girls. In upper middle-class families, meanwhile, parent–child relations were more often "adult-directed" (p. 30); that is, parents provided substantial direction but were comparatively willing for children to engage in creative play. Because upper middle-class parents stressed professional success, they also encouraged high academic achievement, for girls and boys, and often presented themselves as appropriate role models.

The most common family ideology was that presented by lower middle-class families. Most generally, such families attached unusual significance to the family unit. According to Gans, parents supported "cultural values of orderliness, self-reliance, constructive leisure, and above all, the primacy of the home and its moral strictures" (1967, p. 28). Spouses in these families were "closer to being companions" (p. 27) in that they shared a variety of familial duties as well as interests and leisure time. Parent–child relations, meanwhile, were "child-centered" (p. 27); that is, they involved substantial parental discipline, on the one hand, but high levels of child-related play, on the other. Such play was often between siblings and cohorts but often involved parents and adults, too. Finally, while parents of lower middle-class families emphasized academic achievement, they also placed value on interpersonal success and, as such, encouraged both college attendance and friendship development.

An important feature of Gans' analysis is the suggestion that, in many families, spousal sex roles were relatively ambiguous and spousal relations increasingly egalitarian. While Gans (1967) observed that, "even among highly educated Levittowners, the husbands still made the decisions, and women still threatened errant children with 'wait till your father comes home'" (p. 224) and, in his discussion of vitality in Levittown, implied a similar family model, arguing that "mothers get their share of it from the daily adventures of their children and the men get it at work" (p. 201), there is substantial evidence that the integrity of both the "Tarzan" and "Jane" principles had been breached. Not only did Gans observe that "some household roles that were once the woman's monopoly are now shared" (p. 224), he also concluded that "much of the popular talk about an emerging matriarchy strikes me as a misreading of the trend toward greater equality between the sexes—a middle class value which is also being adopted by many working class women these days—and the development of more shared interests, owing to increased (and increasingly coeducational) schooling for women" (p. 224).

This suggests a system of family life and family relations not unlike that proposed in the present inquiry. In some families, especially working-class families, rights and responsibilities appear to have been distributed orthogonally; males assumed a provider role and retained final authority, even in the home where they were otherwise minimally involved, while females fulfilled an exclusively domestic role defined largely by traditional duties associated with childrearing, cleaning, and meal preparation. In such families, children were socialized to "stay out of trouble" so that parent–child relations were rule-governed and children were punished when they violated those rules. In most families, however, adult sex roles appear to have been considerably less distinct. Males typically shared in childrearing as well as other domestic tasks, and females often developed ambitions outside of the family. Spousal and parent–child relations seem to have involved mutual affection, commitment, and interest and, for the most part, to have been relatively egalitarian, although both seem to have acknowledged the husband-father's fundamental authority.

ONTO THE SCREEN: THE FAMILY
ON TELEVISION

From the very outset, domestic comedy has been a staple of commercial television. Families like the Aldriches (*The Aldrich Family*) and Rileys (*The Life of Riley*) were transported from radio and immediately became popular, perhaps because they provided the new viewer a sense of continuity and familiarity, and, by 1951, *I Love Lucy*, featuring the Ricardos, had become the most watched television show in America.

These families and others of the postwar period are important for two reasons. Most basically, they comprise the "Adam and Eve" generation and, as such, are critical to describing and evaluating the development of the family on television. At the same time, popular portrayals, especially those on television, are seen not only to have defined current understanding of real postwar families but are posited to have misrepresented real family life and, so, contributed substantially to the (erroneous) conclusion that the contemporary family is in decay (Coontz, 1992; Jones, 1992; Skolnick, 1991). While this hypothesis is complex, it predicts significant differences between television family life and real family life and, so, can be tested, in part, by assessing the extent to which television portrayals of the period were (in)consistent with what is known or can be inferred about life and relations in real postwar families.

In the most general sense, examination of postwar domestic comedy reveals that, across time, struggling urban families, such as the Goldbergs (*The Goldbergs*), Kramdens (*The Honeymooners*), and the Jones and Stevens families of *Amos'n'Andy*, gave way to prosperous suburban families, like the

Nelsons (*The Adventures of Ozzie and Harriet*), Andersons (*Father Knows Best*), and Cleavers (*Leave it to Beaver*). In the process, apartment renters gave way to homeowners and minority and/or working-class families, often childless, gave way to White, middle-class, child-centered families. Notably, the most popular television family of the period, the Ricardos, narrated many of these trends in a self-contained way, evolving from a lower middle-class couple who rented an apartment in New York city and often found it difficult to pay their bills on time into suburban parents with their own, well-furnished, ranch-style home.

Kozol (1994) argued that *Life* magazine's depiction of postwar America failed to address the experiences of minority families and, thereby, reproduced "a discourse of racism" (p. 54). Clearly, television's exposition of the postwar family was similarly limited and can be criticized as both racist and classist. At the same time, however, the portrayals appear demographically authentic. As broad census data as well as more holistic studies, such as Gans' (1967) analysis of Levittown, show, the postwar population, especially the White, middle-class population, did move to the suburbs and, when they did, many became parents; that is, the suburban experience was, itself, racist and classist and was commonly constructed so as to accommodate children. This is not to suggest that television portrayals should be considered entirely veridical, even at such a general level. In particular, television presented an unrealistically mature version of suburbia; clean neighborhoods, completed houses, schools, shopping centers, parks, manicured lawns, shady trees, and flowers and shrubs in bloom. Not only may this "nothing under construction" vision of suburbia have provided a sense of what neighborhoods could and should become and, so, functioned as a salve to displaced television viewers (Jones, 1992; Spigel, 1992), it also relieved television families of the uncertainty and stress inherent in large-scale, residential development. Nonetheless, contemporary audiences judged the portrayals realistic (Haralovich, 1989; Leibman, 1995), suggesting that, although television distorted the suburban family experience, such distortions may have been overwhelmed by a broader sense of reality and, so, incidental to the familial meanings that viewers constructed. At the very least, within the narrow suburban band of domestic comedy, there does appear to be substantial demographic congruity between real families and those on television.

Power and Affect in the Family

Power and affect in the television family should be examined in the context of tensions that defined life and relations in real postwar families: on the one hand, tension due to the oppositional demands of the strong man and the family man and, on the other, tension produced by the divergent expectations of the educated woman and the happy housewife. These tensions derived most obviously from the Depression and war experiences that had destabilized the family and made images of male strength and female domesticity salient; the postwar emphasis on the family's reconstruction, which encouraged young couples to negotiate their ambitions and identities in the context of marriage and parenthood; and the democratization of education that occurred during the period and produced comparatively large numbers of educated women, particularly among the expanding suburban middle class.

The usual conclusion is that, in television families, these tensions were resolved through a system of family rights and responsibilities that invested males with wide authority, extending explicitly to family life, and allowed females to be articulate and thoughtful but, nonetheless, satisfied with an exclusively domestic role. According to this position, male power derived, in part, from their publicly centered provider role, although even professional achievement was narrated through the family in the form of furnishings, gadgets, and other symbols of domesticity, and emerged, too, from the family itself. Not only were adult males not portrayed without family but they appeared to enjoy their place in the family and their time spent with the family, which was considerable. At the same time, women adhered to a domestic ideology into which a thin intelligence was incorporated, producing a popular image of the wife-mother reminiscent of the Blondie Bumstead model.

These resolutions are apparent in the following advice offered to Harriet Nelson by her friend, Helen, and the subsequent exchange between Harriet and her husband, Ozzie. At the outset of the episode, Helen "stops by" on her way home from the beauty parlor and reflects that "the longer I sat in the beauty parlor, the more I got to feeling sorry for that poor husband of mine . . . Oh, nothing's wrong. I just couldn't stop thinking about him. There I was, getting my hair done, nails manicured. Somebody brought me a sandwich and coffee and practically fed me my lunch. And I suddenly realized what a glorious life we women lead . . . I really mean it. I just couldn't stop thinking about it. The poor guy comes home from work tired and, before he even gets in the door, I start boring him with all my troubles. . . . Big important things; like the difficulty I had picking out a head of lettuce at the market or a magazine salesman who sold me a subscription that's good until 1961. I'm telling you Harriet, that poor husband of mine never gets a minute's rest." She then recounts the story of a friend who, like Harriet, thought that her husband liked "staying home, helping out." "She insisted her husband, Harry, stay home every night. And he did, for eight long years. Then, one night, some girl came to the door selling some new kind of suspenders and, well, Harry hasn't been home since."

As a consequence of this conversation, Harriet invites Ozzie to spend the night with his friends. After trudging around town alone for 4 hours, Ozzie returns home and explains that "all the other men are home with their families where they belong." Harriet, then, admits, "we'd have been much happier if you'd stayed at home with us. The boys and I didn't do as well as you think we did. In fact, we needed your help desperately . . . Ricky couldn't do any of his algebra problems, so that means he'll get a failing mark tomorrow, and David got just about one paragraph of his English composition done. And I've made a complete mess out of the bank balance; comes out different every time I add it up. Honestly, I never saw so many nines and sevens in all my life; I ran out of fingers." The scene closes with Ozzie asking, "Are you sure you aren't saying this just to make me feel happy?"

These interactions are fairly representative of those postwar television families that are most commonly seen to articulate the traditional family, the Andersons, Nelsons, and Cleavers, and map a comparatively complex relational topography. First, there is strain toward a primitive "Tarzan–Jane" dichotomy and, to some extent, the attendant witless wife stereotype; the husbands provide through their strenuous efforts in the workplace, the wives stay home and spend time improving their appearance and dealing, sometimes ineffectively, with low level domestic issues, and Harriet, in particular, is stereotypically unable to perform basic arithmetic functions.

Previous analyses have focused most extensively on this aspect of the postwar television family. Critics have concluded uniformly that popular depictions, including those on television, contrived a family model defined by a gender-based system of rights and responsibilities that promoted conservative revision of both the "Tarzan" and "Jane" principles. Leibman (1995), for example, argued that, in television presentations, "men and boys are associated ideally with strength, intelligence, logic, consistency, and humor, while girls are rendered intuitive, dependent, flighty, sentimental, and self-sacrificing" (p. 174). According to Leibman, television family narrative not only "commands that women and girls marry and that men and boys take responsibility for their actions" (p. 174) but invests males with power, both as a function of their authority inside the family and the way in which action is contextualized, while at the same time trivializing the role of females. For instance, Leibman proposed that television fathers control the distribution of rewards and punishments in the family and are empowered further because family interaction often occurs in male space, the living room, the dining room, and the spouses' bedroom. Television mothers, meanwhile, are seen to

be marginalized both because they can legitimately offer praise and exert discipline only in mundane circumstances, such as those surrounding infant
care, and because they are typically situated in the kitchen where their authority is undermined by the domestic nature of their work (see also Haralovich,
1989; Jones, 1992; May, 1988; Spigel, 1992).

According to this position, television not only articulated a "dominant
male provider–subservient female caregiver" family model but advocated that
model through story lines that repeatedly associated positive consequences,
prosperity, and harmony, with families such as the Andersons, Nelsons, and
Cleavers, who abided by such a system and negative consequences with those
who, in one way or another, violated the mandate (Jones, 1992; Long, 1985).
These revised versions of the "Tarzan" and "Jane" principles would be violated, on the one hand, by a father-husband who was either insufficiently
dominant and/or unable to provide adequately for his family, such as Ralph
Kramden (*The Honeymooners*), and, on the other, by a wife-mother who was
either too assertive and/or unable to nurture her family, such as Lucy Ricardo
(Jones, 1992; Spigel, 1992).

Although such a model is consistent with popular understanding of the
postwar family and offers a reasonable fit with television family interaction,
it places heavy emphasis on spousal relations and, so, is relatively insensitive
to the ways in which sex roles, in particular, and power and affect, in general,
are defined in other family relationships. Moreover, despite its intuitive and
empirical appeal, the model probably overstates the extent to which television
spouses adhered to such primitive role and relational profiles and, as such,
encourages an undifferentiated and potentially misleading sense of life and
relations in postwar families. For example, Jones (1992) described Lucy
Ricardo as "a hapless victim of modern tensions" (p. 70) because her personal
ambition is subverted by her husband, Ricky, who wants "a wife who's just a
wife." Indeed, in that same exchange, Ricky explains to Lucy that "all you have
to do is clean the house for me, bring me my slippers when I come home at
night, cook for me, and be the mother of my children." However, this scene,
which is prompted by Lucy's desire to appear on television, does not end in
ways that confirm either an extreme "Tarzan–Jane" dichotomy or the fatuous,
dependent wife-mother; Lucy is not only successful in her audition but is
offered a television contract which, notably, she does not refuse, suggesting a
considerably more ambiguous family narrative than is ordinarily supposed.

A similar ambiguity is inherent in the sequence from *The Adventures of
Ozzie and Harriet.* Most obviously, the sequence shifts the locus of the
"Tarzan" principle further inside the family so that husband-fathers do not
simply hold authority in the family but function as an integrated part of the

family and accrue power because of their familial expertise. On their visits to Middletown, the Lynds (1937, 1956) observed that males and females shared marriage but, otherwise, moved in separate spheres. In fiction, Dagwood Bumstead enjoyed special authority in family relations as a consequence of his gender but was inexpert in the home, whether the issues involved infant care, children's homework, paying bills, or repairing appliances, and complained that "marriage is a wonderful institution. It teaches a man to be thrifty, patient, persevering, understanding, punctual, and many other things he wouldn't need if he stayed single" (C. Young, 1945–1980, p. 153). In contrast, Ozzie Nelson recognizes, first, that a male's natural place is with his family; he reports to Harriet that "all the other men are home with their families where they belong." What is more, Ozzie is instrumental to family well-being and appears to enjoy his role; not only do none of the family succeed without his help but he does not complain about their dependence and, instead, asks Harriet whether her admission of family failure is simply designed to make him feel happy.

Harriet and her friend, Helen, also articulate a relatively thoughtful version of the "Jane" principle. Although, like Blondie Bumstead, they are economically and, at times, intellectually dependent, these wife-mothers are considerably more self-reflective. They understand the cultural and personal significance of the family and work to maintain family stability. Moreover, their failings are not individual failings but family failings; the wife-mother fails intellectually without her husband, the sons fail academically without their father, and the father fails socially and personally without his wife and children. The lesson, here, is that family is fundamental and needs all of its parts to function effectively so that a wife-mother's place *and* a husband-father's place is in the home.

It is worth noting, first, that domestic revision of the "Tarzan" principle reduced the distance between husband-fathers and wife-mothers, especially to the extent that the "Jane" principle encouraged wife-mothers to be more contemplative. That is, television portrayals suggest that sex roles became more symmetrical in the postwar family. Second, high school students in Middletown had previously indicated that the most desirable attribute in a father and the second most desirable attribute in a mother (second, that is, to "being a good cook and housewife") was "spending time with his/her children" (Lynd & Lynd, 1956), implying that a more involved relationship between husband-father and family was, at the very least, desirable and may have occurred in real families. Third, children were essential to domestic revision of the "Tarzan" principle. Children have previously been considered symbolically important to the postwar family, in part because they signaled a husband-father's virility and success as a provider. May (1988), for instance, has observed that, according to postwar doctrine, fatherhood "tamed the husband's extravagance, making him a responsible provider" (p. 145) so that children "were an identification of a man's potency and ability to provide" (p. 159). Kozol (1994) presented a similar position, arguing that "fatherhood became a defining characteristic of masculinity and maturity" (p. 77). The present analysis suggests that children may also have been significant because they functioned to integrate the potentially divergent role requirements of the strong man and the family man. Not only did the increasingly sentimental view of children (May, 1995; Uhlenberg, 1989) increase the value of parent–child interaction but contemporary childrearing practices emphasized toughness and adventure in young boys (Sears, Maccoby, & Levin, 1957), so that the family involvement of real husband-fathers may have been rationalized on the basis that child care was a significant undertaking and/or that his participation was necessary to moderate the wife-mother's inherent timidity. Certainly, in the Anderson, Nelson, and Cleaver families, spouses repeatedly acted in this way; husband-fathers were both attentive to their children and routinely discouraged wife-mothers from interfering in children's activities, whether those activities were playing sports (the Andersons), riding motorcycles (the Nelsons), or traveling on the train alone (the Cleavers).

It should be made explicit that child-centered revision of the "Tarzan" and "Jane" principles as well as the more general rules concerning the distribution of power and regulation of affect reflected life and relations in middle-class television families. For a variety of reasons, working-class families failed to fulfill that mandate. Some working-class families, like the Kramdens, were childless so that there was no straightforward reconciliation of the strong man and the family man; Ralph Kramden's frustration, his inability to succeed, and his physical threats to Alice can all be read as outcomes of that unresolved tension. In others, such as the Rileys, the husband-father was portrayed as incompetent and bumbling and the wife-mother as responsible and able (Andreasen, 1990; Butsch, 1992; Cantor, 1991; Glennon & Butsch, 1982), producing a quite different family dynamic. Nonetheless, because the working-class family quickly disappeared from domestic comedy, it was a middle-class family ideology that became dominant.

Family Performance

According to Fitzpatrick and Badzinski's extensive reviews of the family literature (1985, 1994), family performance involves a variety of responsibilities, such as conflict management, child socialization, and management of the daily routine. Although the conclusion that the family has decayed across time derives, in part, from the belief that the postwar family performed such tasks more effectively, and although contemporary understanding of the postwar family is often seen to rely on popular portrayals, especially those on television, little has been written about the ability of the Andersons, Nelsons, and other fictional families to perform such tasks.

Previous investigations of family performance in the postwar television family have focused exclusively on conflict and conflict management and argue a system in which spousal relations were conflict-free and parents cooperated to resolve low-level sibling disputes (Cantor, 1991; Lichter et al., 1988; Moore, 1992; Taylor, 1989). Taylor (1989), for example, concluded that "television children of the 1950s and 1960s inhabited a universe in which mild sibling quarrels were quickly but fairly adjudicated by sage, kindly parents equipped with endless reserves of time and patience" (p. 27). Examination of the Andersons, Nelsons, and Cleavers confirms this model. In each instance, wives and husbands appear to share a loving relationship in which disagreements are effectively managed either through amicable negotiation, acquiescence by one partner, or good-natured attribution to the partner's fundamental nature, particularly gender. In these families, conflict involving children, although common, is short-lived and resolved by parents, most often the husband-father, in ways that provide children important personal, relational, and/or civic insights.

The postwar television family also performs effectively in other ways. Children are socialized to value systems that emphasize achievement through hard work, respect for others, including those "less fortunate," commitment to family and community, and self-reliance. Socialization is achieved both actively, through mindfully enacted strategies, and passively, through example. As well, while socialization is most clearly a parent-to-child process, it also occurs between siblings; that is, older siblings generally encourage younger children to perform effectively and frequently provide relevant advice and instruction.

It is important to note, again, that these observations do not generalize to working-class families. In particular, such families appear more conflictual and less able to resolve conflict when it occurs. The Kramdens, for example, appear to share a substantially troubled relationship in which high levels of conflict are ordinary and involve mutually altered speech patterns (for example, raised voices, talk-overs, and interruptions), mutual personal disconfirmation (for example, name-calling and attribution of the other's success to chance), and mutual threat (for example, to deprive or hit the other). Moreover, conflict frequently leaks across content domains and involves past events so that conflict resolution is an untidy process and often relies on the intervention of others.

Relational Satisfaction and Family Stability

According to social exchange theory (Kelley, 1979; Kelley & Thibaut, 1978; Thibaut & Kelley, 1959), relational satisfaction and stability are a function of the relational outcomes that persons experience, their general expectations about appropriate rewards and costs in such a relationship (comparison level), and the extent to which other available relationships offer either increased profits or decreased losses (comparison level for alternatives). Relational satisfaction is determined by comparison of present relational outcomes and comparison level while relational stability is fixed through comparison of present relational outcomes and comparison level for alternatives. To the extent that partners' current rewards-to-costs ratio exceeds what they believe is appropriate or customary, the relationship is satisfying; to the extent that partners' current rewards-to-costs ratio exceeds what is available elsewhere, the relationship is stable.

Domestic comedy has always offered an unrealistically satisfying and stable view of the family; couples do not divorce, even when their marriage appears unhappy, children are not abandoned and do not run away from home, and family members are rarely threatened by serious illness. Likewise, a television family's evolution is severely limited and tied to their popularity so that viewers are generally uninformed about long-term relational satisfaction and family stability. For example, the transition from active parenthood to "empty nest" is absent from domestic comedy, as are the adult lives and relationships of television children and their subsequent commitment to parents and siblings.

Such a narrow and friendly portrayal contributes to an extremely optimistic view of postwar family relations. As is apparent in the exchange between Ozzie and Harriet Nelson, family relationships appear highly satisfying and provide rewards unavailable elsewhere. Indeed, in families like the Nelsons, Andersons, and Cleavers, persons routinely acknowledge that they feel fortunate to be part of such a family. As such, the portrayals imply high relational satisfaction, because persons' current relational outcomes far and explicitly exceed what they believe to be normal, and, because persons are mutually dependent, convey extreme family stability. Ozzie and Harriet Nelson will always love each other and remain together, as will Jim and Mary

Anderson and Ward and June Cleaver; likewise, holiday celebrations will always be family celebrations for these families, parents and children will continue to come together to celebrate their shared familial construction.

CONCLUSIONS AND IMPLICATIONS

Although it has become popular to dismiss the postwar family as an unnatural artifact of government policy and popular culture, considerable evidence suggests an opposite view. Sociological analyses of family life in Middletown (Lynd & Lynd, 1937, 1956) and Levittown (Gans, 1967), together with more particular data concerning persons' relational, professional, and academic choices, suggests that the 1950s family, characterized by gender-based separation of public and private space, increased sharing of a variety of family responsibilities, and child-centered family relations, fits comfortably into a coherent sequence of family change. Indeed, it can be argued that any appearance of abnormality accrues from the two prior decades when deep economic depression and global war suppressed couples' willingness to marry and/or have children and so disrupted normal development and ongoing revision of the family. Likewise, television families of the period, even though they were often situated in contexts that were both demographically and emotionally sterile, were judged by contemporary audiences as fundamentally authentic (Haralovich, 1989; Jones, 1992; Leibman, 1995; Spigel, 1992). Certainly, families like the Ricardos, Nelsons, Andersons, and Cleavers appear to have mapped the complex distribution of power, gender, and age that kept intact the traditional division of spousal roles but placed growing priority on shared parental authority and situated children at the center of the modern family.

Such convergence between the dominant postwar family ideology and the value system reflected by popular television families of the period reinforces the sense of conjunction between real and fictional families. This is a position that those involved in television and even media researchers often disavow, arguing, instead, that domestic comedy is designed simply to entertain and, so, radically distorts the family experience. In his criticism of the film industry, for instance, Rainer (1995, p. 24) complained that, "when some of us are primed for movies that really speak to us about the disarray of modern families, we're fobbed off with movies that resemble big-screen sitcoms," implying that television portrayals bear little or no resemblance to actual family life. However, to the extent that action is cognitively mediated and to the extent that television portrayals influence cognition, as is routinely argued (Andersen, 1993; Brown et al., 1990; Buerkel-Rothfuss & Mayes, 1981; Gans, 1968;

Meadowcroft & Fitzpatrick, 1988; Robinson et al., 1985; Wober & Gunter, 1987), then some connection between real and fictional family relations appears inevitable. Such linkage is suggested, too, by a considerable volume of anecdotal evidence. Breines (1992), for example, has argued that the symbols of rebellion offered by postwar popular culture were, like those in society, gender-biased. Similarly, in her recent analysis of male culture, Faludi (1999) observed that the strong father–son culture of the 1950s was not limited to shows like *Father Knows Best* and *Leave It to Beaver* but was a fixed reality in her own neighborhood and elsewhere.

Again, this is not to argue that television families narrated the postwar audience experience directly. Obvious and important differences separate the real 1950s family from its television surrogate. Nonetheless, the preceding analysis suggests something more than trivial similarity between the family at home and the family on television and, furthermore, suggests that similarity derived not from what the television family looked like but, instead, from how family members acted toward each other and the family's everyday surroundings. That is, the conjunction between real and television families seems not to be demographically based, although the presence of children may be critical, but to accrue, instead, from relational cues and the routine familiarity of day-to-day family life.

Subsequent chapters sought to map the development of television families and, more specifically, to test the "double decay hypothesis." In particular, the investigation sought to assess the extent to which television family life and family relations have become distressed in ways that are seen to characterize the real family experience (e.g., Popenoe, 1988, 1993a, 1993b, 1995, 1996).

Chapter 5

Development of the Television Family:
I. Spousal Relations

In the half-century since the end of World War II, the changing role of women has dominated the development of family life and family relations. Debate about the issue has cascaded through society, igniting concerned discussion about everything from diminished educational achievement among children to the viability of the traditional family. It is not that the familial rights and responsibilities of women had previously been irrelevant to the family experience. Indeed, the history of the American family reveals not only that women repeatedly redefined their publicly assumed nature and place but also that, in doing so, they exerted substantial influence on both family functioning and family relations. Certainly, women's evolving sense of themselves did not escape the Lynds (Lynd & Lynd, 1937), who argued that, as they reconstructed their social identity, women were "incidentally changing significantly the pattern of 'marriage,' 'family life,' 'wife,' and 'mother' in Middletown" (p. 181).

In postwar America, controversy about the familial role of women and its corollary, feminization of the workplace, has simply assumed a larger scale. Skolnick (1991), in fact, has gone so far as to argue that, by the mid-1970s, family life had been devastated by the "third Big One," a strongly feminist ideological upheaval that demolished "structures that had, little more than a decade before, seemed stable and changeless—lifelong marriage, sexual morality, parental authority, the 'traditional' family" (p. 127). According to Skolnick, a gender-based family model was not only anachronistic but, because women were unchallenged and unfulfilled by the day-to-day reality of homemaking and child care, implicitly dysfunctional.

A similar, although less extreme, impression emerges from the third analysis of Middletown (Caplow et al., 1982). Perhaps most fundamentally, Caplow and his colleagues noted that, as had been the case four decades earlier, "a significant majority of the population conformed to the norm by living in a family household composed of a married pair and their unmarried offspring, in a house they owned, on a residential street surrounded on all sides by houses of similar size and value" (Caplow et al., 1982, pp. 14–15). They observed, too, that much of the family routine remained gender specific; child care, housekeeping, and maintaining contact with family and friends were still considered "female" activities while providing the family income and effecting home repair continued to be defined as "male" activities. As such, the researchers concluded that, "Among Middletown's married women, at any rate, the seminal ideas of feminism fall on barren ground" (Caplow et al., 1982, p. 115).

At the same time, however, the investigators reported that most Middletowners believed there had been considerable change in the identity and expectations of women. Not only did contemporary Middletown women look unlike their 1935 counterparts, something that was not true of Middletown men, but many women had begun to think and behave in dissimilar ways, as well. Regardless of class, for example, modern women spent substantially less time performing housework and substantially more time working for pay and/or interacting with their children than had earlier generations. Consistent with this, marriage relations had changed to become more egalitarian so that contemporary spouses talked more frequently and more openly with each other and spent more leisure time together. Perhaps because marriage had altered so dramatically, now involving strong and mutual expectations of companionship, and perhaps because an increased number of women had established some level of economic independence, divorce had become more common, too. By 1975, 59% of Middletown's adult population had experienced at least one divorce in their direct family, leading the researchers to conclude that, "Divorce, like marriage, is a normal part of life; and most people do not expect marriages to last forever" (Caplow et al., 1982, p. 53).

Hence, by the mid-1970s, several broad statements about the family appear justified. First, marriage and family continued to be a potent ambition for many young couples. Although the average age of marriage and of parenthood had increased since the 1950s and although the fertility rate had declined, marriage remained commonplace and, once married, couples were expected to produce children. Second, the implicit marriage contract had changed to accommodate the elevated promise of matrimony, shared decision making, female sexuality, and traditionally female values such as openness, conversational intimacy, and supportiveness. Marriage had also become less fixed. Divorce had lost its stigmatizing bite and was becoming routine, although probably not as widespread as many people imagined (Caplow et al., 1982). Finally, while some women continued to choose a traditional and domestic role, the opportunities available to women extended beyond that narrow confine, and increasing numbers of women were pursuing educational and professional options outside the family context. In a broader sense, even relatively poorly educated and older women were more often seeking employment outside the home.

Clearly, these trends have continued and have continued to influence family life and family relations. Although increasing numbers of people seek alternatives, marriage remains the default choice of the vast majority of Americans. In 1998, 56% of American adults were married and living with their partner and another 10% were divorced; likewise, among persons 25 to 34 years old, 65% were or had been married (U.S. Bureau of the Census, 1998). In the same way, while more and more women have chosen to remain childless, or, at least, to delay pregnancy, parenthood remains the norm. For example, between 1976 and 1990 the percentage of childless women between 30 and 34 years old rose from 16% to 25% (May, 1995); that is, even in 1990, 75% of women in this age group had at least one child. It appears, too, that marriage has continued to be revised toward an egalitarian model. Skolnick (1991), for example, concluded that modern marriage "portrays husband and wife not just as companions but as best friends, emotional intimates, and fulfilling sex partners. It has been infused with feminist as well as 'therapeutic' sensibilities, emphasizing the husband's participation in child care as well as emotional candor and talk about feelings" (p. 191). Similarly, Driscoll (1996) proposed that marriage has come to be based on consensual love and, so, emphasizes negotiation and mutual agreement between partners. Of course, while "marriage, with children, remains the preferred cultural norm" (Skolnick, 1991, p. 220), divorce, too, has become more common. The divorce rate, which, in 1970, was 42.3 divorces per 100 marriages had, by 1990, increased to 54.8 divorces per 100 marriages (The Population Council, 1995), suggesting that marriage had become even more open-ended than in the mid-1970s. Finally, the migration of women into the paid workforce has not simply continued, it has accelerated. According to the Select Committee on Children, Youth, and Families (1987), 47% of mothers worked either full-time or part-time in 1975; by 1985, 69% did so. Moreover, a 1995 survey of 1,502 American women (Friedman, 1995) showed that 45% were employed full-time outside of the home, 15% were employed part-time, and a further 8% were self-employed; only 17% were described as "homemakers."

The redefinition of females' familial role was paralleled by revision of males' family rights and responsibilities. In some instances, male expectations changed as a function of those applied to women. Men, for example, were increasingly expected to provide support and sexual satisfaction and to play some part in childrearing and housekeeping, although both latter activities continued to be associated primarily with women, even those employed outside of the home. In other instances, however, male expectations changed in response to a more general feature of the postwar marriage arrangement.

After World War II, the family experience was increasingly a suburban experience. What is more, not only did many new suburbanites subscribe to a family model that defined the father as provider but, because suburbia routinely separated home and workplace, they inadvertently supported a model that distanced fathers from wives and children. The consequences of such an arrangement have been seen by some as catastrophic. Popenoe (1996), for example, has asserted that, in the immediate aftermath of World War II, "fatherhood again became a defining identity for many men, a fact that was highlighted by such popular television characters as Ward Cleaver and Ozzie Nelson, whose lives beyond the confines of their father role always remained vague and amorphous" (p. 128). Such involvement, Popenoe argues, was incongruent with the role of provider, which narrowed a father's place in the day-to-day routine, placing him at the periphery of family life and eroding family attachments, especially those between father and children.

Working from a quite different set of social assumptions, Faludi (1999) has articulated a similar position. In her analysis of the American male, Faludi argues, first, that the strong father–son relations available in television programs, such as *The Adventures of Ozzie and Harriet* and *Leave It to Beaver,* were reflections of real-life family relations familiar in every suburb. Even more pointedly, Faludi claims that postwar America was "the era of the boy. It was the culture of *Father Knows Best* and *Leave It to Beaver,* of Pop Warner rituals and Westinghouse science scholarships, of BB guns and rocket clubs, of football practice and lettered jackets, of magazine ads where "Dad" seemed always beaming down at his scampy, cowboy-suited younger son or proudly handing his older son the keys to a brand-new tail-finned convertible. It was father–son Eden" (p. 24). According to Faludi, this closeness between fathers and sons together with fathers' rootedness in the family was destroyed because fathers, distracted by the need to provide, "so often seemed spectral, there and yet not there, 'heads' of households strangely disconnected from the familial body" (p. 597).

The similarities between Popenoe's (1996) position and that of Faludi (1999) are apparent. First, both reflect on a brief period during which fathers contributed significantly to life and relations in the postwar family. Second, both argue that fathers became physically and emotionally separated from the family, confined by the limited rights and limiting responsibilities of their role as provider. And, finally, both Popenoe (1996) and Faludi (1999) invoke television portrayals of the time to illustrate and verify their arguments, again suggesting that television families do not function simply as entertainment but, in a variety of ways, may provide insight into real family life.

It should be added that this is especially important because the family experience has become increasingly privatized. Even in Willingboro, where similarities of age, income, and general circumstance induced relatively elevated levels of interaction among the first residents, Gans (1967) reported that there was a limit to persons' openness, that Levittowners subscribed to the social rule that "what people do inside their houses is considered their own affair" (p. 177). Indeed, even formal study of the contemporary family is more often based on examination of family structure than family life (Skolnick, 1991).

TELEVISION FAMILIES: POWER AND AFFECT IN SPOUSAL RELATIONS

Analysis of the ways in which power and affect are manifest in fictional spousal relations will be conducted within a framework that examines separately sex roles, relational supportiveness, and communication. Each of these areas is then divided further: investigation of spousal sex roles involves discussion of dominance/equality and family function; investigation of spousal supportiveness involves discussion of involvement, attraction, including sexual attraction, and receptivity-trust; and investigation of spousal communication involves discussion of the formality of interaction as well as the extent to which spouses use communication to influence each other.

Spousal Sex Roles in Television Families

In general, the relationship between television spouses has become more egalitarian across time. Contrary to intuition, in early portrayals wives seem to have been more competent and more dominant than their male partners. A contemporary critic, for example, concluded that, in such presentations as "'Life of Riley,' 'The Adventures of Ozzie and Harriet,' 'Father Knows Best,' 'Make Room for Daddy,' and numerous others, it is made quite clear that the modern father is an overgrown adolescent, a boob, and a nitwit, who is no match for all the rest of the family" (Hunt, 1955, p. 21).

Such female authority, reminiscent of Blondie's in her marriage to Dagwood, appears to have been short-lived, especially in middle-class television families. In his analysis of domestic comedy during the 1960s, Newcomb (1974) argued that middle-class husbands and fathers governed the family, accruing power, first, from their decision-making ability and, second, from their benevolent wisdom. More generally, Leibman (1995) proposed that, in television families, power is distributed as a function of gender and, to a much lesser extent, age, so that even sons exert more authority than mothers. Husbands and fathers, meanwhile, derive influence from a variety of factors, including their conversational prominence, their overall level of activity, and their granted ability to regulate rewards and discipline in the family.

Middle-class women, of course, quickly came to be defined by their domestic subservience. Perhaps the most extreme example of this willing servility is Samantha Stevens (*Bewitched*), who remained "a contented suburban wifette" (Marc, 1989, p. 135) despite her magical powers, which she subverted in behalf of her husband's career. The tradition, however, was substantially more widespread. Taylor (1989), for example, proposed that even "Lear women" were marginalized by their moral, family imperative. Specifically, Taylor suggested that, unlike men who often acted strategically, such women were constructed to demonstrate that "honesty, integrity, kindness, and social responsibility always pay, while deviousness and mean-spirited behavior are doomed to ignominious failure" (p. 82).

The empowerment of men, and the attendant marginalization of women, did not extend to working-class television families. Instead, husbands such as Ralph Kramden (*The Honeymooners*), Chester Riley (*The Life of Riley*), Lars Hansen (*I Remember Mama*), and, later, Archie Bunker (*All in the Family*), Fred Sanford (*Sanford and Son*), and James Evans (*Good Times*) were portrayed as inept, immature, stupid, lacking good sense, and emotional (Glennon & Butsch, 1982). That is, they were invested with attributes typically associated with television women so that the "composite image is of a demasculinized working-class man whose gender status is inverted" (Butsch, 1992, p. 397). In contrast, working-class wives have been presented in generally positive ways, as relatively intelligent, rational, responsible, and so on, emphasizing the departure from the middle-class model. What is more, there is evidence that this tradition has continued. First, Marc (1989) has concluded that popular culture, in general, and television, in particular, habitually present middle-class characters as "soft-spoken, rational, successful, and fair-minded" but portray working-class characters as "loud, emotional, static" (p. 174). Second, in his more recent analysis of the husband/father character, Walsh (1995) dismissed Dan Conner (*Roseanne*) as an example of the "soft man," arguing that he "seems a strong, hard worker, sensitive and funny, but when it comes to asserting himself in the house, often he disappears, runs, leaving the vital Roseanne to discipline or instruct or nurture" (p. 19). Hence, it does seem that working-class spouses routinely exhibit a gender inversion in which husbands appear inept and relatively powerless and wives appear competent and relatively powerful.

Although there is some disagreement, the balance of evidence suggests that the distribution of power in spousal relations has become more balanced. That is, while some observers have claimed that modern wives continue to promote a passive and traditional image (Silver, 1995) and that modern husbands frequently display an assortment of negative attributes, including oafishness (Zoglin, 1990), rudeness, and sexism (Gates, 2000), more formal analyses advocate a contrary position. Based on her comprehensive review of the television family, Cantor (1991), for example, concluded that spousal relations have become noncompetitive and relatively equal (see also Cantor & Cantor, 1992). Likewise, after showing participant viewers examples of families in domestic comedy, ranging from the Ricardos (*I Love Lucy*) and Andersons (*Father Knows Best*) to the Conners (*Roseanne*) and Taylors (*Home Improvement*), Douglas and Olson (1995) reported that contemporary wives and husbands were judged more equal than earlier couples.

Of course, while the distribution of relational power may be affected by partners' efforts to dominate or influence each other, and while specific attributes and ideologies may predispose a partner to seek or avoid authority, control is embedded in partners' rights and responsibilities, their prescribed functions inside the family. Clearly, those rights and responsibilities have changed dramatically across time.

Early studies consistently revealed that television confined wives to an essentially domestic role and husbands to the role of provider. J. McNeil (1975), for example, reported that female characters were more likely to be associated with family themes, in both their daily work and their interactions, and four times less likely to be presented as the primary provider than male characters. Less than a quarter of the married women in McNeil's sample were employed outside the home and those who were held less powerful positions than their male counterparts. Likewise, Seggar (1975) observed that women were less likely than men to pursue professional careers, and Feshbach, Dillman, and Jordan (1979), Signorielli (1982), and Press and Strathman (1994) noted that wives and mothers were rarely presented in work situations but, rather, were recurrently rooted in the home and family. Consistent with these findings, research has also shown that spousal relations were often portrayed stereotypically so that males acted in instrumental ways and wives in expressive ways (Fitzpatrick, 1987; Reep & Dambrot, 1989; Shaner, 1982). Several authors have taken the position that the roles of nurturer/caregiver and provider are not only value-laden but implicit in the distribution and use of domestic space. Newcomb (1974), for example, proposed a convention in which the kitchen, a place of work, is defined as female space so that inter-action occurring there must be understood as "softer, more 'feminine'" (p. 45). The living room, meanwhile, is defined as male space, a place where husbands and fathers relax and, as such, a symbol of male authority. Similarly, Haralovich (1989) argued that, unlike husbands, wives do not have private space in the home. Their space, and their influence, is restricted to places such as the kitchen and dining room, that is, family or communal space where authority is more ambiguous. Finally, Leibman (1995) suggested not only that domestic space is partitioned as a function of gender but that a husband's power is enhanced because interaction often occurs in male space and, there-fore, in and on male terms. At the same time, a wife's power is undermined by both the narrowness of her space, the kitchen, and the domestic (and, so, unappreciated) work she performs there.

For the most part, more recent analyses suggest that rights and responsi-bilities in the family have become less gender specific. While Frazer and Frazer (1992) concluded that *Father Knows Best* and *The Cosby Show* portrayed spousal gender roles in essentially the same way, implying that wives continue to be placed in a domestic and subservient role, most research promotes the view that, in a wider sense, gender roles have become more elastic. For exam-ple, Cantor's (1991) extensive review indicated that modern women are more likely to work outside of the home (see also, Moore, 1992) and more likely to hold a professional position, although this may be more common among unmarried women (Atkin, 1991; Elasmar, Hasegawa, & Brain, 1999). Nonethe-less, relatively few contemporary women are portrayed as homemakers. In one recent study (Elasmar et al., 1999), only 14% of female characters were classi-fied as homemakers or housewives, and in a second study (Hcintz-Knowles, 2001), fewer than 4% of female characters performed that traditional role.

What television men do inside marriage has also changed. Compared to earlier generations, modern fathers are more frequently involved in domestic life, in general, and child care and parenting, in particular (Heintz, 1992). Indeed, modern spouses appear to share equally in a collection of child-care activities, including putting children to bed, driving children to and from activities, and disciplining children. Modern fathers are even more likely than mothers to console children, although mothers continue to be more often responsible for food preparation and feeding and cleaning up after children (Heintz-Knowles, 2001).

Press and Stratham (1994) have argued that, although modern wives are frequently employed outside the home, they are almost uniformly presented in a domestic context. As such, their accomplishments and status outside of the family is minimized and their identity remains fundamentally domestic. The authors offer the specific example of Clare Huxtable (*The Cosby Show*), who is seen only rarely in the role of attorney and almost always as wife or mother. While this position appears to have merit, two observations should be made. First, the same bias may affect the portrayal of male characters. Not only is Cliff Huxtable shown infrequently in the role of doctor but only two domestic comedies, *The Dick Van Dyke Show* and *Home Improvement*, consistently presented the man-at-work as well as the man-at-home (Walsh, 1995). Second, this tendency may be an artifact of domestic comedy's inherent and, perhaps, unavoidable focus on home and family.

Spousal Supportiveness in Television Families

Following Fitzpatrick and Badzinski (1985, 1994), Douglas and Olson (1995) defined spousal supportiveness to be comprised of involvement, attraction (including sexual attraction), and receptivity and trust. A review of the television family literature reveals few studies dealing with these issues.

Certainly, both formal and informal analyses suggest that spousal relations have become more explicitly sexual. This is not only the opinion of popular critics, such as Barnes (1995) and Jensen (1995), but also the conclusion of Cantor (1991), whose inquiry was both more extensive and more rigorous. In fact, modern couples appear generally more attracted to each other; that is, they are more likely to express their mutual affection both sexually and in other, nonsexual ways (Douglas & Olson, 1995).

In general, television couples seem broadly supportive of each other. Conversation is common among television family members and, in modern families such as the Huxtables (*The Cosby Show*) and Keatons (*Family Ties*), as well as earlier families, such as the Andersons (*Father Knows Best*), couples appear to have developed comparatively open relationships in which they communicate freely and honestly and are willing to listen to each other (Douglas & Olson, 1995). What is more, contemporary couples are more likely to express their mutual affection (Douglas & Olson, 1995), suggesting that, while spouses in general are seen as relatively involved and trusting, modern couples are recognized as more overtly affectionate and, so, especially supportive of each other.

The generalizability of this conclusion may be limited in two respects. First, specific spouses violate the pattern. The Conners (*Roseanne*) and, more especially, the Taylors (*Home Improvement*), for example, have been seen to act in ways that imply low involvement, low receptivity and trust, and reduced attraction for each other (Douglas & Olson, 1995). Second, working-class spouses have been judged substantially less open and involved with each other than their middle-class counterparts. That is, in the same way that working-class husbands have been rated as relatively incompetent and oafish (Glennon & Butsch, 1982), families such as the Ricardos (*I Love Lucy*), Bunkers (*All in the Family*), Jeffersons (*The Jeffersons*), and Conners (*Roseanne*), all of which live outside of the middle-class, appear to involve spousal relations that are comparatively closed (Douglas & Olson, 1995).

Spousal Communication in Television Families

For the most part, examination of communication in television families has been conducted in the context of spousal or family conflict or has been sensitive to interaction between mothers and fathers, rather than wives and husbands. Most fundamentally, this research reveals a recurrent gender effect.

In an early study of communication patterns, Turow (1974) reported that, compared to women, men were more likely to issue commands and provide advice. Likewise, Skill, Wallace, and Cassata (1990) studied interaction in intact, non-intact, and mixed families and determined that, regardless of family type, wives sought out information more frequently than did husbands. Finally, in an analysis of all shows in which the narrative was family dependent, Skill and Wallace (1990) demonstrated that, during conversation, husbands typically rely on expert power, whereas wives are more likely to use a mixture of power and reward strategies. That is, husbands' influence derived most often from their various assumed competencies while wives, perhaps because of their more restricted and largely domestic expertise, also offered rewards in order to "get their way."

Clearly, such findings suggest an underlying traditional model of spousal relations. Issuing commands, providing advice and information, and using personal knowledge or understanding to influence others imply authority and self-efficacy. Following instructions, seeking advice and information, and relying on exchange to achieve interaction goals imply submissiveness and dependence. Hence, although spousal relations have become less formal (Douglas & Olson, 1995), there is considerable reason to suppose that interaction remains gender-biased and, more specifically, continues to reflect a relational model in which husbands are generally active and dominant and wives passive and submissive.

TELEVISION FAMILIES:
PERFORMANCE IN SPOUSAL RELATIONS

Investigation of spousal performance in television families involves separate examination of spousal conflict and spouses' ability to manage the daily routine. The analytical framework suggested by Fitzpatrick and Badzinski (1985, 1994) and used by Douglas and Olson (1995, 1996) includes two additional categories: socialization of family members and cultivation of stable personalities. These, however, appear relevant only to the study of television parents and children, since spouses are not usually assumed to be responsible for such outcomes in one another.

Spousal Conflict in Television Families

Spousal relations appear to have become increasingly conflictual. While Fisher's (1974) early content analysis suggested that television marriages of the period were essentially conflict-free, more recent studies offer substantial evidence that this has changed. Cantor (1991), for example, comprehensively reviewed television family interaction from the 1950s to the 1980s and concluded that, although it was typically resolved quite easily and prosocially, conflict was a stable feature of domestic comedy. Other research further encourages the view that spousal conflict is following an upward trajectory, at least in the most popular television families. Specifically, Heintz (1992) compared the five favorite shows of Chicago-area children in 1980 with those of 1990 and determined that conflict had become more common, especially in spousal interactions. Similarly, Douglas and Olson (1995) examined viewer attributions about relations in a variety of television families popular during the period 1950–1994 and reported that modern couples, like the Winslows (*Family Matters*), Seavers (*Growing Pains*), and Taylors (*Home Improvement*), were judged more conflictual than earlier couples, like the Ricardos (*I Love Lucy*), Andersons (*Father Knows Best*), and Douglases (*My Three Sons*).

The balance of extant research also suggests that working-class spousal relations are particularly hostile. In contrast to Thomas and Callahan (1982), who concluded that happiness, friendliness, and ability to solve problems were inversely related to SES, Douglas and Olson (1995) observed that working-class spouses, like the Bunkers (*All in the Family*) and Conners (*Roseanne*), were judged both more conflictual and less able to resolve conflict than their middle-class counterparts. Similarly, Heintz-Knowles (2001) examined conflict episodes in dual-career couples and reported that conflict was more common among low-status spouses than those of high-status.

Finally, there is some evidence that gender influences the sorts of circumstances that persons find conflictual and the strategies they use to resolve conflict. Heintz-Knowles (2001) distinguished between family-initiated conflict, that is, conflict that occurs when family interferes with work obligations, and work-initiated conflict, that is, conflict that occurs when work interferes with family obligations. Subsequent analysis revealed that men were almost always troubled by family-initiated conflict, whereas women were significantly more likely to be troubled by work-initiated conflict, leading the author to conclude that, "on TV, women's worlds revolved around their families and men's worlds revolved around their work" (Heintz-Knowles, 2001, p. 187).

The traditional family/gender ideology seems manifest, as well, in the conflict resolution strategies that couples use. Skill et al. (1990) examined conflict episodes in a variety of television families and reported that males are generally more likely than females to resolve conflict through reasoning, a stereotypically male attribute. In some family situations, males are also more likely to seek resolution of conflict, whereas females are more often engaged in conflict escalation. This finding is consistent with that of Comstock and Strzyzewski (1990), who observed that, as responders to conflict, husbands make extensive use of integrative strategies, such as initiating problem-solving and stressing commonalities, while wives rely on avoidance.

Spousal Ability to Manage the Daily Routine in Television Families

Very few studies have been directed toward spouses' management of the daily routine of family life. This is likely a consequence of the low visibility of this issue in television family research, where the focus more often relates to changing gender roles, family conflict, and so on. As well, because most research has examined family life in domestic comedy and because those families habitually include children, studies that do offer insight into management of the daily routine normally use the family, rather than the spouses, as the unit of analysis.

One view of the management issue, based on indirect analyses, is that spouses typically manage the daily routine quite well, largely because that routine is non-taxing. It has been argued that television spouses experience few marital difficulties (Cantor, 1991) and solve problems easily (Moore, 1992), in part, perhaps, because television families tend to be isolated from any surrounding context and, so, protected from potentially disruptive out-side influences. More direct analyses, however, suggest that more modern couples may experience more distress.

Only Douglas and Olson (1995) and Douglas (1996) have incorporated spousal management of the daily routine as an explicit dependent measure. In their studies, these researchers required participants to evaluate spousal, parent–child, and sibling relations in an assortment of television families. The spousal measure of "ability to manage the daily routine" comprised the fol-lowing items: the couple managed the daily routine effectively; the couple was unable to cope with day-to-day life; and the couple let life get on top of them (Douglas & Olson, 1995). When these items were combined and used as a sin-gle measure, analyses indicated that early television spouses, specifically the Andersons (*Father Knows Best*) and Douglases (*My Three Sons*), were judged more able to manage the daily routine than more modern families. Further, the most contemporary spouses, the Keatons (*Family Ties*), Conners (*Rose-anne*), and Taylors (*Home Improvement*), were judged least able to manage the daily routine. This pattern clearly indicates a descending trajectory among television spouses, suggesting they have become less organized, less compe-tent, and less able to cope with the mundane and recurrent aspects of day-to-day family life.

TELEVISION FAMILIES: SATISFACTION AND STABILITY IN SPOUSAL RELATIONS

For the most part, television spouses appear satisfied in their relationships and quite willing to continue those relationships. In his early examination of the family in domestic comedy, Newcomb (1974) concluded that the genre necessarily projected "a sense of deep personal love among the members of the family" (p. 48), including husband and wife, and it is this view that con-tinues to prevail.

Spouses who share a traditional relationship appear especially satisfied. Couples who enact conventional gender roles, for example, are seen as more satisfied than couples who divide familial rights and responsibilities in other ways (Perse et al., 1990). Likewise, wives who perform the role of homemaker are happier and share more successful marriages than those who work out-side the home (Durkin, 1985; Manes & Melnyk, 1974). Again, however, such satisfaction may not extend to working-class couples, even when their rela-tionship involves the provider husband and the stay-at-home wife. In their attributional analysis, Douglas and Olson (1995) observed that perceived relational satisfaction was lowest in families like the Bunkers (*All in the Family*), Jeffersons (*The Jeffersons*), and Conners (*Roseanne*), that is, in working-class families that adhered exclusively or intermittently to a traditional model of marriage. Nonetheless, perhaps because the middle-class is pervasive and the traditional, middle-class marriage normative, television spouses seem generally satisfied with each other (Douglas & Olson, 1995).

Not surprisingly, television also promotes the illusion that marriage is highly robust. The intact family is a television staple (Abelman, 1990; Cantor, 1991) and even working-class couples, who often exhibit signs of relational distress, habitually remain together (Overbeck, 1995). Intact families are also more harmonious than other family types. Members of such families are least likely to invoke their authority to influence others, least likely to reject others, and most likely to accommodate to others' views (Skill & Wallace, 1990). Hence, on television at least, couples rarely seek divorce, even couples that are relatively unsatisfied with each other.

TELEVISION FAMILIES: THE FAMILY AND ITS WORLD

Together with its attention to the relational detail of family life, television explicates a broader ideology that informs viewers about the significance and meaning of family and defines the fictional world in which television family life occurs. This ideology is not unique to specific families but is comprised largely of recurrent conventions that have become part of the status quo of television portrayals. Some families, such as those outside of the middle-class, may violate this general ideology but, when this happens, it is the family and not the ideology that is likely to be evaluated negatively. Of course, to the extent that violations are widespread, the ideology may be challenged and revised. In such instances, features that were previously taken for granted, such as the absence of minority families, are made salient and judged more critically.

The Significance and Meaning of Family

Perhaps most fundamental to television's family ideology is the assumption that the family is "the chief haven from worldly cares" (Cantor, 1991, p. 215). For television families, this seems to mean not only that the family is "a harbor of comfort and peace" (Beecher & Stowe, 1869, p. 466) but that it is isolated from a potentially threatening outside world. On the one hand, television homes are physically and emotionally "comfortable" (Newcomb, 1974, p. 47). They exude the physical ease of affluence (Frazer & Frazer, 1992) so that "homes are filled with comfortable furniture, books, paintings, plants, and the most up-to-date modern appliances" (Leibman, 1995, p. 231). They are also affectively therapeutic, filled with the reassuring love of sympathetic parents and good-natured children.

At the same time, the integrity of the family experience is protected by the almost uninterrupted separation of families from each other and from the communities in which they live. Television portrayals rarely include routine or extensive interaction between family members and their neighbors and friends. Nor do television narratives normally integrate the family-at-home and the family-at-work. As such, family life is privatized (Marc, 1989). Television communities are typically made up of "isolated households" (Cantor, 1991, p. 215) inhabited by families unaffected by social or economic dynamics external to the home.

Television's family ideology also advocates the married couple, with or without children, as the standard family model (Cantor, 1991). Although the nuclear family has become less common and single-parent families more common, domestic comedy, in particular, continues to promote the nuclear family as normal (Frazer & Frazer, 1992). In the 1950s, 37% of all television families were comprised of married parents and dependent children, and only 14% were single-parent families; in the 1980s, 26% of all television families were comprised of married parents and dependent children, while 22% were single-parent families (Skill & Robinson, 1994). Nonetheless, more than half of all parents are married (Skill & Robinson, 1994) and the "homogeneous suburban family at home" (Marc, 1989, p. 115) remains an accepted convention of domestic comedy.

The Television World

To a large extent, the television world remains White, male, and middle-class. Heintz-Knowles' (2001) recent content analysis of prime-time programming revealed that 77% of all characters were Caucasian, only 16% were African American, and even fewer were Hispanic, Oriental, or Native American. Similarly, males continue to be represented disproportionately in the television population. Early demographic studies (Lemon, 1977; Miller & Reeves, 1976; Turow, 1974) consistently showed that almost three quarters of regular or significant characters were male. Indeed, Dominick's (1979) review of gender and television indicated that, since the 1950s, approximately 70% of all main characters had been played by men and that this had not changed significantly across time. Nor does it appear to have changed substantially since. A variety of studies have shown that men continue to constitute between 65% and 70% of all television characters (Mackey & Hess, 1982; Signorielli, 1989; Vande Berg & Streckfuss, 1992; Weigel & Loomis, 1981) and recent analyses, by Greenberg and Collette (1997) and Elasmar et al. (1999), have suggested an ongoing, flat-line trend. Greenberg and Collette (1997) categorized all major characters added during a new network season for the period 1966 to 1992. Of the more than 1,700 characters, 65% were male. Likewise, Elasmar et al. (1999) content analyzed 6 constructed weeks of prime-time programming between October, 1992 and September, 1993 and reported that men filled 61% of all speaking roles and 82% of all major roles. Notably, almost 70% of female major characters were situated in domestic comedy.

The television world is also insistently middle-class. Not only are most television families middle-class (Moore, 1992) but middle-class family life is customarily presented in very positive ways (Cantor & Cantor, 1992). Middle-class families are surrounded by the material symbols of privilege but, more important, middle-class adults act in role-appropriate ways, often exceeding role requirements (Glennon & Butsch, 1982), and middle-class family relationships are generally happier, more harmonious, more satisfying, and more stable than those in other families (Douglas & Olson, 1995, 1996). In fact, perhaps because the middle-class is portrayed as principled and benign (Leibman, 1995), the advantages of middle-class family life have long appeared natural and deserved (Haralovich, 1989).

Finally, the television family experience is predominantly a suburban experience. Like their real-life counterparts, television families quickly deserted the inner-city in favor of the burgeoning suburbs. In domestic comedy, in particular, the home-owning, suburban family has become iconic. The story of television's first favorite family, the Ricardos (*I Love Lucy*), may be seen as a narrative of passage, from working-class to middle-class status and from childlessness to parenthood, but also passage from urban apartment renters to suburban homeowners. Real suburbia favored White Americans over minorities, young over old, parenthood over childlessness, and affluence over poverty. These same biases appear to have quickly infiltrated the suburbia of the Andersons (*Father Knows Best*), Stones (*The Donna Reed Show*), and Cleavers (*Leave It to Beaver*) and, in so doing, may have contributed to the enduring narrowness of the television world.

TELEVISION FAMILIES: THE CASE OF SOAP OPERAS

Like so much television programming, soap operas deal extensively with issues of family life and family relations. However, in contrast to other portrayals, which are often deemed realistic, soap operas situate the family in "a fantasy world of changing mates, prohibited loves, and the constant vanishing and reappearing of long-lost or newly discovered family members" (Livingstone & Liebes, 1995, p. 155). Although characters are often linked by associations of family, neither the families nor the family networks correspond to any fact-based model (Pingree & Thompson, 1990).

Nonetheless, in the current context, soap operas are important for two reasons. First, they are seen to articulate a single coherent version of spousal relations that is significant because it describes, to a largely female audience, the "norms and mores about women's place in the social order" (Harrington & Bielby, 1991, p. 130). Second, soap operas explicate a detailed sexual code. This code is especially intimate because of the comparatively extended "shelf life" of soap operas that allows viewers long-term access to the sexual experiences of characters and, in aggregate, provides a sense of the implicit standards of the "community."

Early studies of the family in soap operas suggested a traditional model of spousal relations even though a substantial proportion of female characters worked either full-time or part-time outside the home. Katzman's (1972) analysis of daytime soap operas showed that fully 45% of female characters worked outside the home, some only part-time, and 33% were identified unambiguously as homemakers. However, Ramsdell (1973) argued that, when attention was focused on central characters and salient relationships, the typical soap opera marriage involved "an aggressive, achieving husband and a work-at-home wife and mother" (p. 303). Ramsdell reasoned that the dominance of this traditional family model was a function of soap opera's audience, stay-at-home wives and mothers, and, so, its appeal to sponsors.

Applying a similar logic, Cantor and Pingree (1983) proposed that VCR penetration altered the soap opera audience to include a large number of working women. As a consequence, they argued, sponsors had become less committed to the homemaker, facilitating a fundamental change in the portrayal of married women. Some studies seem to confirm this position. Pingree and Thompson (1990), for example, examined the cast lists of popular soap operas and found that only 4% of female characters were clearly presented as homemakers, whereas 71% worked outside the home. However, more recent analyses have reasserted the dominance of traditional sex roles, suggesting that, although women may be shown to work outside the home, they continue to perform the duties of the homemaker so that their status is ambiguous. Harrington and Bielby (1991), for instance, distinguished between two love mythologies, a traditional mythology that emphasizes life-long commitment and a modern mythology that emphasizes self-development. Their examination of *General Hospital, Ryan's Hope,* and *Beauty and the Beast* led the authors to decide that popular portrayals continue to be constructed around a traditional mythology. In particular, the authors concluded that, "in the realm of power relations or decision-making, men continue to wield authority over women" (Harrington & Bielby, 1991, p. 143). Based on their broader analysis, Livingstone and Liebes (1995) reached a similar conclusion, arguing that soap operas encourage male dominance and female dependence and, as such, are repressive rather than liberating.

The sexual ideology of soap operas is explicit and stands in opposition to the sexually opaque but transparently monogamous code of other types of programming. In a series of studies, Greenberg and his colleagues (Greenberg, Abelman, & Neuendorf, 1981; Greenberg, Brown, & Buerkel-Rothfuss, 1993; Greenberg & Busselle, 1996) have demonstrated that, in soap operas, sexual intimacy is explicit and common, acts of sexual intimacy have become more common across time, and sexual intimacy between partners not married to each other is especially common.

Greenberg et al. (1981) content analyzed relatively small amounts of soap operas aired during 1976, 1979, and 1980. The analysis showed that petting, including long kisses, accounted for 52% of all sex acts, intercourse between unmarried partners accounted for 22% of all sex acts, and intercourse between married partners accounted for only 5% of all sex acts. Additionally, although the average number of intimate acts per hour was relatively stable across the three samples, intercourse between both married and unmarried partners was more common in 1980 than in previous years: in 1976, the rates were .06 and .39, respectively; in 1979, the rates were .05 and .19; in 1980, the rates increased to .14 and .49. That is, not only did acts of intercourse become increasingly common but intercourse between unmarried partners was significantly and consistently more common than intercourse between married partners. It should be stressed, too, that, when partners were defined as "unmarried," this indicated that they were not married to each other. In soap operas, infidelity is not unusual, so a substantial proportion of sexual activity between unmarried partners were acts of unfaithfulness by one or both persons. Even irregular viewers of soap operas are familiar with characters such as Erica Kane (*All My Children*), Dixie Martin (*All My Children*), Reva Bauer (*The Guiding Light*), Blake Marler (*The Guiding Light*), Nikki Newman (*The Young and the Restless*), Victor Newman (*The Young and the Restless*), and others for whom extramarital affairs are commonplace.

Greenberg et al. (1993) content analyzed soap operas popular among adolescents during 1985. This investigation revealed, first, that, on average, the three programs examined showed 3.7 sex acts per hour, a significant increase over each of the years included in the Greenberg et al. (1981) study, where the rates varied between 1.8 and 2.3 sex acts per hour. The investigation also showed that intercourse between unmarried partners occurred twice as often as intercourse between married partners. Intercourse between unmarried partners accounted for 43% of all intimate acts while intercourse between married partners accounted for only 20%.

Greenberg and Busselle (1996) content analyzed 10 episodes from each of five soap operas aired during 1994, including *General Hospital, All My Children,* and *One Life to Live,* each of which had been studied by Greenberg et al. (1993). This inquiry demonstrated that, across the three common soap operas, the average number of sex acts per hour had increased significantly from 3.7 to 5.0. What is more, intercourse between unmarried rather than married partners was even more likely than it had been in 1985. Acts of intercourse between unmarried partners accounted for 37% of all intimate acts, while intercourse between married partners accounted for only 13%; that is, intercourse between unmarried partners was three times more likely to occur than intercourse between married partners.

When all five soap operas were examined together, the average number of sex acts per hour was 6.6. Of these, 36% were acts of intercourse between unmarried partners; 11% were acts of intercourse between married partners. Hence, in both the restricted and complete samples, there was no increase in the rate of intercourse between married partners, but the rate of intercourse between unmarried partners increased from an average of 1.6 per hour in 1985 to 1.8 in the restricted sample and 2.4 in the overall sample. As well, while intercourse, generally, was more likely to be shown than implied in 1994 soap operas, the increase was especially large when it was between unmarried partners. In 1985, there had been a single instance of intercourse between unmarried partners presented visually; in 1994, there were 13 cases in the parallel sample and 32 cases in the total sample.

CONCLUSIONS AND IMPLICATIONS

The American family, in general, and spousal relations, in particular, have been altered in a fundamental and ongoing way by the changing role and expectations of women. Other factors, such as the elevated relational status of children, have exerted substantial influence, too, but women's expanding ambition has been critical. While most Americans continue to take marriage for granted, the modern family experience is dramatically different from that of earlier generations, although the changes appear to follow an established and familiar pattern.

In the broadest sense, the family has continued to be feminized. That is, the female voice has become stronger and increased emphasis has been placed on traditionally female values. Spousal relations have become more egalitarian and more open. Marriage has also become more companionate so that modern spousal relations are characterized by increased intimacy and supportiveness. Spouses have come to spend more time together and talk more to each other. Spouses have also developed heightened sexual expectations, including expectations of mutual sexual satisfaction. At the same time, women have established a more prominent and more heterogeneous place in the paid workforce. Not only are more women pursuing personal ambitions outside the home, many are engaged in high-status professional positions.

Two additional aspects of the family experience deserve mention, in part because of their quite opposite place in television family life. First, the postwar migration to the suburbs has continued despite growing efforts to "reclaim" inner-cities. White, middle-class life, in particular, remains most often constructed around the suburban home and the suburban commute. Second, divorce has become more common for all Americans, suggesting that modern couples define marriage as less binding than earlier generations. As Caplow et al.'s (1982) study of Middletown revealed, divorce has intruded into the life of most Americans, at least indirectly.

In many ways, television families exhibit the same changes. The postwar middle-class model of family relations, in which rights and responsibilities were distributed primarily as a function of gender and wives remained second to their husbands, has given way to a more gender-ambiguous system. Spousal relations on television, like those of real couples, have become more symmetrical so that wives and husbands tend to share rights and responsibilities. Additionally, television spousal relations have become more open and more supportive. Contemporary spouses are both more talkative and more attentive to each other than were their earlier counterparts. Spousal relations on television have also become more intimate as couples have become increasingly affectionate and more explicitly sexual. As well, television women are rarely depicted as homemakers but, rather, are more and more often portrayed as part of the paid workforce, often holding high-status positions such as a doctor, attorney, or corporate executive.

Like the real family experience, that of television families remains largely suburban. Families continue to be presented in quasi-small town contexts, away from the clutter, noise, and tacit threat of urban America. In contrast, divorce, which is common among real couples, is a relatively infrequent occurrence on television. In domestic comedy, in particular, spouses simply do not divorce, even when relational and/or economic stress appears acute. Nonetheless, television couples have become more hostile toward each other and less able to manage the daily routine, suggesting that, while divorce is uncommon, television marriages have, to some extent, become distressed.

In summary, analysis of spousal relations suggests, first, that real family life and family relations have progressed coherently along a trajectory defined most significantly by the changing ambitions of women. Second, the analysis offers support for the claim that the experience of television families is not independent of real family life. Indeed, relations between television spouses appear to reflect closely the relational experience of real spouses. Finally, the analysis provides some suggestion that the television family is relatively distressed, although this should not be overstated. Modern television spouses are relatively conflictual and do seem to manage family life less capably than earlier couples. However, contemporary spouses also appear more affectionate and more supportive than previous iterations, suggesting a comparatively complex emotional context.

Chapter 6

Development of the Television Family: II. Parent–Child and Sibling Relations

Over the course of the 20th century, the family is seen to have become more and more child-centered (Calhoun, 1945; Key, 1909) so that the apparent value now placed on children is substantial. In a recent survey of almost 2,000 American parents (National Family Opinion Inc., 1994), for example, 77% agreed with the statement, "my children are the most important part of my life," 71% agreed with the statement, "I have a tremendous amount of trust in my kids," and a majority agreed that "a family isn't a family without children." To some extent, this "sentimentalized view of children" (May, 1995, p. 38) probably derives from reduced infant mortality, which has encouraged stronger emotional ties between parents and children, and reduced parental mortality, which has made orphanhood comparatively uncommon. In 1900, for example, the probability of a child surviving to his/her 15th birthday was .79, the probability of at least one child in a family dying by that age was .62, and the probability that one or both parents would die by a child's 15th birthday was .24. Finally, the likelihood that neither parent would survive to see a child reach middle age was .52. By 1976, those probabilities were .98, .04, .05, and .14, respectively (Uhlenberg, 1989). Such dramatic changes, it is argued, contributed to the construction of "childhood" and "adolescence" (Aries, 1962), the separation of "middle-age" from surrounding life stages (Sheehy, 1976), and the redefinition of "old age" (Fitzgerald, 1987).

At the same time, of course, there is considerable evidence that the system of family support and parental nurturing has ruptured, leaving many children in relatively deprived circumstances. Not only do an overwhelming majority of American adults continue to believe that the quality of life for children has declined since their own childhood (Mellman et al., 1990; Whitman et al., 1996) but broad sociological data appear to confirm that belief, at least indirectly. First, an increasing proportion of marriages end in divorce. In 1970, the divorce rate was 42 divorces per 100 marriages; by 1990, the rate was almost 55 divorces per 100 marriages (The Population Council, 1995). Second, larger numbers of children live with a single parent, usually the mother, than ever before. In 1960, 9.1% of all children lived with one parent; by 1970, that figure had risen to 11.9%; by 1980, 19.7% of all children lived with only one parent; by 1990, 24.7% did so; and, by 1998, 27.7% of all children lived with a single parent (U.S. Bureau of the Census, 1999). Both divorce and single-parenthood are seen to be inherently injurious to children (e.g., Coontz, 1995; Stacey, 1995). Third, in 1990, four out of ten fathers were delinquent in payment of child support (The Population Council, 1995), fostering the prolonged impoverishment of other family members. It is unsurprising that Abelman (1990) has concluded that, "things look fairly grim for the American family, particularly in terms of size and stability" (p. 168). Indeed, although explanations vary, there is wide agreement among critics that the familial condition of children has deteriorated. Some, like Coontz (1995), have argued that family systems detrimental to children, such as single-parenthood and divorce, are more common because they are rooted in impoverishment, which afflicts an ever-increasing number of families. Between 1972 and 1994, the median income of men aged 25 to 34 years fell 26% so that the proportion with an income below the poverty level increased from 16% to 32%. According to Coontz, such expanded need is necessarily damaging to the family, in general, and children, in particular, because "Poor individuals are twice as likely to divorce as more affluent ones, three to four times less likely to marry in the first place, and five to seven times more likely to have a child out of wedlock" (Coontz, 1995, p. 14). Caplovitz (1979) has taken a similar position, reasoning that elevated financial anxiety produces increased marital conflict, especially at low SES levels. That conflict, in turn, produces an array of negative relational outcomes, including divorce.

Other observers have situated the cause of children's attenuated welfare more clearly inside the family. Popenoe (1988, 1993a, 1993b, 1995, 1996), Blankenhorn (1995), and others have argued that the modern family is structurally and functionally unable to meet the explicit priority placed on children. More specifically, their position maintains, first, that there has evolved an increased cultural commitment to children that remains an active promise in most contemporary families; second, families of the 1950s, for whom "reproduction became a national obsession" (May, 1995, p. 18), kept this promise; and, third, for a variety of reasons and in a variety of ways, modern families have betrayed the promise so that children's familial experience has become severely depleted.

Fundamental to this argument is the claim that there exists essentially universal consensus that contemporary children have the "right . . . to have a happy, stable home with devoted parents" (Popenoe, 1993a, p. 528). Although lacking direct support, such a claim is consistent with views expressed by others (e.g., Calhoun, 1945; Key, 1909; May, 1995; Mintz & Kellogg, 1988), and Uhlenberg's (1989) observations regarding parent and infant mortality as well as a host of media reports and daily conversations that emphasize the "sanctity of childhood," the essential usefulness of "staying together for the kids," and a host of negative consequences that children are seen to suffer as a function of parental neglect, including "premature sexuality and out-of-wedlock births; deteriorating educational achievement; depression, substance abuse, and alienation" (Popenoe, 1996, p. 3). Indeed, there can be little doubt that, in today's society, children are seen as special and endangered and, as such, both deserving and in need of parental love and protection. According to Popenoe (1993a, 1996) and May (1995), in particular, postwar families actualized this child-centered ideology. Not only were the 1950s characterized by elevated marriage and birth rates, low divorce rates, and family togetherness (Popenoe, 1993a) but children became crucial to the development of adult identities (May, 1995). On the one hand, motherhood confirmed a female's inherent womanhood and, so, her social identity as nurturer and caregiver. In a little more than a decade, the average number of children per family increased by a third (May, 1995); between 1940 and 1957, the fertility rate rose by a half, the birth rate of third children doubled, and of fourth children tripled (Breines, 1992); and, by the end of the 1950s, 70% of all women were married by age 24, almost 50% were married by age 20, and almost a third had delivered their first child before age 20 (Breines, 1992). Additionally, whereas 27% of women born between 1885 and 1915 remained childless, only 10% of women born between 1915 and 1930 did so, leading May (1995) to conclude that, "virtually everyone was having children" (p. 3). At the same time, of course, fatherhood became "a new badge of masculinity" (May, 1995, p. 135), establishing a male's responsibility and commitment to family. Even in popular culture, the entrepreneurial model, which presented men's professional status as personal triumph, was replaced by a corporate-suburban model in which success was achieved in the family (Long, 1985). In television, for example, the workplace became, in most cases, invisible so that the work-related accomplishments of fathers like Ozzie Nelson (*The Adventures of Ozzie and Harriet*), Jim Anderson (*Father Knows Best*), and Ward Cleaver (*Leave It to Beaver*) were expressed indirectly through the family's economic, physical, and emotional well-being.

Such widespread endorsement of parenthood produced an assortment of consequences. Most obviously, parenthood became a standard of both womanhood and manhood, conferring "not only full adult status, but also evidence of socially sanctioned heterosexuality and patriotic citizenship" (May, 1995, p. 3). Second, children became more common and, paradoxically, their significance also increased. Postwar America was "an enormously child-centered era, an era in which preoccupation with the needs and interests of children was paramount" (Popenoe, 1996, p. 129). Finally, children became the defining feature of family. As May (1995) has demonstrated in her expansive analysis of childlessness, there arose "a new priority in adoption policy: the creation of nuclear families" (p. 142). That is, young married couples simply did not constitute a family; a child or, preferably, several children were required.

The demise of this fragile system has been presented in several ways. In the most general sense, it has been cast in terms of a change from one set of family priorities to another. Elkind (1995), for instance, has discussed the transition from the modern family, which emphasized sexual and relational exclusivity, life-long commitment, women's instinct toward motherhood, and the priority of the family (Shorter, 1975), to the postmodern family, which emphasizes equality, relational impermanence, individual choice, and personal ambition. Children are believed to be especially vulnerable in such an arrangement because their competence is assumed rather than nurtured and because their "needs for limit-setting, guidance, and value-modeling are not being met" (Elkind, 1995, p. 28). Bernstein (1964) has made similar arguments in his discussion of the shift from the positional family to the personal family, a shift that is seen to involve a move away from gender-specific sex roles and values such as conformity and obedience to authority, to values that promote individualism, sensitivity to others' feelings and motives, and decision making through negotiation. It is worth noting, too, that a large majority of the public appears to agree with Elkind's (1995) assertion that contemporary parents fail to regulate their children sufficiently. In a national poll (Marks, 1996), 76% of more than 1,000 adults agreed that parents' willingness to keep their children under control has weakened in the past decade.

The destruction of the traditional family, together with parents' reduced commitment to their children's welfare, has been described in substantially more specific terms by Popenoe (1988, 1993a, 1993b, 1995, 1996) and others. According to these authors, children's tenuous circumstances derive from the fragmentation of the family, in general, and collapse of long-term marriage, in particular.

Popenoe (1995), for example, has argued that "Absent fathers, working mothers, distant grandparents, anonymous schools, and transient communities" (p. 16) have contrived to minimize the amount of time modern children spend with adults. As a consequence, children are often unmonitored, and, so, tacitly encouraged to behave sometimes in extravagantly antisocial ways, and routinely denied the support and sense of connectivity necessary to develop stable relationships, both inside and outside the home.

Children are seen to be at risk, more straightforwardly, as a combined function of decreased marriage rates and increased divorce rates that force a large and rising number of children to be raised in single-parent homes (Popenoe, 1993b, 1995, 1996). Indeed, in 1960, 7.1% of White children, 21.9% of African American children, and 9.1% of all children lived with one parent; by 1998, those figures had risen to 22.8%, 54.8%, and 27.7%, respectively (U.S. Bureau of the Census, 1999). This situation is problematic for children, in part, because it increases significantly the likelihood that a child will grow up in poverty and, in part, because mothers and fathers not only bring dissimilar areas of expertise to parenthood but it is enormously difficult for one to mimic the attributes of the other (Popenoe, 1996).

Children's family environment is posited to be diminished further because an increasing number of mothers choose not to fill the traditional role of stay-at-home nurturer/caregiver but, instead, integrate a reduced form of that role with their work outside the home (Popenoe, 1995; Samuelson, 1996). This absence from the home harms children because they are left in the care of others or themselves, neither of which, it is argued, provide the guidance, attention, or love necessary to induce development of socially functional action. For example, children who are placed into a full-time or near full-time, continuous day-care environment during infancy exhibit the highest levels of aggression toward peers and the highest levels of disobedience toward adults (Belsky, 1995). Likewise, single-parenting is associated with increased (Greenberg et al., 1987; Medrich, Roizen, Rubin, & Buckley, 1982) and relatively unregulated television viewing (Brown, Childers, Bauman, & Koch, 1990), the effects of which are frequently harmful, both relationally and cognitively (e.g., Desmond, Singer, & Singer, 1990; Singer & Singer, 1983, 1986; Singer, Singer, Desmond, Hirsch, & Nicol, 1988).

Feminist scholars have long argued that the modern American family is often "father-absent" (Leupnitz, 1988; Weingarten, 1991). That is, fathers are frequently uninvolved, inconspicuous, or distant from family life, a situation that is necessarily harmful to family relations. This appears congruent with public opinion. In a recent survey of almost 2,000 adults (National Family Opinion, Inc., 1994), only a small minority believed that contemporary fathers and children share a close relationship and an even smaller minority believed that contemporary fathers share equally in parenting responsibilities.

Popenoe (1996) has proposed that father absence is rooted in the demise of marriage. Like Blankenhorn (1995) and Samuelson (1996), Popenoe (1996) has posited the emergence of a relational ideology that emphasizes self-fulfillment and, as such, undermines partners' commitment to marriage and family. Specifically, Popenoe has argued that marriage has become less satisfying and more conflictual (see also, Glenn, 1991; Glenn & Weaver, 1988) and, because it is no longer constructed around responsibility and obligation to others, has caused a "devaluation of children . . . an alarming weakening of the fundamental assumption, long at the center of our culture, that children are to be loved and valued at the highest level of priority" (Popenoe, 1996, p. 14).

Destruction of the traditional family is presumed to have diminished the family experience in a mixture of ways. Popenoe (1993a) proposed that, since the postwar period, the family has become less able to perform essential functions, such as the socialization of children, less able to maintain authority over its members, and less able to provide care, affection, and companionship. As well, Popenoe concluded that family relations are comparatively unsatisfying and unstable. Others have made similar arguments. Faludi (1999), for example, has suggested that, because they live in "parallel universes" (p. 44), contemporary fathers are poor role models for their sons who must often "search for how to be a man in a fatherless landscape" (p. 532). May (1988), too, has argued that, in modern families, parents provide "ambiguous role models for children" (p. 217) so that effective socialization is unlikely.

In summary, while society appears to place high priority on children's welfare, there is wide agreement that the family experience of children has worsened since the 1950s. In particular, many families are thought to be inadequate, unable to achieve important family outcomes, ranging from effective socialization of children to establishment and maintenance of fulfilling family relations.

Some critics have posited that television's portrayal of family life and family relations contributes to the public's sense of decline in real families. Stacey (1995), for example, has proposed that fictional families are often more compelling than real families and, so, substantially influence our real-world beliefs. Whitman and colleagues (1996), too, have attributed pessimism about a variety of issues, including the state of the modern family, to television content. Certainly, a mechanism such as television appears necessary in order to reconcile what seem to be contradictory public sentiments about the contemporary family. That is, on the one hand, opinion polls routinely reveal that large majorities of respondents believe their family to be their chief priority, believe family life to be emotionally and relationally satisfying, and believe their involvement with family to be psychologically essential. On the other, public opinion habitually endorses statements that are extremely critical of families in general, charging that the American family is incapable of performing basic functions associated with parenting and has become a hostile environment for children, in particular.

For the most part, the analysis of parent–child and sibling relations in the following section proceeds in the same way as the investigation of television spouses. Issues associated with power and affect, performance, satisfaction and stability, and the family and its world are examined independently. However, special attention is not paid to soap opera portrayals, although examination of television parents and children does involve separate analysis of the attributional studies conducted by Douglas and Olson (Douglas, 1996; Douglas & Olson, 1995, 1996). Not only do these studies frequently rely on discriminant function analysis, so that variables such as involvement (an issue of relational power and affect), socialization (an issue of relational performance), and satisfaction (an issue of relational satisfaction and stability) often become amalgamated and, so, lose their conceptual integrity, but they also encourage an essentially opposite set of conclusions to much content-centered research.

TELEVISION FAMILIES: POWER AND AFFECT IN PARENT–CHILD AND SIBLING RELATIONS

Investigation of power and affect in parent–child and sibling relationships is conducted within a framework that examines sex roles, relational supportiveness, and communication. As in the study of spousal relations, each of these areas is divided further: investigation of sex roles involves discussion of dominance/equality and family function; investigation of relational supportiveness involves discussion of involvement, attraction, and receptivity-trust; and investigation of parent–child and sibling communication involves discussion of the formality of interaction as well as the extent to which parents and children use communication to influence each other.

Parent and Child Sex Roles in Television Families

Formal analyses of parent and child sex roles in television families have generally suggested a traditional family model (Skill, Robinson, & Wallace, 1987;

Robinson & Skill, 2001) in which parents and children are encouraged to behave in complementary ways, as are female and male family members. Parents, for example, are more likely to exhibit concern (Shaner, 1982) and more likely to provide reassurance and instruction (Skill et al., 1990); children are more likely to seek support and attention (Shaner, 1982). Children also typically rely on parents to resolve problems, both inside and outside the family (Newcomb, 1974). Indeed, although some families, especially nontraditional families, may reflect a system characterized by reduced role differentiation and relative equality between parents and children (Cantor, 1991), most television families appear still to rely on a model of parental wisdom, authority, and control (Cantor, 1991; Lichter et al., 1988; Newcomb, 1974).

Extant research suggests, as well, that, in television families, rights and responsibilities are divided on the basis of gender. While fathers are involved habitually in family problem-solving (Newcomb, 1974) and family discipline (Leibman, 1995), mothers are more often associated with issues of domesticity and nurturance (Feshbach et al., 1979; Press & Strathman, 1994; Signorielli, 1982). Even in television families in which both spouses work outside the home, few mothers are employed full-time. Heintz-Knowles (2001), for example, reported that less than a third of her sample of prime-time mothers were fully employed and the working status of another 50% was unclear because the characters were engaged exclusively in domestic tasks such as child care and meal preparation. Finally, television fathers seem to enact more instrumental behaviors, whereas television mothers enact more expressive behaviors (Dail & Way, 1985), again suggesting a traditional and gender-stereotypic parental model.

Children appear to act in similar ways. Based on their analysis of intact, non-intact, and mixed families, Skill et al. (1990) noted that, compared to sisters, brothers less commonly sought information and advice, less commonly provided reassurance, and less commonly denied the other's argument. Similarly, brothers more frequently used both reasoning and commands and more often disparaged the other or attacked the other's motives (Skill et al., 1990). Additionally, like their adult counterparts, male children seem more likely than female children to display aggression, whereas female children seem more likely to exhibit affection (Heintz-Knowles, 1995).

In contrast to these formal studies, more popular analyses often conclude that parents violate their traditional roles, either because of incompetence or opposition. In an early critique, Hunt (1955) argued that, "exemplified by *Life of Riley, The Adventures of Ozzie and Harriet, Father Knows Best, Make Room for Daddy,* and numerous others, it is made quite clear that the modern father is an overgrown adolescent, a boob, and a nitwit, who is no match for all the rest of the family" (p. 21). More recent reviewers have judged television parents similarly. Zoglin (1990), for example, advocated that modern television fathers are "slobs or oafs" (p. 85) while modern television mothers are unfriendly and aggressive toward other family members and, too, typically are unable to perform traditional female duties such as food preparation. Likewise, Waters (1993) characterized television fathers as collectively incompetent and television parents, in general, as "overgrown kids" (p. 50). Critics are inclined to view children in the same unkind way. In particular, Zoglin (1990) described modern television children as "bratty and disrespectful" (p. 85).

Hence, while formal analyses suggest that television parents and children continue to abide by a traditional model in which rights and responsibilities are distributed on the basis of gender and age, popular critics are considerably more likely to claim the destruction of that model as a function of parental inability and unwillingness to meet the various role requirements. Likewise, explicit study of television families encourages the view that television parents and children share an orderly and effective system of family governance. In contrast, more intuitive summaries, which tend to evaluate family life holistically, more often conclude that television family roles are ambiguous and muddled.

Parent and Child Supportiveness in Television Families

Again, investigation of family supportiveness, this time in relations involving parents and children, will be based on the argument that supportiveness is comprised of involvement, attraction, and receptivity and trust (Fitzpatrick & Badzinski, 1985, 1994), each of which can be examined separately.

Although few studies have examined involvement in parent–child relations, those that have suggest relatively high shared involvement between television parents and their children. In their circumplex analysis of television family systems, for example, Bryant et al. (2001) concluded that modern families exhibited moderately high levels of parent–child cohesion, that is, mutual involvement, emotional closeness, and recognition of relational boundaries. Indeed, contemporary parents and children appeared more involved than some earlier generations. Likewise, modern parent–child relations were judged mutually respectful. That is, television relationships involving parents and children were deemed effective, especially in more modern families.

Other analyses have suggested a similar but less undifferentiated conclusion. For instance, Akins (1986) compared family presentations aired during 1980 with those of 1960 and observed that members of more modern families showed more support for each other. At the same time, however, 1980 families were more likely to engage in affectively negative displays, such as opposing, ignoring, and evading others and withdrawing from other family members. Heintz-Knowles' (1995) analysis of children on television yielded similarly ambiguous results. Examination of children's motivations revealed that children, especially young children, are often motivated by family relationships (15% of all child acts were entirely or partially family-motivated). However, children are more commonly motivated by relationships with friends or romantic partners (52% of all child acts were entirely or partially friend/romantic partner-motivated) and a desire to help themselves (79% of all child acts were entirely or partially self-motivated).

Nor do television family members appear equally likely to provide support to others. Mothers are especially likely to behave in supportive or nurturing ways (Dail & Way, 1985) although both mothers and fathers routinely provide support, whereas sons and brothers rarely perform such a function (Greenberg et al., 1980). Although television mothers are particularly supportive of other family members, television children seem more responsive to the attention of fathers (Dail & Way, 1985). One potential explanation for this is that, as in real families (Kotelchuck, 1976; Lamb, 1977; Parke & Tinsley, 1987; Yogman, 1981), father–child interactions are more often a site of physical play than are mother–child interactions and, so, more likely to prompt response from the (child) play-partner(s).

In contrast to shows of supportiveness, which may often be disparate across family members, mutual love is seen to be a constant feature of television family life. In his landmark investigation, Newcomb (1974) concluded that the "real basis for domestic comedy is a sense of deep personal love among the members of the family" (p. 48). More recently, Cantor (1991) and Cantor and Cantor (1992) have reaffirmed this position, arguing that, in domestic comedy at least, parents and children invariably exhibit an obvious and abiding love for each other, even during conflict, which is habitual in programming of this type.

Although receptivity-trust has not been examined directly, there is reason to suppose that television families are usually characterized by attributes such as trust, sincerity, and openness, each of which is an indicator of the larger construct. Most obviously, television children recurrently volunteer their problems to parents and to each other. What is more, those problems are discussed honestly as both parents and children display a willingness to listen to each other. Indeed, when evaluated clinically, television families appear uniformly open, self-disclosive, mutually respectful, and willing to listen attentively to what each other has to say (Bryant et al., 2001). Family members are also empathic (Bryant et al., 2001) although this may be more true of parents than children (Shaner, 1982), again suggesting openness and receptivity for others.

In summary, television families seem generally supportive. Although, compared to earlier iterations, modern families are more likely to enact distancing behaviors, such as evading and ignoring, they also exhibit higher levels of mutual involvement. Parents, and, more particularly, mothers are predisposed to provide support to others and love seems pervasive and enduring. There is also indirect evidence that receptivity and trust is common among contemporary television families. Such families are disclosive, open, honest, willing to listen to each other, empathic, and mutually respectful, implying a responsive and trusting family environment. It should be noted that television children appear less supportive than their parents. Not only are sons unlikely to offer support to other family members but children, both sons and daughters, are more often motivated by concern for themselves or friends than concern for family.

Parent and Child Communication in Television Families

Studies of parent and child communication have focused almost exclusively on the issue of communicative influence. Little or no attention has been directed toward other aspects of interaction, such as conversational formality.

Influence attempts are common in television families as parents and children try to resolve differences, establish understanding, or simply "get their own way." Although family members appear to have access to a wide variety of compliance-gaining strategies, they seem to rely on comparatively few. Haefner and Comstock (1990), for example, content analyzed a random selection of prime-time programming and reported that two strategies, commanding and reasoning, accounted for half of all influence attempts and two others, requesting and hinting, accounted for an additional quarter. Such reliance on a relatively small number of strategies may be a consequence of the immediate success of a large majority of efforts. In fact, 81% of all compliance-gaining attempts were successful at the first trial so that family members were rarely forced to invoke alternative approaches. Notably, parents were somewhat more likely to exert influence than were children, although both parents and children were more likely to be successful than unsuccessful, and fathers were more likely than mothers to seek influence, although they were proportionally no more successful. That is, influence was slightly biased as a function of family role, and influence seeking was biased as a function of an interaction between family role and gender.

Influence may be achieved in ways that are, on the one hand, more systemic and, on the other, more creative. Systemic power accrues to family members because of the rights associated with their family role and because other family members act cooperatively to affirm those rights. Parents, for example, are more likely than children to provide information and direction (Greenberg et al., 1980) and more likely to use commands and offer reassurance (Skill et al., 1990). Children, meanwhile, more often seek information and are least likely to provide direction (Greenberg et al., 1980). Likewise, parents are substantially more likely to act as problem solvers while children typically are unable to resolve problems, even their own (Cantor, 1991; Newcomb, 1974). Hence, the relationship between parents and children is, in some critical respects, repetitively complementary such that children play a submissive role that requires that they endorse parents' power and influence over and over again.

Family members may also influence each other in more conversationally creative ways. Children, for example, appear to violate their general passivity by initiating and sometimes dominating family interaction (Abelman & Ross, 1986; Akins, 1986). In this way, it is possible that television children establish a conversational agenda that others are encouraged to follow. Television fathers may also use conversation to exhibit and, perhaps, reinforce the authority they derive from a gender-based division of rights and responsibilities. On religious television, where a traditional family model dominates, fathers control and direct conversation (Neuendorf & Abelman, 1987). Likewise, time series analysis of the Huxtables (*The Cosby Show*), a family that adheres to a traditional family model despite the wife/mother's successful career as an attorney (Frazer & Frazer, 1992; Mellancamp, 1986), revealed that the husband/father was demonstrably the most talkative family member (Honeycutt, Wellman, & Larson, 1997).

TELEVISION FAMILIES: PERFORMANCE IN PARENT AND CHILD RELATIONS

Like analysis of television spousal relations, investigation of performance in parent and child relations involves separate examination of parent and child conflict and parent and child ability to manage the daily routine. Additionally, the investigation includes examination of two additional categories, socialization of family members, and cultivation of stable personalities. These categories are part of the analytical framework suggested by Fitzpatrick and Badzinski (1985, 1994) and used by Douglas and Olson (1995, 1996) and appear relevant to the study of parent and child relations. In contrast, spouses are not usually assumed to be responsible for such outcomes in one another.

Parent and Child Conflict in Television Families

Although television family relations have been labeled *conflict free* (Fisher, 1974), most researchers have reached a quite different conclusion. For the most part, investigators have argued that, while members of television families are more likely to behave affiliatively than oppositionally (Larson, 1993, 2001; Weiss & Wilson, 1990), even in families like the Simpsons, who are often assumed inherently hostile (Larson, 1993), and while most conflict is easily resolved (Cantor, 1991; Moore, 1992; Newcomb, 1974; Taylor, 1989), disagreements and disputes are a standard feature of television family life.

Weiss and Wilson (1990) content analyzed episodes of each of the five highest rated situation comedies among child viewers and reported that, although positive affect was more common than negative affect, the difference was only slight. Negative emotion was expressed by 47% of characters and was more ordinarily displayed by featured characters in the main plot than by non-featured characters or in the secondary plot. What is more, the great majority of those who experienced negative emotion were unable to resolve their feelings. It is not unreasonable to suppose that negative affect may be especially salient to viewers given such character/plot centrality and ongoing presence.

Much television conflict, however, is deemed benign. Even in parent–child relations, which are highly disputative (Comstock & Strzyzewski, 1990), arguments are usually settled through talk and to the satisfaction of all involved (Lichter et al., 1988). Nonetheless, while parents rarely use coercion (Skill & Wallace, 1990) they do appear often to rely on strategies that retain and emphasize their power in the family (Skill & Wallace, 1990).

Television parents and children also appear often willing to damage family relations. Comstock and Strzyzewski (1990) examined the use of prosocial and antisocial strategies during family conflict. As initiators of conflict with their children, fathers were found to use distributive strategies, such as blaming, rejecting the other(s), hostile questioning, and hostile joking. Because such strategies emphasize personal goals (e.g., "winning" the argument) over relational goals (e.g., helping others retain face), they are considered relationally damaging. In contrast, mothers are most likely to employ integrative strategies when they are the initiators of parent–child conflict. Strategies of this kind, which are posited to be relationally constructive, include emphasizing commonalities, exhibiting empathy, accepting some amount of responsibility, and making situation-relevant disclosures. As responders to conflict, parents make even wider use of distributive strategies. In this role, mothers are most likely to use distributive strategies, regardless of child gender, while fathers are most likely to use distributive strategies when involved in conflict initiated by sons but prefer integrative strategies when the cointerlocutor is a daughter.

In the same study, sons were found to rely on integrative strategies during conflict with their parents, whether the sons were initiators or responders. Daughters, meanwhile, displayed a fairly complex strategy use that was a function of both personal role (initiator, responder) and parent gender (mother, father). When they were the initiators of parent–daughter conflict, daughters were most likely to invoke distributive strategies against both mothers and fathers. However, when they were responders, daughters were most likely to use avoidance in conflict with mothers and distributive strategies in conflict with fathers. Like distributive strategies, avoidance strategies are normally relationally problematic because they are not intended to resolve conflict so that the potential for further disagreement remains. Examples of avoidance are shifting the conversational topic, denial of the conflict, and focusing on issues tangential to the conflict, such as the language of the other person(s). That is, only sons appear consistently to place priority on family relations during parent–child conflict; other family members, particularly daughters, seem willing to contribute to situations in which relations are jeopardized.

Sibling relations are also frequently hostile. Whereas television children of the 1950s and 1960s "inhabited a universe in which mild sibling quarrels were quickly but fairly adjudicated by sage, kindly parents" (Taylor, 1989, p. 27), modern children seem to enjoy less friendly relations. Based on comparison of sibling interactions in *Leave It to Beaver, The Adventures of Ozzie and Harriet,* and *Father Knows Best* with those in *The Cosby Show, Growing Pains,* and *Family Ties,* Larson (1991) concluded that, while children had become more central to the television family experience, their interactions were comparatively less affable.

A more extensive examination conducted by the same author suggests, again, that sibling relations have followed a downward affective trajectory. Larson (2001) compared sibling interactions from the 1950s, 1960s, 1980s, and 1990s and determined that, while a majority of sibling interaction remained friendly, an increasing proportion was conflictual. Although this conclusion must be interpreted with some caution because of potential problems associated with the selection of television families, the analysis is consistent with Larson's (1991) earlier study as well as more intuitive statements about television siblings.

There is also reason to suppose that siblings, and most especially sons, are significantly less conciliatory and less able to resolve disagreements with each other than with parents. As in parent–child conflict, where daughters routinely invoke relationally destructive strategies (i.e., distributive and avoidance strategies), sisters rely most extensively on distributive strategies in sibling conflict, whether they initiate the conflict or not. In contrast, whereas sons consistently use relationally constructive strategies (i.e., integrative strategies) in parent–child conflict, they use distributive strategies when they instigate conflict with brothers and sisters and, when responding to conflict started by others, use distributive strategies against sisters and avoidance strategies against brothers (Comstock & Strzyzewski, 1990).

Hence, extant research provides a somewhat inconsistent view of parent and child conflict. Many researchers have dismissed television family conflict as trivial. While acknowledging that conflict episodes are common and that issues prompting conflict have become more serious (Lichter et al., 1988), critics often argue that disagreements are uniformly resolved easily, in ways that satisfy each of those involved, and in ways that routinely include humor (Moore, 1992). At the same time, other studies have shown that parent–child and sibling interactions involve a substantial amount of negative affect and hostility and that both television parents and children commonly use conversation strategies that, in real families, are relationally dysfunctional.

Parent and Child Socialization in Television Families

While few studies have examined parent–child and sibling socialization in television families, those studies offer little consensus and, once again, the primary division is between formal analyses and more popular criticism.

In his extensive examination of domestic comedy, Jones (1992) claimed that "*Father Knows Best* preached many basic lessons: Fulfill your promises; respect others; don't lie to your parents; always do your best" (p. 98), suggesting that, in the Anderson family, children were socialized to satisfy contemporary middle-class mores. The same can probably be said about other television families of the period. The Nelsons (*The Adventures of Ozzie and Harriet*), Cleavers (*Leave It to Beaver*), and Douglases (*My Three Sons*), for example, each appear to have enacted a family narrative in which children were gratefully socialized, by both parents and older siblings, to comply with a value system constructed around integrity, responsibility, and love of family. Heintz-Knowles' (1995) content analysis suggests that more modern television families also socialize children effectively. Although a majority of children examined in the study engaged in antisocial behavior, they were more than twice as likely to behave prosocially and, when they did behave in ways that were judged antisocial, they typically did not achieve their objective. Notably, boys were substantially more likely than girls to fail when performing goal-related sexual and/or romantic acts, implying that, like their real-life counterparts (see, e.g., Knapp & Vangelisti, 2000), television males are socialized by a process that leaves them less relationally competent than television females. Nonetheless, according to academic analyses, social training in both early and more recent television families appears generally successful.

In contrast, popular reviews yield the impression that the socialization of television children is hopelessly inadequate. Zoglin (1990) has argued that, in television families, children are ill-mannered, disrespectful, and annoying, a position supported by Rapping (1994), who has proposed that television children are inactive, apathetic, undisciplined, and disorderly. Clearly, to the extent that such views are veridical, contemporary television parents and siblings are unable and/or unwilling to socialize young children appropriately.

Parent and Child Management of the Daily Routine in Television Families

Again, the ability of parents and children to manage the routine of television family life has attracted little research interest. However, studies that have provided insight suggest that television families are essentially untroubled by the inherent instability of day-to-day life.

Most generally, television families are seen to be affected by only minor problems and even those are resolved easily and amicably (Cantor, 1991; Cantor & Cantor, 1992; Lichter et al., 1988; Newcomb, 1974; Taylor, 1989). Similarly, while modern television women are commonly presented as part of the paid workforce, more problematic social changes, such as single parenthood, the feminization of poverty (Moore, 1992), and parental dependence on day care for children (Heintz-Knowles, 2001) are typically absent. That is, available literature implies that television parents and children manage the mundane turbulence of family life quite effectively. The same appears to be true of siblings.

Using Bank and Kahn's (1975) typology of sibling-to-sibling functions, Larson (1991) content analyzed episodes of *The Adventures of Ozzie and Harriet*, *Father Knows Best*, and *Leave It to Beaver*. Although the scheme defines four functions, two functions, direct service and mutual regulation, accounted for 95% of all sibling interactions. Providing direct services includes such behaviors as lending money or possessions and teaching new skills and accounted for 66% of all interactions; 97% of these were defined as affectively positive.

Mutual regulation includes such behaviors as allowing a sibling to test the usefulness or coherence of new ideas and accounted for 29% of all interactions; 22% of these were defined as affectively positive. That is, acts that served to reduce a sibling's distress or uncertainty were common among brothers and sisters and, for the most part (74%), were characterized by apparent mutual affection.

TELEVISION FAMILIES: SATISFACTION AND STABILITY IN PARENT–CHILD AND SIBLING RELATIONS

Despite the recurrent disagreements that occur between television parents and children and between television siblings, a large segment of television content portrays those relationships as both loving and fulfilling (Cantor & Cantor, 1992). Early television families were shown to be happy and stable (Jones, 1992; Taylor, 1989), and this characterization appears to have continued. Television families are, for the most part, intact (Abelman, 1990; Cantor, 1991) and, even in modern families, the vast majority of television children live with both biological parents (Heintz-Knowles, 1995). Finally, there is some evidence that both television family satisfaction and television family stability is influenced by a class effect. Specifically, based on their analysis of prime-time families, Thomas and Callahan (1982) concluded that working-class families displayed higher levels of family sympathy (i.e., unity or stability) and relational happiness (i.e., satisfaction) than did higher SES families.

TELEVISION PARENTS AND CHILDREN: THE CASE OF ATTRIBUTIONAL STUDIES

In a series of studies, Douglas and Olson (Douglas, 1996; Douglas & Olson, 1995, 1996; Olson & Douglas, 1997) examined viewer attributions about a variety of families presented in domestic comedy. In overview, these researchers studied television families that had appeared in the "top 20" annualized viewer ratings during the period 1950–1997; that is, families were selected on the basis of prominence. This criterion yielded a group of 17 families; the Ricardos (*I Love Lucy*), Andersons (*Father Knows Best*), Douglases (*My Three Sons*), Clampetts (*Beverly Hillbillies*), Stevenses (*Bewitched*), Bunkers (*All in the Family*), Sanfords (*Sanford and Son*), Cunninghams (*Happy Days*), Jeffersons (*The Jeffersons*), Huxtables (*The Cosby Show*), Keatons (*Family Ties*),

Bower-Micellises (*Who's the Boss?*), Conners (*Roseanne*), Winslows (*Family Matters*), Tanners (*Full House*), Seavers (*Growing Pains*), and Taylors (*Home Improvement*).

Participants in the studies were shown sample episodes, determined by viewer "experts" to be representative of the program as a whole, and required to make judgments about family power and affect, family performance, and family satisfaction and stability. Participants made separate judgments about spousal, parent–child, and sibling relationships. Only the analyses of parent–child and sibling data are reported here.

Parents and Children on Television

Viewer attributions about the relationship between television parents and children appear complex. On the one hand, parent–child relations were judged relatively more conflictual in contemporary families and contemporary parents were also seen to socialize children less effectively than their earlier counterparts. As well, modern parents and children were judged relatively less able to manage the day-to-day routine of family life. At the same time, parent–child relations seem to have become generally more cohesive; that is, modern parents and children were perceived as more mutually involved, more trusting of each other, more attracted to each other, and more relationally satisfied. Finally, according to viewers, parents and children performed increasingly similar functions in the modern television family.

Two families, the Conners and Taylors, violated this general model. Relations between parents and children in these families appeared not only highly conflictual but were characterized by levels of cohesiveness and role similarity more like early television families. The analyses suggested that the Conners, in particular, were substantially unable to perform functions associated with child socialization and family management and that relations between parents and children were flagrantly hostile, nonsupportive, and unsatisfying. Parents and children in *Home Improvement* were evaluated in similar ways, although the level of distress was considerably lower than in *Roseanne*.

Attributional studies, then, support two versions of parent–child relations. One coincides, at least in tone, with studies of television content and suggests emotional closeness although, even in this model, modern parents are seen to exert less authority, socialize their children less effectively, and be less able to cope with the stresses of family life than earlier couples; the other proposes a substantially distressed model in which parent–child relations have become oppositional so that modern parents and children are not only affectively remote from each other but also significantly less able to achieve outcomes normally expected of families, such as those associated with child socialization and family management.

Siblings on Television

In overview, attributional analyses suggest that sibling relations have evolved along a trajectory of increasing distress. According to viewers, contemporary siblings, such as those in the Conner, Winslow, Seaver, and Taylor families, are less trusting, more hostile, less able to manage and resolve conflict, and less able to socialize each other appropriately than were siblings in families like the Andersons, Douglases, Cunninghams, Huxtables, and Keatons. Modern siblings also appear not only to like one another less and to be less happy in their relationships but less involved with each other and less likely to become or remain close and supportive in the future. That is, sibling relations were judged to have become relatively ineffective, emotionally unrewarding, and unlikely to endure.

Relations between television siblings also appear more impoverished than other family relationships. Spouses, for example, were seen as more involved and more attracted to each other, less fixed on dominating or influencing each other, more trusting and more open, less conflictual, and more able to manage conflict than were children. Spousal relations were also rated as more satisfying and more stable. Likewise, compared to sibling relations, those between parents and children were seen as significantly less conflictual and more cohesive, implying that relations between siblings are moderated by parental involvement. Modern parents were also judged more effective role models than siblings and more likely to encourage academic and social success in children. Specifically, parents' perceived socializing ability has remained stable while that of siblings has decayed sharply across time so that, in earlier families (i.e., the Andersons to the Keatons), siblings were seen to outperform parents whereas, in more contemporary families (i.e., the Conners to the Taylors), that pattern was reversed.

Clearly, attributional analyses suggest that, in television families, sibling relations have deteriorated and have become considerably distressed. Modern siblings scored relatively poorly on a variety of performance measures and were judged less able than both other family members and earlier generations of television children to construct and maintain mutually satisfying relationships. This contrasts with content-based studies which suggest that children are often motivated by concern for each other and continue to share generally positive relations inside the family.

TELEVISION FAMILIES:
THE FAMILY AND ITS WORLD

Television portrayals of parent–child and sibling relations are embedded in a larger context that offers insight into at least two issues; the significance and place of children in television families and the nature of the suburban world that television families quickly populated. Examination of these issues is important because both children and suburban America became incorporated as standard features of television family narratives and, as such, their study enlarges our understanding of television families and the communities in which they lived.

The Significance of Children to the Television Family

Children have become a stable component of television families. In domestic comedy, in particular, children are ubiquitous (Cantor, 1991; Heintz-Knowles, 1995) so that families such as the Andersons (*Father Knows Best*), Huxtables (*The Cosby Show*), and Conners (*Roseanne*) are often the vehicle for child-centered narratives (Rapping, 1992). The prevalence of children also means that parent–child and sibling interaction is common in television families (Abelman, 1990) and, because children appear most frequently in primary roles, especially as they grow older (Heintz-Knowles, 1995), issues associated with parent–child and sibling relations may be salient and defining features of the television family experience.

At least until the recent past, the "fertility rate" of television families has increased. Skill and Robinson (1994) examined almost 500 television families and observed, first, that only 17% of families were childless during the 1980s compared to 25% during the 1950s, and, second, that the average number of children per family had increased from 1.8 in the 1950s to 2.2 in the 1980s. Similarly, Robinson and Skill (2001) studied "all prime-time fictional series that employed a family configuration as the primary story vehicle on the commercial networks (ABC, CBS, FOX, NBC)" (p. 143) and reported that both the number and the proportion of television families with children had increased. Married parents with children, which remained the modal family type, accounted for 38% of all families between 1990 and 1995. In contrast, married couples without children, which accounted for approximately 25% of all families during the 1950s and more than 10% in the 1980s, accounted for less than 2% of all families between 1990 and 1995. During the same period, the average number of children per family increased to 2.45, a new high-water mark.

Notably, since the mid-1990s, television children may have become, at least temporarily, less commonplace. During this time, domestic comedies, in which the narrative relies on parents and children, have lost much of their popularity. At the same time, situation comedies, such as *Seinfeld, Friends,* and *Frazier,* in which the narrative is constructed around adult–adult relationships, have gained significant visibility (Larson, 2001).

Analysis of A. C. Nielsen's "top 20" rated shows between 1950 and 2000 supports the same conclusion. During this period, there appear to have been four "generations" of domestic comedy (Douglas & Olson, 1995); the first lasted from 1950 to 1956, the second from 1957 to 1970, the third from 1971 to 1983, and the fourth from 1984 to 2000. Comparison of the average number of children in each generation reveals that family size increased across the first (average number of children = 2.14, *n* of families = 7), second (average number of children = 3.63, *n* of families = 19), and third generations (average number of children = 3.92, *n* of families = 12), but decreased during the fourth (average number of children = 2.73, *n* of families = 15). Although these data are specific to domestic comedy, they, nonetheless, provide further evidence that children have become less central to television programming.

The Suburban World of Television

The postwar period was characterized, in part, by rapid and expansive suburban development and the migration of American families to their mass-produced suburban homes. While young, White, middle-class parents and children were welcomed into these new communities, others were excluded. As Spigel (1992) observed, "People of color, lesbian and gay people, unmarried people, homeless people and senior citizens were simply written out of these spaces" (p. 110). So it was on television. Families like the Nelsons, Andersons, and Cleavers gave no hint of social or sexual nonconformity and, after the demise of *Amos'n'Andy,* the minority family disappeared from television for more than a decade.

Real communities, however, are constructed piece by piece. Streets, houses, schools, shopping centers, and parks appear as if parts of ongoing but unsynchronized circles. Likewise, gardens take time to grow and young families accumulate the trappings of home slowly. This was not so on television. The opening sequence of *The Adventures of Ozzie and Harriet, Father Knows Best, Leave It to Beaver,* and other shows repeatedly presented viewers with images of mature communities, familiar and friendly neighbors, picket fences, shade trees, and manicured lawns. As Jones (1992) noted, "No 'suburban' sitcom ever really showed the blank, barren developments, populated by recent strangers" (p. 100). Instead, as Spigel (1992) argued, the television's fictional, surrogate neighborhoods "provided an illusion of the ideal neighborhood— the way it was supposed to be" (p. 129).

CONCLUSIONS AND IMPLICATIONS

The analysis of real and fictional parents and children suggests that the American family has continued to develop along a path marked by increased parental absence from the home and diminishing family performance. Compared to previous generations, modern mothers and fathers are both more likely to work outside the home. Critics argue that this is problematic for two reasons. First, it derives from an altered ideology that emphasizes personal ambition and achievement rather than family life and family relations. Second, it erodes parental ability to provide children with the attention, care, and support implicitly promised to them. Indeed, the "latch-key" experience is seen to produce a long list of child-related problems, ranging from teenage pregnancy and drug abuse to decreased academic performance and depression to the demise of the traditional family and the emergence of what might be labeled the "scattered family." At the same time, critics have proposed that the contemporary family is relatively unable to perform functions routinely expected of families, such as the nurturing and socialization of children, regulation of family members, and construction of satisfying and stable family relations.

This position is supported by public opinion polls, which routinely show that large majorities of respondents believe the family experience has deteriorated, and deteriorated in ways that center on the treatment of children. However, those same polls also reveal that similarly large majorities believe *their own family* is unaffected by such problems. Some observers have invoked television as an explanation for this discrepancy, arguing that television presents a troubled view of the family that significantly and negatively influences viewers' sense of the *family in general.*

Traditional studies of the family on television provide minimal support for this position. Content-based investigations suggest that the family experience of modern parents and children is functional and mutually satisfying and shows few signs of distress. For example, such analyses encourage the conclusion that parents and children cooperate to sustain a traditional family model and adhere to the gender-based division of rights and responsibilities characteristic of adult–adult relationships. According to this position, parent–child relations and sibling relations are mutually supportive, mutually loving and attentive, mutually trusting, and, even in modern television families, happy, satisfying, and stable. Additionally, while parents and children routinely seek to influence each other, success usually is straightforward because other family members commonly acquiesce willingly and easily. Content-based studies also indicate that, although relationships involving parents and children have become highly conflictual and although members may use relationally problematic strategies during family disputes, conflict is generally resolved easily and amicably. As well, modern television families are seen to fulfill significant functions, especially those involving socialization of children and management of the daily routine. Hence, traditional analyses suggest that television parents and children continue to share largely warm, secure, and effective relationships and, as such, yield no evidence of conjunction between the television family experience and that posited to characterize real families.

Less formal evaluations, together with audience-based studies of the television family, offer a quite contrary impression. First, popular reviews have contended that modern parents and children fail to maintain a traditional family model because both lack the requisite relational and task skills and, too, seek personal outcomes, independent of others. Those reviews have also argued that contemporary television families typically fail to socialize children effectively and point to widespread antisocial behavior among children as evidence of this failure. Attributional studies suggest more expansive family distress. According to these investigations, parent–child relations have remained relatively positive and mutually fulfilling, although, in modern families, coordinated action is more often a consequence of negotiation than parental mandate, parents and children are comparatively conflictual and less able to regulate everyday events, and parents tend to socialize children relatively ineffectively. Moreover, compared to earlier sibling relations, those in modern television families are seen to be less trusting, more hostile, less involving, less satisfying, and less likely to endure. Notably, modern siblings were also rated significantly less effective socializers of each other, more often seeking to disadvantage brothers and sisters.

Clearly, both informal and attributional analyses suggest broad convergence between the depleted contemporary family, proposed by Popenoe and others, and the television family. While divorce is rare among television families and while topics such as academic achievement and teenage pregnancy receive little attention, viewers do appear to conclude that television families are relatively unable to achieve an assortment of relational outcomes, including constructing a nurturing family environment, socializing children effectively, regulating family members social and family behavior, and establishing happy and lasting family relationships.

Chapter 7

Minorities on Television:
A Tale of Two Groups

This chapter considers the television portrayal of two minority groups; African Americans and the aged. Until recently, both groups occupied minor and often negative roles on television, largely as a function of public sentiment.

Certainly prior to television, the history of African Americans in popular culture is an uninterrupted procession of stereotypic and racist caricatures. The minstrel tradition was constructed, initially, around enslaved African Americans, who were depicted as indolent, emotionally immature, and happy, and their free counterparts, who were portrayed as inept and unhappy outside the plantation's order and menial labor (Kibler, 1999).

When the minstrel show was revived around the turn of the century, these characters, together with their topsy-turvy opposition, had been rewritten. While the obedient and contented, although incompetent, male slave was retained in the figure of "Jim Crow," the list of players had been expanded to include a female slave figure, the "mammy," a free African American male, "Zip Coon," and a misrepresentation of African American children, the "pickaninny." The "mammy" was defined by her large size and deep blackness and by her devotion and dependability. Although established in vaudeville, the "mammy" would become a familiar aspect of early (White) television families through characters such as Beulah (*Beulah*) and Louise (*Make Room for Daddy*). Accompanying the slave figures were "Zip Coon," a self-absorbed and foppish extension of the free Black man, long a standard part of the minstrel show, and the "pickaninny," an unruly, disheveled, and simple-minded parody of African American children.

In comics, African Americans were essentially absent and, when involved, typically portrayed as "thick-lipped, wide-eyed caricatures" (Gordon, 1998, p. 61). More specifically, the presentation of African Americans in comics moved from "Sambo," a nonthreatening childlike character, to a wider variety of harsher and more elaborate depictions. For example, a paneled illustration for the back page of *Puck*, published in 1896, showed two adult African Americans in conversation. The male, Mr. Johnson, is trying to court the female, Miss Jackson, and implicitly offers to take her to the circus, a place that Miss Jackson apparently adores. Faced by a potentially expensive outing, however, Mr. Jackson "recalls" that he will be out of town and, so, unable to take Miss Jackson to the circus. As Gordon, (1998, p. 61) has argued, this exchange "associates a voracious appetite for excitement and limited generosity with Black women and men respectively." The portrayal of African Americans was also often menacing. In "The New Bully," for instance, Outcault's title character was a powerful and fierce African American youth who carried (and, presumably, used) a cutthroat razor. Likewise, in "Pore Lil Mose," Outcault showed Mose daydreaming of affluence. His dream included himself dressed as a dandy as well as a family coat of arms made up of a cutthroat razor, a set of dice, and a slice of watermelon. In summary, Outcault, and others, "depicted African Americans as superstitious, lazy, violent, and shiftless individuals who loved to eat watermelon, wielded razors, and had pretensions to refinements such as religion and Shakespeare" (Gordon, 1998, p. 63).

Finally, African Americans were a popular part of a radio's relatively diverse although small ethnic community. African American families were featured in the hugely popular *Amos'n'Andy Show* (discussed separately, later) and *The Johnson Family*. The other featured African American was Beulah, a Black maid who, like the characters in the *Amos'n'Andy Show*, would prove sufficiently popular to make the transition from radio to television.

In general, radio portrayals were no friendlier than earlier presentations in vaudeville and comics. African Americans continued to be presented in stereotype and the narratives continued to be constructed around familiar figures, such as "Zip Coon" and the "mammy," and, so, familiar sequences and contexts, such as get-rich-quick schemes and domestic service.

The elderly were even less visible than African Americans. However, like other minorities, when they were incorporated into popular culture, they were most often depicted in negative ways. Unlike concert saloons, vaudeville soon sought to establish a female audience base so that performance content became feminized. In order to attract female customers, sketches focused strongly on courtship and domesticity, although not in ways that required elderly family members. Early narratives typically dealt with courtship, often courtship opposed by the young woman's father, but developed to include a wider variety of relational circumstances, such as spousal conflict and everyday family life. These topics, however, were habitually enacted in the context of the young couple or the emerging family so that, again, there was no natural place for older performers.

In comics and radio, too, the elderly were peripheral. In both the comic and radio versions of *Blondie,* for example, older characters were uncommon and, when included, were presented negatively. Dagwood's family opposes his marriage to Blondie, preferring, instead, a more affluent and more socially adept partner. In so doing, they become anachronistic, champions of a previous ideology. Moreover, they are depicted as substantially overweight, especially female family members who grow larger with age. Likewise, Dagwood's boss, Mr. Dithers, although endowed with power and professional success, is also significantly overweight, constantly disheveled, highly emotional, and often ineffectual in his dealings with Dagwood and others. Perhaps because the domestic comic-strip as well as family radio concentrated on courtship and marriage and childbirth and child-rearing (O'Sullivan, 1990), the elderly were used primarily to frustrate and hinder the young couple and the young family.

AFRICAN AMERICANS ON TELEVISION: THE GREAT REAPPEARING ACT

Two events form the immediate baseline from which the development of the African American family, both off and on television, can be understood. The first is the experience of young Black couples during the postwar, suburban migration; the second is the destiny of fictional Black families in the postwar rush to populate the surrogate suburbs of television, especially following the cancellation of *Amos'n'Andy.*

The Case of Willingboro

When Lynd and Lynd (1937) revisited Muncie in the 1930s, they concluded that African Americans were "the most marginal population" (p. 465) in the city and occupied "a more exposed position . . . than before the depression" (p. 465). African Americans, who accounted for less than 6% of Middletown's population, lived in two areas of the city; one, on the northeastern outskirts, was almost exclusively Black and, the other, to the south of the city, was populated by a mixture of Black and poor White families.

Gans' (1967) account of life in Levittown III (Willingboro) suggests that little had changed a quarter of a century later. William Levitt, who had not previously sold homes to African Americans, pursued the same policy in Willingboro. Despite a state law prohibiting racial discrimination in the sale of federally supported housing, Levitt's "salesmen refused to sell to Negroes and assured whites . . . that the community would be as lily-white as other Levittowns" (Gans, 1967, p. 14). The policy effectively excluded African American families who comprised less than 1% of the 3,000 families who moved into Willingboro between October 1958, when the development opened, and June 1960.

Shortly after the opening of Willingboro, however, an African American couple, who had been refused housing, filed suit against the homebuilder, contending that the FHA mortgage insurance, which was available for homes in Willingboro, was an example of federal support. The case languished until late 1959 when an Appellate Court ruled that the State Division Against Discrimination could hold public hearings. Levitt appealed to the New Jersey Supreme Court, at the same time promising that, if the lower court ruling was upheld, he would voluntarily desegregate Levittown III. Although the state Supreme Court issued a stay in the case until April, in late March Levitt held a series of meetings with community leaders and, on Sunday, March 29, local ministers announced to their congregations that William Levitt "had decided to desegregate voluntarily and asked the community to prepare itself to welcome Negro residents" (Gans, 1967, p. 375).

In fact, there was no straightforward admission of African Americans into Willingboro. First, on the basis of a consultant's report and consistent with Levitt's design, African American applicants were carefully screened to verify their membership in the middle-class. Second, Levitt instructed sales personnel to distribute African American buyers through the community. Ideally, this meant a single family per block but, under no circumstances, should African American families be allowed to purchase adjacent homes. Third, in developing communities, Levitt offered African American families the opportunity to buy premium lots, such as those that backed onto woods. Because such lots were situated along the edge of these communities, this strategy had a scattering effect, further contributing to the isolation of African Americans and implicitly discouraging other African Americans from moving to Willingboro.

It is unlikely that the case of Willingboro is unusual. Other builders adhered to the same policy so that the experience was more probably widespread. In fact, Levitt argued that he could not act in opposition to other builders (i.e., desegregate Willingboro) without substantial financial loss. Furthermore, their anticipation of routine unkindness and numerous other social difficulties must have tacitly motivated many African Americans to live elsewhere. And, of course, African Americans were commonly disadvantaged by the menial employment and low wages available to them so that frequently there was no choice.

The Case of Amos'n'Andy

Against a backdrop of increased awareness of civil rights and the racial divide in American society, increased postwar membership in the NAACP and the organization's sensitivity to racial stereotyping, and the instant popularity and presumed power of television, CBS sought to create a television version of *Amos'n'Andy*. While the radio version had been "a national sensation" (Jones, 1992, p. 19), accounting for two thirds of the listening audience while compelling grocery store managers to pipe the program into their stores and cinema managers to alter movie schedules in order to retain customers, the television version was troubled from the beginning.

Unlike its radio counterpart, the television version of *Amos'n'Andy* used an all-Black cast, except for transient characters, who were often White. In addition, the network hired a racial consultant, Flournoy Miller, an African American entertainer widely recognized as a social activist, to vet scripts and rehearsals. Despite these actions and despite support from some parts of the African American community, who recognized the important opportunity for Black actors to occupy center stage and/or the significance of a coherent Black presence on television, the program was met with substantial and organized opposition, even before it aired. For the most part, disapproval centered on the perceived stereotypic and negative depiction of Black women and men. Many African Americans were offended by images of the "Black matriarch, the castrating Black female, the domineering, overpowering Black women" as well as men who were "classical minstrel types" (Cummings, 1988, p. 76). In particular, African Americans were outraged by George Stevens, the "Kingfish," a character who was not only "very much the coon" (Jones, 1992, p. 55) but, like J. J. Evans (*Good Times*), quickly became the show's primary comedic vehicle.

Opposition to the program was organized by the NAACP, who encouraged members both to write letters of complaint to CBS and to boycott the program sponsor, Schenley Distilleries/Blatz beer. Although widespread, the extent to which these protests were instrumental in the cancellation of *Amos'n'Andy* is unclear. Jones (1992) has attributed the cancellation to poor ratings, arguing that the NAACP exerted little influence. Brooks and Marsh (1981), too, have asserted that, as in previous conflicts over racial stereotyping, the NAACP's efforts were "to little avail" (p. 36). However, in contrast to Jones (1992), these authors have reasoned that the show was not abandoned as a ratings failure but, rather, was viewed by "sizable audiences" (p. 36). Indeed, the show finished 13th in the annualized Nielsen ratings for 1951/ 1952 and 25th in the following year (McNeil, 1984, p. 821), suggesting that viewership, alone, probably did not account for the show's demise.

It is likely that a mixture of factors contributed to the cancellation of *Amos'n'Andy*. First, despite quite substantial viewership, the television version never approached the success enjoyed by *Amos'n'Andy* on the radio and, as such, must have represented a disappointment to CBS. Second, the significant drop in ratings during the second year must have reduced network confidence in a show already surrounded by controversy. Third, Schenley Distilleries withdrew its sponsorship after the second year, switching to *Four Star Playhouse,* a dramatic anthology that never achieved the ratings of *Amos'n'Andy* but which involved none of the conflict associated with that show.

Regardless of the reasons, CBS cancelled *Amos'n'Andy* at the end of its second season and, in so doing, unknowingly marginalized the African American television family for more than a decade. In particular, the African American family disappeared from domestic comedy and did not reappear until 1968, 15 years later, in the form of *Julia,* the culturally stereotypic story of a widowed Black mother and her son and their adventures in an unrealistically integrated and friendly world. *Julia* met with minimal resistance although, because the show failed to portray an African American experience in an African American culture, both the show and its star, Diahann Carroll, were criticized by some in the African American community. Later presentations were condemned for a variety of reasons. Reminiscent of *Amos'n'Andy*, *Sanford and Son* was accused of articulating a racist narrative, and *Good Times* was censured specifically for the transformation of J. J. from urban artist to ethnic stereotype and, more generally, because it implicitly asserted that "Blacks are oversexed. Black mamas are big, earthy tubs of desire. Single Black women are easy. Young Black men are penises on the make" (Jones, 1992, p. 220).

Like their real-life counterparts, African-American television families were late and often unwelcome residents of television's middle-class suburbs. The public reaction to *Amos'n'Andy* had discouraged networks from establishing and maintaining a minority family presence on television, while potential sponsors were unwilling to become associated with the controversy they now believed inevitable. Ultimately, of course, this would change. However, not until the Huxtables (*The Cosby Show*) did the African-American family become both culturally distinctive and an integrated part of the television family community.

The Development of the African American
Television Family

There appears little doubt that early television portrayals of African Americans and African American families relied on familiar but narrow stereotypes. Often, Black characters were presented not only in service of middle-class, White families but, at the same time, absent from any apparent personal family relations. Characters such as Beulah (*Beulah*) and Louise (*Make Room for Daddy*), both comforting domestics, and Rochester (*The Jack Benny Show*) and Willie (*Trouble With Father*), both helpful but uneducated handymen, provided menial aid to White employers rather than love and support to families of their own.

CBS sought, unsuccessfully, to present African Americans in a recurrent family context in *Amos'n'Andy.* Indeed, as previously discussed, the controversy that surrounded *Amos'n'Andy* contributed not only to the cancellation of the show but also to the prolonged absence of African American families from television. *Amos'n'Andy* was taken off the air in June, 1953; *Julia*, the next attempt to articulate a family-based African American narrative, was first aired in September, 1968 (McNiel, 1984). That is, across the course of a decade and a half, as a variety of White families came and went, establishing a collective television-social history, minority families, in general, and African American families, in particular, remained invisible and, so, marginalized in the most fundamental way.

Julia, together with programs that appeared soon after, such as *Sanford and Son* and *Good Times*, were rebuked for at least two reasons. First, they each presented an incomplete family structure. Julia was a widowed mother, Fred Sanford was a widowed father, and, although the Evans family initially involved married parents and dependent children, internal disagreement regarding the (in)appropriateness of J. J. soon transformed the family into "a fatherless Black family, the very image of Black cultural dysfunction" (Jones, 1992, p. 219) after John Amos (James Evans, the father) was released from his contract. By the following season, Esther Rolle (Florida Evans, the mother) had also resigned in protest so that the Evans family was reduced to three parentless children, "headed" by the eldest son, J. J.! Second, Cummings (1988) and Dates and Stroman (2001) have argued that the shows relied on stereotypic conventions, such as "the 'coon'" and "loud but lovable 'mammy' types" (Cummings, 1988, p. 78), that derived from the minstrel tradition (Dates & Stroman, 2001). According to Cummings (1988), such conventions were not only intrinsically problematic but, because they were instrumentally benign, allowed portrayals to rely on characters and interactions that were comfortable to White viewers. Significant but potentially threatening aspects of African American culture were made harmless in other ways, too. In *Good Times,* for example, the confrontational ideology of the Black Panthers was voiced through Michael Evans, the family's young son, a strategy that allowed the show to include an obviously important feature of the Black experience but functioned, as well, to minimize the issue's tacit menace.

More generally, the television community remains predominantly White. Studies of early television content (Poindexter & Stroman, 1981; U.S. Commission on Civil Rights, 1977) reinforced the "chilling effect" of *Amos'n'Andy,* suggesting that African Americans appeared infrequently and typically occupied minor roles on television. This position is consistent with Greenberg and Collette's (1997) later analysis, which showed not only that African Americans accounted for only 10% of all major characters between 1966 and 1992 but, more specifically, that between 1966 and 1983, African Americans were even more severely underrepresented, accounting for less than 8% of all major characters. It was not until the early 1990s that African Americans' television representation (11% of all prime-time characters) approximated their representation in the general population (12%; Greenberg & Brand, 1994) although, quite obviously, an overwhelming majority of television characters and television families remained White (Skill & Robinson, 1994).

Over the past decade, television's ethnic imbalance appears to have stabilized. Mastro and Greenberg's (2000) recent content analysis of prime-time network programming, for example, revealed that 16% of characters were African American and 80% were Caucasian. Approximately half of each group occupied a main role in the program. In contrast, Heintz-Knowles and Chen (2000) coded characters from sample shows broadcast on ABC, CBS, NBC, Fox, UPN, and WB during the Fall of 1999 and reported that only 14% of leading roles were played by African Americans; 82% were played by Caucasians. In a broader sense, however, Heintz-Knowles and Chen observed that only 13% of all characters were African American and 80% were Caucasian, suggesting a similar level of ethnic diversity as Mastro and Greenberg (2000). Likewise, Robinson and Skill (2001) examined all prime-time, fictional series broadcast by ABC, CBS, Fox, and NBC during the period 1950–1995 and concluded that, while minority families had become more common across time, there was no evidence of ethnic or racial diversity. In particular, between 1990 and 1995, 14% of all families were African American, and 81% were White. Heintz-Knowles and her colleagues (Heintz-Knowles, 2001; Heintz-Knowles & Chen, 2000; Heintz-Knowles, Chen, Miller, & Haufler, 2000; Heintz-Knowles et al., 2001) reported similar ethnic configurations. Heintz-Knowles (2001) investigated family-related programs aired by ABC, CBS, NBC, Fox,

WB, and UPN during March, 1998, and reported that 16% of all adult characters were African American and 77% were Caucasian. Heintz-Knowles and Chen (2000), meanwhile, content analyzed three episodes of each prime-time entertainment series shown on the same networks during Fall, 1999, and determined that 13% of characters were Black and 80% were White. A more limited analysis of leading roles revealed little difference; 14% of characters were Black and 82% were White. Heintz-Knowles et al. (2001) conducted a similar analysis of shows aired during Fall, 2000, and observed that 17% of characters were African American while 75% were Caucasian. Likewise, analyses of television children have revealed the same disparity. Even in domestic comedy, a type of programming likely to feature African Americans (Dates & Stroman, 2001; Harrison, 2000; Heintz-Knowles & Chen, 2000; Mastro & Greenberg, 2000), Heintz-Knowles (1995) determined that only 16% of child characters were Black, whereas 77% were White.

In summary, African American families have come to comprise a larger and more visible part of the television community. Nonetheless, television neighborhoods remain ethnically distorted. Not only are White families grossly overrepresented, but groups other than African Americans remain essentially absent.

The portrayal of African Americans has been investigated in two broad ways. First, researchers have compared African Americans to one another. Studies of this kind are usually designed to assess change across time, although some have been cross-sectional and, as such, descriptive of a specific period. Second, researchers have compared African Americans to other groups, typically Whites. Studies of this kind are usually cross-sectional and, so, assess the relative state of African American families and family members at a single point in time.

Within-group analyses encourage the conclusion that, until recently, African Americans have been presented in stereotypic and substantially negative ways. Certainly, until the very late 1980s, African American television families were generally non-intact and female-dominated (Berry, 1980; Greenberg & Atkin, 1978). Additionally, adult African American males were portrayed as lazy, untrustworthy, and unintelligent (Gunter, 1998), and systematically placed in low-income, low-status occupations (Gunter, 1998; Poindexter & Stroman, 1981) such as laborer, gardener, or itinerant worker. Further, African American television families were habitually impoverished (Dates & Stroman, 2001) and unable to care adequately for themselves (Comer, 1982) so that African American males were emasculated both by personal weakness, a violation of the White, middle-class ethic, and inability to provide for their families, a fundamental breach of the father/provider role. The familial competence of African American television wives/mothers was undermined more indirectly. Not only did early depictions often present African American women as disconnected from any family of their own (e.g., Beulah) but subsequent portrayals showed the African-American family to be unloving towards children (Berry, 1980) and isolated from close relatives (Greenberg & Neuendorf, 1980). Such emotional sterility clearly implies a mother's inability to fulfill the mandate of nurturer/caregiver.

More recent within-group analyses suggest that contemporary portrayals of the African American family are more positive and more culturally authentic. Both Stroman, Merritt, and Metabane (1989–1990) and Dates (1993) examined an assortment of family presentations and observed that modern African American television families are more usually depicted as intact and middle-class. Similarly, Merritt and Stroman (1993) examined *The Cosby Show, 227,* and *Charlie & Co.* during the 1985–1986 season and concluded that parents were loving, supportive, and involved and treated children in considerate ways. Specifically, the researchers noted that, in these shows, "both husband and wife (are) present; . . . spouses interact frequently, equally, and lovingly with each other; and children are treated with respect and taught achievement-oriented values. All of this takes place in an atmosphere that harbors little conflictual behavior" (Merritt & Stroman, 1993, pp. 497–498). Finally, Cummings (1988) has pointed to artifacts such as paintings, clothes, and music preferences in the Huxtable home (*The Cosby Show*) as articulation of a unique and unmistakable African-American culture.

Between-group studies are less encouraging. Sweeper (1984) compared the portrayal of Black and White characters in 93 episodes of family comedy and drama series between 1970 and 1980 and determined that Black characters and Black families were more negatively portrayed across a variety of attributes. Black characters were more likely to come from broken homes, and Black families were more likely to be headed by a single female and were also more conflictual than White families. Black males were rated more hostile, more self-centered, less reliable, more vain, and more pompous than White males, and Black females were more obese than White females. Moreover, Black characters, in general, exhibited lower educational achievement and lower occupational status than their White counterparts.

While more contemporary investigations suggest that ethnic bias has weakened, some may overestimate the change because of the television families that were examined. For example, Frazer and Frazer (1992) compared the Andersons (*Father Knows Best*) and Huxtables (*The Cosby Show*) and concluded that, despite superficial differences, the families were alike in that both shows promoted a view of the nuclear family as normal, both families were affluent, both excluded potentially disruptive influences external to the family, and, most notably, both portrayed gender roles and family relationships in essentially the same way, placing women in a domestic and subservient role. Likewise, Larson (1993) compared communication patterns in the Simpsons (*The Simpsons*) and Huxtables (*The Cosby Show*) and concluded that spousal interaction was common in both families and both families were significantly more affiliative than conflictual. These studies imply close similarity between African-American and Caucasian television family life but should be interpreted cautiously. First, the repeated use of *The Cosby Show* is potentially problematic because the program was a conscious attempt to situate the Black family in middle-class America (L. Fuller, 1992) and, as such, may be anomalous. Second, Frazer and Frazer's (1992) research demonstrates that the Huxtables would not have been out of place (except as a function of their color) in the postwar television community. The research does not demonstrate that contemporary African American families are an integral part of a mainstream television family narrative. Third, Larson's (1993) selection of *The Simpsons* is troublesome because the show presents the experience of a cartoon family and, as such, provides a distorted account of family life. For example, the program necessarily lacks all aspects of the family experience associated with the aging of family members and the impact of aging on family life and family relations. If the Simpson children aged naturally, it seems likely that parent–child communication would be substantially *less* affiliative, reflecting the conflict between parents and children that frequently occurs as children pass through adolescence.

A more comprehensive analysis conducted by Mastro and Greenberg (2000) compared African American, Latino, and Caucasian television characters across a mixture of personal and social dimensions and suggests that African Americans continue to be portrayed in relatively negative ways. Although perceived income, intelligence, weight, and loudness did not vary as a function of ethnicity, African Americans were judged the most lazy and least respected of the groups. African Americans were also seen to be more provocatively and less professionally dressed than Caucasians and less well groomed than Caucasians. Finally, conversations between African Americans were rated the most relaxed and most spontaneous.

A series of studies conducted by Heintz-Knowles and others (Heintz-Knowles, 2001; Heintz-Knowles & Chen, 2000; Heintz-Knowles et al., 2000; Heintz-Knowles et al., 2001) also produced mixed results. Characters of color were more likely than White characters to be portrayed narrowly (i.e., either at home *or* at work/school *or* in public places), and 76% of African American characters were never shown at home (Heintz-Knowles et al., 2000). As well, African American characters were relatively less likely to be employed in professional careers, although the differences were potentially small. For example, while Heintz-Knowles and Chen (2000) reported that, among recurring prime-time characters, 18% of Black characters but 28% of White characters were portrayed as professionals, an additional 15% of Black characters were depicted as small business owners. No White characters were depicted in this way. Similarly, while Heintz-Knowles et al. (2001) reported that Black characters were approximately half as likely as White characters to be depicted as professionals, that gap diminished significantly when attorneys, physicians, executives and CEOs, media professionals, and teachers were added to the list of professional occupations. Within this enlarged definition, the occupations of 20% of Black characters and 26% of White characters could be considered professional. Moreover, African-Americans, both male and female, were *more* likely than their White counterparts to be judged successful, good, and competent, and African Americans, as a group, were depicted as better problem solvers than Whites (Heintz-Knowles et al., 2000). Hence, in contrast to within-group studies, which suggest wide improvement in the portrayal of African-Americans across time, between-group analyses are less conclusive. While some of the most negative attributes appear no longer a stock part of the African American television character, and while African Americans may, in some instances, be depicted more positively than their White counterparts, African Americans continue to be presented as lazy, undeserving of admiration, and frivolous.

One difficulty inherent in the study of African Americans on television is that they are often portrayed as working-class. Analyses of early depictions, in particular, have routinely concluded that African American males were placed in low-income, low-status occupations and/or that African American families were shown as poor. Because working-class males, in general, are presented as inept, stupid, emotional, and so on (Butsch, 1992; Glennon & Butsch, 1982), SES may confound the examination of African Americans, especially African American males. That is, the negative portrayal of African American males may be a function of their working-class status rather than their ethnicity. Consistent with this position, when African American males are presented as middle-class, as was the case with Cliff Huxtable (*The Cosby Show*), they appear articulate, competent, successful, and able to provide comfortably for their families.

THE ELDERLY ON TELEVISION:
PLAYING IN THE MARGINS

Aging Americans participated only minimally in the postwar suburban migration. For the most part, they, like African Americans and other ethnic groups, understood that the emerging communities were intended for young White couples and their newly born or soon-to-be-born children. Gans (1967), for example, reported that almost 80% of Willingboro's male residents were under 40 years of age and almost half were between 30 and 40 years old. Additionally, 17 out of every 20 couples had school-age children, 1 in 5 families included three children, and more than 1 in 10 families included four or more children. Older couples may have been discouraged further by a growing sense of ideological and social isolation. According to Gans (1967), a few women "found surrogate mothers among friends or neighbors, but chose women only slightly older than themselves, and rarely consulted elderly neighbors. As for the husbands, they were, to a man, glad they had moved away from parents and in-laws" (p. 169). Such age-biased predispositions minimized social interaction across levels of age so that older residents were often friendless and lonely. In particular, little contact occurred between the old and the very young, encouraging both the elderly and children to view one another as "strange" (p. 169). Nor did Gans believe this social disjunction was limited to Willingboro, arguing instead that "change in America has been so rapid that the ideas and experiences of the elderly are often anachronistic" (p. 169). Butler (1969) took an even wider view, proposing that American culture has consistently "valued pragmatism, action, power, and the vigor of youth over contemplation, reflection, experience, and the wisdom of age" (p. 243), producing a "deep seated uneasiness on the part of the young and middle-aged—a personal revulsion to and distaste for growing old, disease, disability, and fear of powerlessness, 'uselessness,' and death" (p. 243).

Unsurprisingly, the same biases appear to have emerged when people gathered around the television. Hess (1974) has reasoned that, in postwar America, extreme mobility among young families made the aged less familiar and aging more undesirable so that, on television, older Americans quickly became associated with "hair darkeners, laxatives, denture adhesives, ... wrinkles, gray hair, lack of zap, and irregularity" (Hess, 1974, pp. 80–81). Because of their limited commercial value, elderly Americans were, and for the most part remain, unappealing to advertisers, as well. This, according to Davis (1984), has affected television content in two ways. First, programmers have been unwilling to feature older characters and, second, when they have been included, the elderly have been portrayed in distorted and negative ways.

Portrayal of the Elderly on Television

Studies of the elderly on television have been guided by three issues; the extent to which the elderly are underrepresented, determination of the attributes typically associated with elderly characters, and the extent to which portrayal of the elderly varies as a function of gender.

Two early studies generated widely discrepant estimates of the frequency with which older characters appeared on television. On the one hand, Petersen (1973) examined evening programming and reported that 13% of the characters could be classified as elderly. On the other, Aronoff (1974) categorized almost 3,000 prime-time characters on the basis of perceived age and determined that the elderly comprised less than 5% of the sample. Later studies have, for the most part, generated estimates closer to those offered by Aronoff, although there remains some inconsistency, even in contemporary analyses.

Northcott (1975), for example, coded a single week of network programming and deemed that less than 2% of all characters were over 65 years of age. Likewise, Greenberg, Korzenny, and Atkin (1979) examined prime-time programs during the period 1975–1977 and concluded that only 3% of characters were at least 64 years old, and Gerbner, Gross, Signorielli, and Morgan's (1980) examination of network programming during the period 1969–1978 showed that older characters represented a little more than 2% of all characters and a little more than 1% of weekend daytime characters. Similarly, Harris and Feinberg (1977) coded an assortment of non-prime-time programming and determined that less than 8% of all characters were between the ages of 60 and 70, and less than 1% were older than 70. Older characters also appear rare in cartoons. Bishop and Krause (1984), for example, evaluated cartoons aired by ABC, CBS, and NBC during 1981. Only 7% of characters were defined as "old," that is exhibiting signs of old age, such as wrinkled skin, white hair, and/or a cracking voice. Additionally, only one plot-line, of more than 100, centered on the "old" and this involved a robotic maid considered too old for her job. Finally, "old" characters enacted only 7% of all positive actions and only 11% of all negative actions, far less than "adults" who enacted half of all positive actions and 85% of all negative actions, again emphasizing the comparative invisibility of the elderly.

Recent studies yield a less consistent impression. Greenberg and Collette (1997) categorized over 1,700 major characters added during each new season to network television during the period 1966–1992. Seven percent were found to be between 51 and 64 years old whereas only 2% were over 65. In comparison, 7% were under 13 years of age, 13% were between 13 and 19, 43% were between 20 and 35, and 28% were between 36 and 50. Heintz-Knowles (2001), too, examined prime-time characters on six major commercial networks and reported that "seniors" (characters over 65 years of age) comprised only 2% of the television population. In contrast, "adults" (characters between 30 and 50 years of age) comprised 53% of the population and "young adults" (characters between 18 and 30 years of age) comprised 32%. These estimates stand in stark contrast to those generated by Heintz-Knowles et al. (2001). These researchers classified more than 2,000 prime-time characters on the basis of age. All characters appeared in programs aired during 2000 on the six major commercial networks. Almost 14% were categorized as "older adults" (characters between 50 and 69 years of age) and another 3% were categorized as "elderly" (characters over 70). The complete analysis showed that 3% of all characters were children, 8% were adolescents, 19% were between 19 and 29 years old, 32% were between 30 and 39 years old, and 21% were between 40 and 49 years old.

There is inconsistency, too, regarding the extent to which older characters are present in soap operas. An early study suggested that older adults were commonly featured in this type of programming. Cassata, Anderson, and Skill (1980) examined a 2-week sample of 13 daytime serials aired during 1979 and reported that 16% of all characters were judged to be over 55 years of age. However, not only did Harris and Feinberg (1977) observe that older characters were especially uncommon in soap operas but Elliot's (1984) content analysis of daytime serials revealed that only 8% of characters were over 60 years of age.

Despite variability across studies, the bulk of evidence encourages the conclusion that the elderly are not widely present on television and become less visible as they grow older. Even most contemporary investigations suggest that the elderly are not routinely featured on television, regardless of whether the analysis deals with prime-time programming, non-prime-time programming, or children's programming. Finally, family circumstances common to older people seem rare. For example, Robinson and Skill (2001) studied all family configurations depicted in prime-time fictional programming aired on ABC, CBS, NBC, and Fox beginning in 1979 and observed that depictions of "empty nest" couples were extremely uncommon, accounting usually for zero percent of annual portrayals and, maximally, for less than 2%.

Another research focus has been the depiction of the elderly. Perhaps based on the assumption that portrayal of the elderly has followed a similar trajectory to the portrayal of other marginalized groups, a common belief among many observers is that age is associated inversely with a variety of positive attributes and associated directly with a wide range of negative attributes. For example, in his extensive examination of the elderly and television, Davis (1980) concluded that, because audiences valued attributes such as youth and virility and because television relied on stock characters such as the "silly fluttery maiden lady, the dirty old man . . ., the autocratic and rigid older boss" (p. 68), the elderly were not only shown infrequently but were habitually depicted in negative ways. Others, like Cirillo (1994), Hanlon, Farnsworth, and Murray (1997), Rowles (1994), and Williams and Coupland (1998), have more recently made similar arguments.

Empirical evidence is less conclusive. Certainly, a number of investigations have provided evidence that viewers define older characters negatively. Old age has been associated with incompetence, disability and ill-health, and emotional narrowness (Harris & Feinberg, 1977; Marshall & Wallenstein, 1973). Age has also been related inversely to happiness, benevolence, self-efficacy and active problem-solving, importance, and power (Aronoff, 1974; Elliot, 1984; Gerbner et al., 1980; Signorielli & Gerbner, 1978). Additionally, Elliot (1984) remarked that elderly characters were most likely to enact passive behaviors, such as looking and listening, and least likely to enact sexual displays. The latter observation is congruent with that of Harris and Feinberg (1977), who reported that older characters were almost never involved in developing romantic relationships and, while they were sometimes married, those marriages were not depicted as loving or sexual. Indeed, the authors concluded that, "television clearly perpetuates the myth of the sexless, boring oldster whose inner life is unworthy of interest" (p. 465).

At the same time, however, the elderly have been characterized in quite opposite ways. For example, older characters have been seen as affluent, competent, healthy and attractive, strong and independent, active, involved, and optimistic (Cassata et al., 1980; Dail, 1988; Harris & Feinberg, 1977; Peterson, 1973; Signorielli & Gerbner, 1978). Likewise, the elderly on television have been described as "valued advisors-in-residence with their children and grandchildren" (Ramsdell, 1973, p. 302) and, compared to younger characters, more likely to provide advice and directions, more likely to be nurturing, and less likely to be verbally aggressive or generally angry (Elliot, 1984).

Portrayal of the elderly may be especially positive in programs popular among older viewers. Bell (1992) examined older characters in five such shows, *Murder She Wrote*, *The Golden Girls*, *Matlock*, *Jake and the Fatman*, and *In the Heat of the Night*, and reported that older characters were judged affluent, healthy, active, admired, powerful, and sexy.

Two additional studies require mention because, in comparatively indirect ways, they further suggest that older people are portrayed positively. First, Bishop and Krause (1984) compared the portrayal of young, adult, and elderly characters in cartoons aired by the three major networks during 1981. Analyses indicated, in part, that the young enacted 43% of all positive characterizations and 4% of all negative characterizations; that is, a positive/negative ratio of 10.75. Adults, meanwhile, enacted 50% of positive and 85% of negative characterizations, yielding a positive/negative ratio of 0.59. Finally, the elderly enacted 7% of positive and 11% of negative characterizations, yielding a positive/negative ratio of 0.64. Hence, while the elderly were less salient than other groups and were depicted significantly less positively than children, they were portrayed as favorably as younger adults. Second, Dail (1988) categorized the talk and actions of older prime-time characters appearing on the three major networks during 1984. Content was classified as positive cognitive behavior (e.g., appropriate mental orientation and interaction), negative cognitive behavior (e.g., inappropriate mental orientation and interaction), positive physical behavior (e.g., mobile and physically active), negative physical behavior (e.g., hospitalized and infirm), positive health-related behavior (e.g., non-problematic functioning), negative health-related behavior (e.g., ongoing care and assistance), positive social behavior (e.g., socially active), negative social behavior (e.g., reclusive), positive personality behavior (e.g., happy, optimistic), or negative personality behavior (e.g., sad, irritable, anxious/fearful, depressed). Older characters were found to enact significantly more positive than negative behavior across all categories. In fact, elderly characters rarely engaged in negative behavior of any kind. Specifically, negative behaviors comprised less than 2% of all cognitive acts, 4% of all physical acts, 6% of all health related acts, less than 3% of all social acts, and 7% of all personality acts. That is, the elderly were presented in overwhelmingly positive ways.

Again, despite inconsistency across analyses, a large amount of research suggests that the elderly often are depicted positively. Contrary to popular belief, older people are frequently portrayed in ways that imply activity, independence, optimism, and virility. Moreover, elderly characters appear, in a larger sense, to act appropriately. Not only do they appear aware of social conventions, they also appear able to enact a wide range of normative displays. This appears to be especially true in programs designed to attract older viewers.

The third major research focus has been the extent to which portrayal of the elderly varies across levels of gender. This research tends to deal with two issues; the interaction between characters' gender and age/visibility and the interaction between gender and the attributes associated with elderly characters.

In brief, female characters appear generally younger than their male counterparts and to comprise a smaller proportion of television's elderly population. In his early analysis of the elderly in prime-time, Aronoff (1974) estimated that, on average, television females were 10 years younger than television males. Likewise, while Peterson (1973) noted that 13% of his sample could be considered elderly, older female characters accounted for only a little more than 1% of that contingent. That is, older males were more than nine times more common than older females, a distribution also observed by Davis and Davis (1985) in their extensive review of the elderly on television.

More recent studies have produced similar results. Elliot's (1984) examination of daytime drama, for example, showed that the age of characters in the sample varied systematically as a function of gender. Specifically, 60% of females were aged between 20 and 39, 24% were aged between 40 and 59, and 7% were over 60; meanwhile, 48% of males were aged between 20 and 39, 35% were aged between 40 and 59, and 9% were over 60. That is, not only were females generally younger than males but older female characters were less common than older male characters. Finally, both Greenberg and Collette (1997) and Elasmar et al. (1999) have pointed to the youth bias among female television characters. Greenberg and Collette's (1997) longitudinal analysis revealed that 71% of major female characters introduced since 1966 have been 35 years old or younger, while Elasmar et al.'s (1999) study of prime-time programming indicated that almost 60% of female characters were in their late 20s and 30s.

In general, television females also appear to age less well than television males. Among television women, old age has been associated with inability to achieve goals (Aronoff, 1974; Gerbner et al., 1980), loss of occupational status (Downing, 1974), decreased esteem and authority (Harris & Feinberg, 1977), and diminished physical attractiveness (Beck, 1978). Older television men, meanwhile, are more likely to be portrayed as interesting, appealing, and socially adept (Beck, 1978), powerful (Beck, 1978; Harris & Feinberg, 1977), successful (Gerbner et al., 1980), and respected (Harris & Feinberg, 1977). Additionally, as television characters age, females become less likely to offer advice to others whereas, among males, advice giving increases (Harris & Feinberg, 1977).

Hence, there is broad agreement that female characters are generally younger than males, female characters comprise a comparatively smaller proportion of television's elderly population, and older women tend to be portrayed in negative ways, whereas older men are portrayed positively. Clearly, such a gender bias is not unique to portrayal of the elderly but it does emphasize that, to the extent that viewers learn from television, women are likely to view aging as a debilitating process and viewers, in general, are likely to develop aversive expectations that may influence the probability of voluntarily interacting with elderly women and interpretation of elderly women's actions.

CONCLUSIONS AND IMPLICATIONS

Examination of the depiction of African-Americans and the elderly suggests, first, that, as in Middletown and Willingboro, both groups were marginalized in the White, middle-class, and relatively young communities that were a staple of early television. Furthermore, although African Americans and the elderly have both come to occupy an enlarged and more visible presence, they remain a relatively small part of the television population and, too, continue to be portrayed in ways that are, at best, ambiguous and, at worst, stereotypic and hostile.

African Americans, for example, may no longer be portrayed as overweight, unintelligent, incapable of performing anything other than low-level work, and inherently poor, and the Huxtables (*The Cosby Show*) may have placed the African American family on television's main street. Nonetheless, reminiscent of "Zip Coon," African Americans continue to be seen as lazy as well as provocatively and unprofessionally dressed, and no African American family has assumed the place and role of the Huxtables so that the African American family's wide visibility has been short-lived.

The portrayal of the elderly has also been ambiguous. On the one hand, they have been presented in ways that suggest the elderly are physically active, in good health, strong, and independent. At the same time, other depictions have implied that the elderly, and most especially older women, are incompetent, passive, and unhappy. The elderly are also underrepresented on television, a discrepancy that increases as the American population becomes older.

Clearly, to the extent that these trends continue, minority groups are likely to feel disenfranchised, threatened, and/or alienated. As the "baby-boom" generation ages, it is probable that older characters, at least, will become more common and their portrayal more positive, in part because networks are likely to air more age-sensitive programming, that is, programming in which the elderly are depicted positively. The future of African Americans and the African American family is less clear. It is possible that African Americans will become a more economically powerful group, which may translate into increased attention to issues important to the African American community and a more varied and, in aggregate, more positive presentation of African Americans and the African American family experience. This, however, is far less certain than the accommodation to aging baby-boomers, evidenced already in everything from the reincarnation of postwar television families, such as the Cleavers (*Leave It to Beaver*), to the widespread syndication of television families, such as the Bunkers (*All in the Family*) and Petries (*The Dick Van Dyke Show*) previously popular among that age group.

Chapter 8

Is Something Wrong in Suburbia?

This analysis was designed to trace the evolution of the family on television and yield insight into the confused relationship between life and relations in fictional and real families. The investigation was also intended to assess the present state of the television family and test the specific hypothesis that the television family has become distressed in ways that are sometimes seen to define the real family experience.

Television's family lexicon emerged from the conventions of vaudeville and its focus on the family that encouraged portrayal of routine family life and family relations. Vaudeville also provided a cast of stock characters, including the shrewish wife and the old maid, and stock sequences, such as courtship and marriage, that remained popular even on television. Additionally, vaudeville articulated a family sociology that defined marriage as a female institution and women as irresponsible and superficial and, too, implied that infidelity was common.

Because newspapers and magazines, like vaudeville, sought an enlarged female readership, comic strips also soon placed a priority on relational issues, in general, and family issues, in particular. Hence, a variety of strips often depicted scenes from courtship, marriage, and parent–child relations, especially those between mother and child(ren). Unlike vaudeville, which had a rather narrow family focus, comic strips presented an expansive version of the family experience and quickly situated that experience in a traditional family model. *Blondie* represents an example of this convention and indicates, as well, that comic strips frequently exhibited an inherent authenticity. First, although *Blondie* originated as a courtship serial, it developed into a much richer narrative, dealing with the transition from courtship to marriage, gender and marriage, parenthood, and a host of other family topics. At the same time, the fictional vignettes were constructed around characters and events that must have been familiar to readers, at least to those of Muncie, Indiana. For example, comparison of *Blondie* and life and relations in Middletown (Lynd & Lynd, 1937, 1956) revealed a broad similarity. For example, both advocated an ideology of marriage based on mutual love and emphasized the need for young men to demonstrate their independence although, once married, to subvert any competing ambitions in order to provide effectively for their families. Likewise, because they were most likely to lead to a "good" marriage, both promoted attributes such as physical attractiveness, emotionality, and illogic as appropriate for young women but assumed that marriage would direct women's sexuality to childbearing and release their innate ability to establish a nurturing and caring home environment.

Such narratives, rich in their detail of day-to-day family life, together with their attendant conventions and ideology migrated to radio and, then, television. Families like the Bumsteads (*Blondie*), Jones' and Stevens' (*Amos'n'Andy*), Aldriches (*The Aldrich Family*), and Rileys (*The Life of Riley*) defined radio family culture and transported that culture to television. Hence, television families inherited a tradition deeply rooted in the domestic narrative and characterized by social and ethnic diversity, commitment to the traditional family, and embedded, at least episodically, in the real family experience.

DEVELOPMENT OF THE TELEVISION FAMILY

The television family landscape changed almost immediately, becoming more homogeneous and substantially suburban. Ethnic families, working-class families, and minority families, together with the elderly and childless, disappeared to be replaced by young, White, middle-class families. Families like the Nelsons (*The Adventures of Ozzie and Harriet*), Andersons (*Father Knows Best*), and Cleavers (*Leave It to Beaver*) inhabited television suburbia and demonstrated their intrinsic value not only through their easy affluence but also as a function of their peaceful and fulfilling family life. Each of these families, like others of that generation, adhered strictly to a family model that mandated gender-specific rights and responsibilities, parental authority, mutual love, and the ideological priority of home and family.

Across time, spousal relations have become more egalitarian so that wives and mothers are infrequently portrayed as homemakers and modern fathers are often involved in domestic life, especially child care and parenting. Spousal relations have also become explicitly sexual and, while contemporary couples are more likely than their postwar counterparts to engage in argument, they are also more likely to express their affection for each other, suggesting an ideology of increased expressivity in marriage. However, spousal interaction appears still to be governed by rules that empower males and marginalize females. For example, conversation continues often to conform to a traditional, gender-based model in which husbands offer advice, provide instruction, and influence others as a consequence of their own expertise while wives more commonly seek advice, require instruction, and rely on exchange strategies to influence partners. Similarly, husbands more often seek to resolve hostility while wives more frequently engage in acts that increase both the intensity and the magnitude of conflict. In particular, husbands tend to rely on integrative strategies, such as emphasizing commonality, whereas wives engage in avoidance strategies, increasing the likelihood that any disagreement will continue to infiltrate the relationship. Compared to their earlier counterparts, contemporary couples also seem less organized, less competent, and less able to manage the mundane and recurrent issues of family life. Nonetheless, like their predecessors, modern middle-class couples appear to develop enduring relationships that provide both wives and husbands high levels of friendship, happiness, and satisfaction.

Working-class couples seem not to enjoy such relational outcomes. In families like the Kramdens (*The Honeymooners*), Bunkers (*All in the Family*), Evans' (*Good Times*), and Conners (*Roseanne*), not only are gender roles inverted, so that both wives and husbands habitually violate the nurturer/ provider dichotomy fundamental to middle-class families, but spousal relations are characterized by repetitive and sometimes acute hostility. Compared to their white-collar counterparts, working-class husbands are more likely to threaten or imply violence (e.g., "To the moon, Alice") and both husbands and wives more frequently use divisive strategies, such as personal insult and derisive labeling (e.g., "You dingbat"). Additionally, working-class couples appear to viewers less able to manage the routine of family life, perhaps because they are surrounded by the trappings of hardship; their jobs are menial and offer severely limited expectations, their homes untidy and dour, their furniture dowdy, and their personal appearance often unattractive. Finally, in contrast to middle-class couples, working-class spouses seem unhappy and discontented, even though their marriages are generally stable. Hence, television portrayals of spousal relations explicitly advocate the merit of the middle-class experience, suggesting not only that middle-class couples enjoy a more comfortable life together but also that they develop more effective, more affectionate, and more satisfying relationships.

Although soap opera portrayals are less rooted in ordinary family life than other types of programming and often present family relations that are quite unreal, they nonetheless offer explicit and unique insight into the issue of sex and the family. Because of their long-term episodic structure, soap operas also encourage viewers to enter into the social and personal histories of their community and characters so that viewers may accrue a storehouse of knowledge about a variety of issues, including characters' sexuality.

In general, soap operas indicate that sexual intimacy between married partners has become more common. This is consistent with evidence from other programming that shows that, compared to earlier spouses, modern couples are more likely to express their affection and more likely to engage in low-level sexual intimacy, such as kissing and engaging in sexual talk. Infidelity, however, is even more common. Intercourse between persons not married to each other occurs approximately three times more often than intercourse between married couples. That is, soap operas depict a sexualized family experience in which adulterous relationships are common, suggesting that television spousal relations have become more openly emotional but, at the same time, less able to contain persons' sexual expressiveness.

The evolutionary trajectory of television parent–child relations is less clear. Content-based studies encourage the view that parents and children continue to develop and maintain mutually supportive and caring relationships, while attributional analyses and informal criticism argue that relations between parents and children have deteriorated across time so that modern relations are substantially troubled. Specifically, content-based studies suggest a traditional relational model in which parents and children act cooperatively to sustain separate, although egalitarian, roles. Parents, for example, provide reassurance and support, show concern, and are watchful and attentive to their children. Children, meanwhile, frequently depend on parents to solve problems and habitually seek parental attention. At the same time, the relationship between television parents and children appears to have become rooted more in negotiation than parental authority so that coordinated action in contemporary families relies more on family-wide discussion and compromise than parental mandate. Likewise, while fathers may dominate family conversation and family decision-making on religious television and while parents, generally, may exert slightly more influence than children, it has become common for children to express their opinions and to influence family life in substantial ways.

For the most part, conventional investigations, as well as some more holistic studies (e.g., Bryant et al., 2001), also imply that television parents and children have established an ongoing tradition of mutual supportiveness and openness. According to such studies, parent–child relations continue to be defined by deep emotional closeness, mutual involvement, and mutual respect. Indeed, mutual love between parents and children is posited to be a staple in television families, including contemporary families. At the same time, the relationship between parents and children is seen to be mutually candid, especially in modern families. Children volunteer their problems and admit their misdeeds to parents while parents share their opinions and talk openly about child-related issues such as school, athletics, and friendships.

Other content-based studies are less conclusive, suggesting, for example, that, while families have become more supportive of each other, modern family members are also more likely to ignore, oppose, and/or evade one another (Akins, 1986). In the same way, despite the love and respect they hold for parents, contemporary television children are significantly more often motivated by friends, romantic partners, and/or desire to help themselves than by any desire to help parents or conform to parental wishes or rules (Heintz-Knowles, 1995).

Conventional studies of the television family also suggest that, although parent–child conflict is habitual, and although both parents and children sometimes use relationally problematic strategies during their disagreements, conflict is usually resolved easily and amicably. For the most part, parent–child opposition is relatively superficial and does not extend across episodic boundaries. That is, content-based investigations provide the impression that even contemporary television parents and children manage conflict capably.

Such investigations also support a model of effective parental socialization. Television parents continue to act as useful role models, demonstrating appropriate ambitions and facilitating actions, and routinely encourage their children to emulate or surpass their own accomplishments. Likewise, content-based analyses suggest that, for the most part, parents and children continue to manage mundane aspects of the family experience with little difficulty so that problems appear minor and fail to disturb the procession of day-to-day life. It is unsurprising that such research typically concludes that television family relations, both between parents and children and among siblings, are mutually satisfying and likely to endure into adulthood.

In summary, content-based inquiries argue that, in television families, parent–child and sibling relations have developed along trajectories marked by mutual love, mutual supportiveness, and shared involvement. Moreover, according to this view, television family relations are purposive, that is, they achieve outcomes expected of families such as limitation and resolution of conflict, successful socialization of children, and effective management of day-to-day life. Finally, television parents and children are seen to construct relationships that are mutually satisfying and robust.

In contrast, both more popular analyses and attributional studies of the television family suggest that family relations have become more or less distressed. For example, viewer-based investigations indicate that spousal relations are often confused because many couples, especially working-class couples, violate traditional gender roles either as a function of their own shortcomings (e.g., working-class fathers) or because of ideological oppositions (e.g., mothers who work outside the home). Informal analyses also suggest that, in contemporary television families, parents are insufficiently invested in their children. As a consequence, modern parents are unable to socialize children effectively so that contemporary television children are commonly disrespectful, hostile, undisciplined, and inactive.

Attributional studies encourage an even more extreme conclusion. Such studies argue that contemporary television parents and children are more mutually involved, display greater mutual trust, and are more attracted to each other than their earlier counterparts. Parent–child relations also seem to have become happier and more mutually fulfilling. However, attributional analyses also indicate that parents and children have become more conflictual and less able to manage the daily routine of family life and, at the same time, that modern parents are less able to socialize children appropriately. That is, attributional studies suggest, on the one hand, that issues associated with power and affect, together with those associated with relational satisfaction and stability, are conducted more successfully by modern families than by those from prior generations. On the other hand, family performance appears to have deteriorated across time so that, compared to television families such as the Andersons (*Father Knows Best*), Douglases (*My Three Sons*), and Cunninghams (*Happy Days*), the Conners (*Roseanne*), Seavers (*Growing Pains*), Taylors (*Home Improvement*), and others are less able to achieve ordinary and expected socialization and family management goals.

Attributional studies also indicate substantial distress in modern sibling relations. According to this research, television siblings have become less trusting and less involved in each other. Siblings are also seen to have become not only more hostile but also less able to resolve conflict and, too, less willing and less able to socialize each other effectively. Finally, contemporary siblings are posited to be mutually unfulfilled and unlikely to remain close. That is, viewers rate modern television siblings relatively poorly in regard to issues of relational power and affect, relational performance, *and* relational satisfaction and stability. Indeed, as in real families, television sibling relations are more impoverished and less effective than any other family relationship.

In summary, there is substantial disagreement regarding the television family's evolution. Content-based studies encourage the conclusion that television family life remains orderly and capably managed while television family relations, although comparatively conflictual, are characterized by mutual love and respect and remain mutually fulfilling. In contrast, viewer-based studies, as well as more popular analyses, provide evidence of significant deterioration. This literature suggests that, while spouses have become more argumentative, perhaps as a function of increased use of negotiation to decide rights and responsibilities inside the family, and less able to manage day-to-day life, spousal relations remain mutually satisfying and, moreover, have become more egalitarian, more important, and more demonstrably affectionate. Parent–child and sibling relations, meanwhile, are seen to have become seriously distressed. Modern parents and children, for example, are more hostile toward each other and less able to cope with family life than their predecessors, and modern siblings share relations that are severely and uniformly distressed.

The argument can be made that content-based studies yield more reliable insight into the television family experience than do other approaches. First, content analysis is the most common method of investigating television families and, as such, offers researchers a performance history. Second, studies that have focused on television content have tended to produce similar results and, so, present a coherent narrative of television family life. Third, audience-based studies can be criticized because they either rely on the potentially idiosyncratic conclusions of a single investigator or the judgments of student participants. These assertions, however, appear less compelling than the case in favor of audience-based analyses.

Because examinations of the television family have tended to rely on content analysis, they are unlikely to reflect a received view of family life and family relations and, in particular, may underestimate the attributional impact of negative family action. While content analysis yields a clear indication of the objective aspects of television family life, viewers often infuse portrayals with information that is not explicit but, nonetheless, affects their interpretations (Dambrot & Reep, 1988; Livingstone, 1990). Moreover, while content analysis implicitly treats all coded acts as attributionally equivalent, viewers are likely to be influenced more substantially by negative acts. In interpersonal situations, negative information exerts significantly more affect on the judgments that persons make about others (e.g., Fiske, 1980; Hamilton & Huffman, 1971; Hamilton & Zanna, 1972) and both Abelman (1986) and Comstock and Strzyzewski (1990) have speculated that the same effect obtains during television viewing. As such, viewers may develop negative impressions of television families (i.e., see them as distressed) even though the majority of family action is pro-social. At the very least, limitations associated with content analysis suggest that the method may provide only limited access to the impressions that audiences develop about television families. Hence, the conclusion of this investigation is that the television family has not evolved along a single trajectory although, in general, the television family has become explicitly distressed. Spousal relations appear comparatively robust. Although television wives and husbands have become more conflictual, they are also more candid and more openly affectionate toward each other. A similar unevenness permeates parent–child relations. Modern parents and children seem more emotionally involved in each other than earlier generations but, at the same time, less able to achieve important family objectives. In particular, parents and children have become less able to perform functions associated with conflict management, child socialization, and management of family life. In contrast, sibling relations appear to have become extensively troubled. Contemporary television siblings exhibit relatively low levels of liking and trust, poor socializing and management skills, and weak and unhappy attachment.

Likewise, working-class television families appear never to have enjoyed either the economic or relational comfort of middle-class life. Family relations are more hostile and their ability to function effectively is lower. Minority families are portrayed in much the same way, although concern has typically been with the individual so that, for example, more is known about the depiction of African American men and women than life and relations in African American television families.

Two additional issues are relevant to the development and status of the television family. First, television family size has decreased and, second, domestic comedy has become less popular while ensemble adult friend groups have increased in popularity. As a consequence, children have become less numerous and so, too, have television families. Although speculative, it is possible that such changes indicate that both children and the family have become less relevant to modern viewers. Certainly, Americans are marrying and having children later in life and divorcing significantly more often than their postwar counterparts, suggesting that friends, coworkers, and independence may assume a more dominant place in the priorities of many television viewers than children, family, and marriage.

TELEVISION FAMILIES AND REAL FAMILIES

Most obviously, the congruency between television families and real families is not absolute. Television families in general are demographically unlike real families, and those in domestic comedy and soap opera, two primary vehicles for the family narrative, enjoy unusually good fortune. They are rarely troubled by academic failure of children, poverty, spousal and child abuse, serious illness, and a host of other negative events that regularly permeate the experience of many real families.

Nonetheless, there is no doubt that television family life and family relations resemble life and relations in real families. First, television families often comprise the lexicon used to discuss real families. For example, reminiscent of George Bush and Dan Quayle during the 1992 presidential campaign, a recent examination of the family began:

> Just imagine what would happen if June and Ward Cleaver were negotiating family life these days. The scenario would go something like this: they meet at the office (she's in marketing, he's in sales) and move in together after dating for a couple of months. A year later, June gets pregnant. What to do? Neither feels quite ready to make it legal and there's no pressure from their parents, all of whom are divorced and remarried themselves. So little Wally is welcomed into the world with June's last name on the birth certificate. A few years later June gets pregnant again with the Beav. Ward's ambivalent about second-time fatherhood and moves out, but June decides to go ahead on her own. In her neighborhood, after all, single motherhood is no big deal; the lesbians down the street adopted kids from South America and the soccer mom next door is divorced with a live-in boyfriend. (Kantrowitz & Wingert, 2001, pp. 46, 48)

Likewise, Popenoe (1996) has used television fathers, such as Ozzie Nelson and Ward Cleaver, to illustrate the nature of real fatherhood during the 1950s and 1960s. Faludi (1999), too, has invoked fictional father–son relations, like those depicted in *The Adventures of Ozzie and Harriet, Father Knows Best*, and *Leave It to Beaver*, to characterize real fathers and sons of the period. Notably, both authors explicitly acknowledge the authenticity of such portrayals and, moreover, use television family life and television family relations more holistically to demonstrate changes that have occurred in the experience of real families during the past 50 years.

The repeated use of fictional families in the debate about the American family is significant because it implies that television families and real families conform to a common relational model. Moreover, the model is attributionally rich, allowing statements about everything from parenting styles to spousal sexuality to parent–child relations.

Second, television families are frequently seen to narrate, or even cause, changes in real family life. For example, Quayle (2001) recently not only reasserted his "Murphy Brown" argument but also posited that modern family life is characterized by "extraordinary turmoil and dysfunction" (p. 52), in part because popular culture, in general, and television, specifically, depict family life and family relations in negative ways. Others, of course, have argued that television depictions reflect the experience of real families and, as such, the changes that are seen to have occurred in family life and family relations. For example, Mayerle (1991) asserted that viewers recognize television characters and situations because they are similar to the characters and situations in their own lives. The same author has also affirmed that, "the more significant realism (of television families) lies in the interaction of the characters" (Mayerle, 1991, p. 82). Such claims are common and suggest that a fundamental realism permeates television family life and, too, that the most productive focus of television family research is on relationships and not the attributes of individual characters. Arguments of this sort are bolstered by the inherent authenticity of vaudeville, radio, and even comics. Like television, vaudeville soon became immersed in the day-to-day routine of family life, dealing with a rash of issues relevant to its core audience of married and ready-to-marry females. This domestic tradition was incorporated into radio and comics, both of which continued to infuse their portrayals with a deep-rooted sense of the familiar. Furthermore, because of their repetitive schedule, both radio and comic strips endowed their families with a shared history which, together with the more extended format of radio and comics, functioned to expand the family narrative to include an increasing variety of issues unavailable to vaudeville. *Blondie*, for example, articulated detailed ideologies associated with courtship, marriage, and family and made those ideologies manifest through an assortment of relational events ranging from trials of courtship to gender-based views of the wedding ceremony and life together to parent–child relations to the inadequacy of the husband-as-handyman. Readers saw Blondie and Dagwood eating in their kitchen, sitting in their living room, lying in their bed, watching over their children, walking along the street, and in the company of friends and family. Readers also heard Blondie and Dagwood talking about meal preparation, their children's homework, and their love for their children and for each other. Readers overheard Blondie and Dagwood's disagreements, heard Dagwood complain about Blondie's fiscal irresponsibility, and watched as Blondie encouraged the children and accepted Dagwood's obvious shortcomings. Immersed in such extensive ordinariness, the strip's story lines must have resembled a broader reality and reminded readers of their own lives and the lives of those around them.

Television depictions of the family experience appear to have been guided by the same priorities. The family model that emerged after World War II reasserted the trends that had defined the American family's development across the previous two centuries. Postwar government policy again encouraged families to divest themselves of tasks once considered fundamental so that agencies external to the family, such as governments and schools, assumed responsibility for family welfare, housing, and education. The tasks that remained collected around two issues, the family's economic well-being and the family's—and most especially the children's—emotional and relational well-being. Hence, inside the family, the father's authority continued to diminish as his role collapsed around the provider function while the mother's role remained centered on child-bearing, child care, and providing support to her husband.

This (traditional) family model was supported by a large majority of Americans prior to the outbreak of war, and the Lynds' (1937, 1956) analyses of Middletown revealed wide adherence to the model and enthusiastic advocacy of the associated ideology. Similarly, Gans' (1967) study of Willingboro showed that, even in the mid-1960s, the provider father, nurturer/caregiver mother, and dependent children remained the dominant family model although, by this time, it had evolved to include increased spousal equality, some ambiguity regarding child care, and greater emphasis on parent–child negotiation.

On television, the same sorts of families with the same sorts of values and ambitions quickly became the norm. Blue-collar families gave way to middle-class families, the city apartment gave way to the suburban ranch-style home, and ethnic minorities, the elderly, and the childless gave way to a population of young White couples with dependent children. Moreover, inside families like the Nelsons (*The Adventures of Ozzie and Harriet*) and Andersons (*Father Knows Best*), life and relations were governed by the same principles that guided the experience of real families. Both Ozzie Nelson and Jim Anderson worked to provide for their families and, across time, became more involved in the moral/ethical education of older children, in particular. Likewise, both Harriet Nelson and Mary Anderson were stay-at-home mothers who constructed and maintained a supportive, nurturing family environment for their children and husbands. In both families, children showed respect for their parents and, while sometimes oppositional, never violated the boundaries placed on them. As Jones (1992) has remarked of Ricky Nelson, he was "rebellious and ill tempered and full of himself—yet he never really rocked the family boat. When push came to shove, he was a good kid" (p. 93).

By the late 1950s and early 1960s, television families had been revised to some extent. The Cleavers (*Leave It to Beaver*) and Douglases (*My Three Sons*), for example, continued to adhere to the traditional family model, especially after Steve Douglas remarried (although, the prior presence of his father-in-law as domestic had served to give the family a normative relational logic). As well, like the families in Willingboro, those on television became more child-centered. Family size increased and children, often young children, assumed an enlarged significance. Not only were plots more routinely built around the everyday events and problems that children experience but children were more likely to be featured as they tried, frequently unsuccessfully, to resolve their difficulties alone or with the help of siblings and/or friends. The relationship between spouses and between parents and children also changed. Spousal relations became more egalitarian as fathers became more involved in tasks associated with child care and socialization. Both Ward Cleaver and Steve Douglas were commonly shown in the company of their children, providing friendship, support, instruction, and advice. Too, fathers and mothers appeared more sensitive toward their children's feelings and opinions than did the previous generation, so that, while children remained respectful and, on important issues, obedient, parent–child interactions included more child talk and more often produced a mutually acceptable outcome.

For example, in an episode of *Leave It to Beaver* ("Cat out of the bag," 1958), in which the children, Wally and "the Beav," lose and recover a cat for which they are responsible, sibling conversation comprises 39.5% of total family interaction time, more than that between any other family configuration. Additionally, spousal conversation, which accounts for 32.3% of total family interaction time, is entirely dedicated to talk about "the boys" and is generally consultative and reassuring. Likewise, interaction involving all family members accounts for 22.4% of total family interaction time and follows a dual pattern of parental inquiry/child response, on the one hand, and shared discussion about children's experiences and concerns, on the other. Finally, while the mother, June, is never alone with the children, interaction between the father, Ward, and the children comprises almost 6% of total family interaction time. That is, even cursory examination of family talk demonstrates the child-centeredness of the Cleaver family as well as the extent and nature of parental involvement. Not only are Wally and "the Beav" visibly available for more than two thirds of all interaction time but, even when physically absent, they are the sole topic of parental conversation. It is worth observing, too, that Ward's conversational involvement with the children is extensive and, at least on this occasion, exceeds that of June. Furthermore, Ward's conversation performs two functions: an instructional or socializing function and a problem-solving function. He advises the children and helps them out of difficulty when asked. He does not punish the children for their mistakes nor does he impose his own solution on them. Instead, he discovers that Wally and "the Beav" have voluntarily resolved the issue in accord with his preferences. That is, the episode appears to capture the more child-centered and more demo-cratic family ideology that Gans (1967) felt permeated Willingboro in the early 1960s.

THE STATE OF THE TELEVISION FAMILY

The final objective of the current investigation was to assess the extent to which television families have become distressed, particularly in ways thought to characterize the real American family. Critics of the modern family, such as Blankenship, Popenoe, Samuelson, and others, have argued that childhood has become a relatively impoverished experience, a position supported by a majority of Americans. In particular, Popenoe (1993a) pro-posed that contemporary parents fail to socialize children effectively, cannot maintain authority nor impose discipline, and are unable to provide care, affection, and companionship. Additionally, Popenoe (1993a) asserted that family relations have become comparatively unsatisfying and unstable so that parents and children are unhappy and unlikely to remain committed to each other.

Both content-based studies and clinical research strongly suggest that tele-vision families are not distressed. Although family relations, in general, and sibling relations, in particular, may have become more conflictual and spouses less able to manage routine family life, other aspects of family climate have become more positive. For example, modern spouses are more explicitly affectionate and more egalitarian than their predecessors while contemporary parent–child relations are characterized by mutual involvement, mutual re-spect, and emotional closeness. Even sibling interactions contain a majority of positive behaviors. Finally, contemporary family relations are seen as both satisfying and stable.

As previously argued, however, these conclusions derive from research that relies on content analysis which, almost always, is sensitive to the frequency of specific acts and insensitive to their attributional or relational weight. As well, the bulk of content-based studies are narrowly focused (e.g., on conflict reso-lution strategies, exhibitions of jealousy, the positivity/negativity of particular conversational exchanges) and, as such, are not equipped to assess family life and family relations in a coordinated way. Attributional studies and less for-mal holistic reviews, however, are not only substantially more likely to capture an integrated and received view of the television family experience, they also encourage the conclusion that television family life and family relations have become more or less distressed.

According to these analyses, spousal relations have remained largely positive. In fact, although conflict has become more common between married couples, so have explicit expressions of love and sexual attraction. In contrast, parent–child relations and, more especially, sibling relations have become considerably troubled. Among parents and children, achievement of expected performance outcomes, such as effective socializing and effective management of the day-to-day family routine, has become less common. However, modern parents and children deal with affective issues more effectively than earlier television families. For example, in contemporary families, parents and children are more mutually involved, more trusting, happier, and more likely to express their love for each other. Sibling relations, however, appear to have deteriorated significantly and, what is more, the deterioration appears to permeate all aspects of the relationship. Contemporary siblings, for example, are hostile and untrusting, poor socializers of younger brothers and sisters, less involved with other siblings, and both relatively unhappy and unlikely to remain emotionally close.

Notably, this characterization conforms closely to the charges advanced by Blankenship, Popenoe, Samuelson, and others regarding real families. In general, critics of the modern family argue that, although families usually "adopt" a child-centered ideology and although parents often articulate a primary commitment to their children, families routinely fail to adhere to these promises so that the family experience of many children is relatively depleted. According to critics, this occurs because parents have become more invested in personal ambition and individual achievement and substantially less sensitive to the family life and the welfare of family members. Children, in particular, are seen to be vulnerable to a range of negative consequences, ranging from lack of care and attention to insufficient parental discipline to ineffective socializing. Further, critics charge that, as a result of increased emphasis on the self, family relations have become less satisfying and less stable.

Clearly, audience-based research has yielded considerable evidence that many television families are distressed in precisely these ways. Furthermore, there is indication that children, in particular, and the family, in general, have become less compelling constructs to television viewers. Studies of television family demographics show that children have become less common on television, especially in programs that attract large and stable audiences. Even in domestic comedy, where children and their problems and relationships are fundamental, family size has decreased during the recent past. As well, family-based programming has been replaced by shows such as *Friends, Frazier,* and *Seinfeld* that, for the most part, involve unmarried and childless adults and, so, deal with adult themes.

In summary, the present investigation suggests that television families have evolved along a diminishing trajectory so that many contemporary families are perceived as distressed. Further, the distress apparent in fictional families, which gathers around the eroded experience of children, corresponds closely with the supposed experience of real families, lending a sense of validity to audience-based research. Moreover, while critics of the real family rely on external indicators, such as the rate of divorce, the current inquiry implies that, even in intact families, family relations—especially those between siblings—may be significantly troubled.

FUTURE DIRECTIONS

Fictional family life and family relations are intrinsically significant so that examination of television families will inevitably continue. The only uncertainty is in relation to the topics and methods of analysis. In the past, family issues have often been studied in an enclosed way and investigations have tended to rely on some form of content analysis. Such research should not stop. Demographic studies, dealing with issues such as the extent to which television populations are ethnically diverse or the frequency and nature of television characters' sexual activity, have obvious merit. So do studies of conflict episodes, the positivity/negativity of sibling interactions, and influence-seeking in families, as well as studies in which the individual is the unit of analysis, like those that examine the attributions made to specific characters on the basis of ethnicity, gender, or age. However, the research agenda should also include more expansive analyses and analyses that place priority on the viewer's sense-making rather than objective content elements.

Perhaps most obviously, future inquiry should be directed toward the study of minority families. Extant research has focused almost exclusively on African Americans (although that does not amount to a great volume of research) and has tended to examine the way in which study participants define individual characters. This leads to evaluative studies in which attributions of African Americans are compared across time or attributions of Black males are compared with those of Black females or attributions of Black males/females are compared with those of White males/females. While society's and popular culture's tradition of stereotypic bias invests such research with transparent significance, future studies should also investigate television's portrayal of minority groups, in general, and, more especially, the portrayal of minority families.

At present, overrepresentation of White families leaves little room for de-piction of other groups. However, given current demographic shifts and the expanded options that accrue from cable, Latino and Oriental families, in par-ticular, are likely to become more common on television. Nonetheless, regard-less of ethnicity, the focus of future research should shift from the individual to the family. Not only is almost nothing known about either minority family life on television or the status of fictional relationships involving minorities but the African American family, in particular, has often been singled out by critics who argue that the prevalence of the single-parent family and the absent father is necessarily dysfunctional. Such issues point to a host of re-search topics, ranging from straightforward description of life and relations in minority families to between-group family comparisons to more global com-parison of the experience of real families with that of families on television.

Second, television research should become more sensitive to issues sur-rounding the process of aging. Certainly, this means looking more closely at the elderly on television but should include, too, examination of the general effects of aging, even among infants and young adults. As is the case with other minority groups, little is known about the family experience of tele-vision's elderly. For the most part, research has sought to document the pro-portion of older characters in television's population or identify the sorts of attributions that audiences make about the elderly. Hence, almost nothing is known about the relational experience of older couples, including the model that the elderly use to distribute family rights and responsibilities and the extent to which they define gender roles uniquely, the sexuality of elderly characters, their ability to cope with life, and the extent to which they remain satisfied with each other. Additionally, no attention has been paid to the rate of occurrence and the ability of television's elderly to manage events, such as the "empty nest," retirement, illness, and diminishing marital satisfaction, which routinely invade the lives of real older couples.

Aging, however, has a broader impact on families simply because all members are becoming older. While this may appear both obvious and in-consequential, in real families the effects can be profound. The most familiar circumstance is adolescence. When children pass through adolescence, they typically exhibit increased independence, decreased satisfaction with family relations, decreased involvement in family relations and family affairs, and increased involvement in peer relations and peer affairs. Because other family members have competing priorities, this frequently leads to substantially increased conflict, particularly between parents and adolescent.

Aging may produce other family problems. For example, it is not unusual for children (in both real and fictional families) to complain that they are treated less favorably than one or more siblings, suggesting parental inconsistency across children or across time. That is, the conclusion of favoritism may derive from either parents treating children differently as a function of dissimilar levels of affection ("You don't like me as much as her") or couples changing their parenting style as a consequence of previous child-related experiences ("I wasn't allowed to do that when I was his age"). Sometimes these claims are veridical. On other occasions, however, the presumed inconsistency is illusionary and accrues from the "unfavored" child's limited temporal perspective. Research (Dunn & Plomin, 1986; Dunn, Plomin, & Daniels, 1986; Dunn, Plomin, & Nettles, 1985) indicates that parents generally interact with and treat children of similar age in similar ways. When *any* child in the family is in pre-school, parents invoke their "guide to parenting a pre-schooler"; when *any* child in the family is in junior high school, parents invoke their "guide to parenting a junior high schooler"; and so on. As such, parents may act consistently but appear to the child who feels out of favor as grossly inconsistent only because children of *different* ages are being treated in *different* ways. The logic of television parenting remains unclear. There is an absence of longitudinal analysis of parent–child relations and the extent to which adult parenting varies across time and/or children. Nonetheless, parental inconsistency is discouraged in real families because it often creates an ambiguous and stressful environment for children. Moreover, of course, television portrayals are almost universally assumed to function as a model so that it is important to determine the sort of implicit instructions offered to couples with children. More straightforwardly, inconsistency among modern parent–child relations would imply further that the contemporary television family is relatively distressed. Third, it is important that future television research examine family performance variables as well as other, more salient, features of family life. Real families, regardless of their composition, are expected to achieve performance outcomes such as effective socializing of children and effective management of the day-to-day routine. Furthermore, such outcomes are critical to the long-term well-being of the family. Television family research has tended to focus on more salient and more discrete issues such as conflict and conflict management. This is not to assert that such studies yield no insight into television family life and family relations, it is a reminder that the family environment is complex and that significant parts of that environment may be widely diffused across episodes. A host of parent behaviors are not intended to socialize others but, nonetheless, are necessarily endowed with that capacity. For example, shouting during conflict or hugging a child who is upset or attending a child's basketball game, have primary implications for conflict and conflict management, supportiveness, and involvement, respectively, but also perform a socializing function, signaling to children actions that are "appropriate" or "desirable" or "most effective."

In a more general sense, these proposals for the content of subsequent research advocate more varied methods of analysis. Studies of minority family life and family relations, aging and the elderly, and family performance each require methods that are sensitive to the expansiveness of television family experiences. Likewise, because the family routine is written into both strategically constructed content and what has been labeled the "taken-for-granted" (that is, content that is included because it fits a specific context in an automatic or mindless way), such studies must reflect a holistic approach. Both of these considerations argue the merits of methods that place priority on viewers rather than content. Unlike content-based methods, audience-based methods focus on the meanings that viewers construct and, because viewers assimilate integrated content, are more likely to deal with television programming coherently. Viewers do not attend solely to conflict, for example, nor is such content likely to be installed into memory as a sovereign sequence separate from all other sequences, nor is such content, once in memory, likely to be associated with a single aspect of family life. Instead, viewers make sense of television content as a whole, they expect and understand the interrelatedness and compound relevance of action and, too, are likely to incorporate (not necessarily knowingly) the taken-for-granted aspects of family life, family relations, and the family home, especially when those features are recurrent and familiar.

Two final recommendations are in order. First, selection of television families should be guided by a clear logic. That logic might be the widespread and extended popularity of particular television families, like those in domestic comedy, or the unique insights offered by specific families, such as those in soap operas. Families might be chosen because they allow expansive analysis of topics, such as aging and the aged, or because they foreground socially significant families not featured elsewhere, such as minority families. That is, family selection may be guided by a variety of considerations, but those considerations must be made clear so as to prevent selection on the basis of momentary popularity, the acute absurdity of the depiction, or something even more vague.

Second, researchers should admit to and seek to make sense of the tangled relationship between real families and those on television. Not only is it impossible to talk about one without, sooner or later, talking about the other but it is also likely that examination of fictional families would be informed by (real) family theory and research. Whether it is politicians running for office, persons chatting at a party, or students in classroom discussion, real families and television families soon become joined in their talk. Television families allow persons to communicate about the family in apparently substantive ways although they may rarely use terms such as "renegotiation of gender roles," "mutual affection," "involvement," or "relational satisfaction." Families like the Nelsons (*The Adventures of Ozzie and Harriet*), Ricardos (*I Love Lucy*), Bunkers (*All in the Family*), Bundys (*Married With Children*), and Conners (*Roseanne*) have been used repeatedly to illustrate distress in the (real) modern family, shortcomings associated with the (real) postwar family, the lack of mutual respect between parents and children in (real) contemporary families, and so on. Similarly, researchers of the television family habitually use the logic of real families to guide or lend significance to their analyses. Demographic studies continue to assess the disparity between television's representation of various groups and their real-world representation. In other analyses, such as those conducted by Bryant et al. (2001) and Douglas and Olson (1995, 1996), researchers have either applied to fictional families diagnostic instruments commonly used to assess the clinical dysfunctionality of real families or constructed an investigative framework based on family theory.

Television families insinuate their way into our lives. Their doors are always open to us and, despite the apparent fiction, we recognize their experience, sometimes because it reminds us of our own and sometimes because it reinforces and extends our sense of life and relations in families unknown to us. Although we are rarely surprised, we watch them regularly and with interest. They are our companions. Mapping their ordinary lives is a significant and difficult undertaking because, like us, they inhabit a complex environment, made more opaque by its familiarity.

References

Abelman, R. (1986). Children's awareness of television's prosocial fare: Parental discipline as an antecedent. *Journal of Family Issues, 7,* 51–66.

Abelman, R. (1990). From "The Huxtables" to "The Humbards": The portrayal of family on religious television. In J. Bryant (Ed.), *Television and the American family* (pp. 165–184). Hillsdale, NJ: Lawrence Erlbaum Associates.

Abelman, R., & Ross, R. (1986). Children, television, and families: An evolution in understanding. *Television & Families, 9,* 2–55.

Akins, G. (1986). An analysis of family interaction styles as portrayed on television. (Doctoral dissertation, University of Georgia, 1986). *Dissertation Abstracts International, 47,* 2013A.

Andersen, P. A. (1993). Cognitive schemata in personal relationships. In S. Duck (Ed.), *Individuals in relationships* (pp. 1–29). Newbury Park, CA: Sage.

Anderson, D. R., Lorch, E. P., Field, D., Collins, P., & Nathan, J. (1986). Television viewing at home: Age trends in visual attention and time with television. *Child Development, 57,* 1024–1033.

Andreasen, M. S. (1990). Evolution of the family's use of television: Normative data from industry and academe. In J. Bryant (Ed.), *Television and the American family* (pp. 3–55). Hillsdale, NJ: Lawrence Erlbaum Associates.

Aries, P. (1962). *Centuries of childhood: A social history of family life.* New York: Knopf.

Aronoff, C. (1974). Old age in prime time. *Journal of Communication, 24,* 86–87.

Atkin, D. (1991). The evolution of television series addressing single women, 1966–1990. *Journal of Broadcasting & Electronic Media, 35,* 517–523.

Bank, S., & Kahn, M. (1975). Sisterhood-brotherhood is powerful: Sibling subsystems and family therapy. *Family Process, 14,* 311–337.

Barnes, J. A. (1995, July 12). Television's loss of innocence. *Investor's Business Daily,* pp. A1, A2.

Beck, K. (1978). Television and the older woman. *Television Quarterly, 15,* 47–49.

Becker, S. (1959). *Comic art in America.* New York: Simon & Shuster.

Beecher, C. E., & Stowe, H. B. (1869). *The American woman's home: Principles of domestic science.* New York: J. B. Ford & Co..

Bell, J. (1992). In search of a discourse of aging: The elderly on television. *Gerontologist, 32,* 305–311.

Belsky, J. (1995). A nation (still) at risk? *National Forum, 75,* 36–38.

Berger, A. A. (1973). *The comic-stripped American: What Dick Tracy, Blondie, Daddy Warbucks, and Charlie Brown tell us about ourselves.* New York: Walker & Co..

Berger, C. R., & Bradac, J. J. (1982). *Language and social knowledge: Uncertainty in interpersonal relationships.* London: Arnold.

Berger, C. R., & Calabrese, R. J. (1975). Some explorations in initial interaction and beyond: Toward a developmental theory of interpersonal communication. *Human Communication Research, 1,* 99–112.

Berkman, D. (1993). Sitcom reality. *Television Quarterly, 26,* 63–69.

Bernstein, B. (1964). Social class and psychoterapy. *British Journal of Sociology, 15,* 54–64.

Berry, G. L. (1980). Television and Afro-Americans: Past legacy and present potrayals. In S. B. Withey & R. P. Abeles (Eds.), *Television and social behavior: Beyond violence and children* (pp. 231–248). Hillsdale, NJ: Lawrence Erlbaum Associates.

Beuick, M. D. (1984). The vaudeville philosopher. In C. W. Stein (Ed.), *American vaudeville as seen by its contemporaries.* New York: Alfred A. Knopf.

Bishop, J. M., & Krause, D. R. (1984). Depictions of aging and old age on Saturday morning television. *Gerontologist, 24,* 91–94.

Blankenhorn, D. (1995). *Fatherless America: Confronting our most urgent social problem.* New York: Basic Books.

Blum, J. J., Catton, B., Morgan, E. S., Schlesinger, A. M., Stampp, K. M., & Woodward, C. V. (1968). *The national experience: A history of the United States since 1865.* New York: Harcourt, Brace, & World.

Bower, R. T. (1973). *Television and the public.* New York: Holt, Rinehart, & Winston.

Bower, R. T. (1985). *The changing television audience in America.* New York: Columbia University Press.

Brody, G. H., Stoneman, Z., & Sanders, A. K. (1980). Effects of television viewing on family interactions: An observational study. *Family Relations, 29,* 216–220.

Breines, W. (1992). *Young, White, and miserable: Growing up female in the fifties.* Boston: Beacon Press Books.

Bronfenbrenner, V. (1970). *Two worlds of childhood: U.S. and U.S.S.R.* New York: Russell Sage Foundation.

Brooks, T., & Marsh, E. (1981). *The complete directory to prime time network TV shows, 1946–present.* New York: Ballantyne.

Brown, D., & Bryant, J. Effects of television on family values and selected attitudes and behaviors. In J. Bryant (Ed.), *Television and the American family* (pp. 253–274). Hillsdale, NJ: Lawrence Erlbaum Associates.

Brown, J. D., Childers, K. W., Bauman, K. E., & Koch, G. G. (1990). The influence of new media and family structure on young adolescents' television and radio use. *Communication Research, 17,* 65–82.

Bryant, J., Aust, C. F., Bryant, J. A., & Venugopalan, G. (2001). How psychologically healthy are America's prime-time television families? In J. Bryant & J. A. Bryant (Eds.), *Television and the American family* (2nd ed., pp. 247–270). Mahwah, NJ: Lawrence Erlbaum Associates.

Buck, J. (1992, September 27). Television's versions of family values. *The Wichita Eagle,* p. 6E.

Buck, R. (1988). Emotional education and mass media: A new view of the global village. In R. P. Hawkins, J. M. Wiemann, & S. Pingree (Eds.), *Advancing communication science: Merging mass and interpersonal processes* (pp. 44–76). Newbury Park, CA: Sage.

Buerkel-Rothfuss, N. L., & Mayes, S. (1981). Soap opera viewing: The cultivation effect. *Journal of Communication, 31,* 108–115.

Burke, K. (1973). The second study of Middletown. In K. Burke (Ed.), *The philosophy of literary form: Studies in symbolic action* (pp. 407–411). Berkeley: University of California Press.

Butler, R. N. (1969). Age-ism: Another form of bigotry. *Gerontologist, 9,* 243–246.

Butsch, R. (1992). Class and gender in four decades of television situation comedy: Plus ça change. *Critical Studies in Mass Communication, 9,* 387–399.

Buxton, J. (1998). *Ending the mother war.* London: MacMillan.

Calhoun, A. W. (1945). *A social history of the American family* (Vol. 3). New York: Barnes & Noble.

Cantor, M. G. (1991). The American family on television: From Molly Goldberg to Bill Cosby. *Journal of Comparative Family Studies, 22,* 205–216.

Cantor, M. G., & Cantor, J. M. (1992). *Prime-time television: Content and control.* Newbury Park: Sage.

Cantor, M. G., & Pingree, S. (1983). *The soap opera.* Beverly Hills, CA: Sage.

Caplovitz, D. (1979). *Making ends meet* (Vol. 86). Beverly Hills: Sage Library of Social Research.

Caplow, T., Bahr, H. M., Chadwick, B. A., Hill, R., & Williamson, M. H. (1982). *Middletown families: Fifty years of change and continuity.* Minneapolis: University of Minnesota Press.

Cassata, M. B., Anderson, P. A., & Skill, T. D. (1980). The older adult in daytime serial drama. *Journal of Communication, 30,* 48–49.

Cirillo, L. (1994). Verbal imagery of aging in the news magazines. In D. Shenk & W. A. Achenbaum (Eds.), *Changing perceptions of aging and the aged* (pp. 173–178). New York: Springer.

Comer, J. (1982). The importance of television images of Black families. In A. W. Jackson (Ed.), *Black families and the medium of television* (pp. 87–98). Ann Arbor, MI: University of Michigan Press.

Comstock, G. (1993). The medium and the society: The role of television in American life. In G. L. Berry & J. K. Asamen (Eds.), *Children and television: Images in a changing sociocultural world* (pp. 117–131). Newbury Park, CA: Sage.

Comstock, J., & Strzyzewski, K. (1990). Interpersonal interaction on television: Family conflict and jealousy on primetime. *Journal of Broadcasting and Electronic Media, 34,* 263–282.

Coontz, S. (1992). *The way we never were: American families and the nostalgia trap.* New York: Basic Books.

Coontz, S. (1995). The way we weren't: The myth and reality of the "traditional" family. *National Forum, 75,* 11–14.

Cummings, M. S. (1988). The changing image of the Black family on television. *Journal of Popular Culture, 22,* 75–85.

Dail, P. W. (1988). Prime time television portrayals of older adults in the context of Family life. *Gerontologist, 28,* 700–706.

Dail, P. W., & Way, W. L. (1985). What do parents observe about parenting from prime time television? *Family Relations, 34,* 491–499.

Dambrot, F. H., & Reep, D. C. (1988). In the eye of the beholder: Viewer perceptions of TV's male/female working partners. *Communication Research, 15,* 51–69.

Dates, J. L. (1993). Fly in the buttermilk. In J. L. Dates & W. Barlow (Eds.), *Split image: African-Americans in the mass media* (pp. 267–329). Washington, DC: Howard University Press.

Dates, J. L., & Stroman, C. A. (2001). Portrayals of families of color on television. In J. Bryant & J. A. Bryant (Eds.), *Television and the American family* (2nd ed., pp. 207–225). Hillsdale, NJ: Lawrence Erlbaum Associates.

Davis, R. H. (1980). *Television and the aging audience.* Los Angeles, CA: University of Southern California Press.

Davis, R. H. (1984). TV's boycott of old age. *Aging, 346,* 12–17.

Davis, R. H., & Davis, J. A. (1985). *TV's image of the elderly: A practical guide for change.* Lexington, KY: D. C. Heath and Company.

DeGrane, L. (1991). *Tuned in: Television in American life.* Urbana and Chicago: University of Illinois Press.

Desmond, R. J., Singer, J. L., & Singer, D. G. (1990). Family mediation: Parental communication patterns and the influences of television on children. In J. Bryant (Ed.), *Television and the American family* (pp. 293–309). Hillsdale, NJ: Lawrence Erlbaum Associates.

Dominick, J. R. (1979). The portrayal of women in prime time, 1953–1977. *Sex Roles, 5,* 405–411.

Dorr, A., Kovaric, P., & Doubleday, C. (1989). Parent-child coviewing of television. *Journal of Broadcasting & Electronic Media, 33,* 35–51.

Douglas, W. (1996). The fall from grace? The modern family on television. *Communication Research, 23,* 675–702.

Douglas, W., & Olson, B. M. (1995). Beyond family structure: The family in domestic comedy. *Journal of Broadcasting and Electronic Media, 39,* 236–261.

Douglas, W., & Olson, B. M. (1996). Subversion of the American family: An examination of children and parents in television families. *Communication Research, 23,* 73–99.

Downing, M. (1974). Heroine of the daytime serial. *Journal of Communication, 24,* 130–137.

Driscoll, M. (1996, March 24). Single-minded. *The Sunday Times,* p. 15.

Dunn, J., & Plomin, R. (1986). Determination of maternal behavior towards three-year-old siblings. *British Journal of Developmental Psychology, 4,* 127–137.

Dunn, J., Plomin, R., & Daniels, D. (1986). Consistency and change in mother's behavior towards young siblings. *Child Development, 57,* 348–356.

Dunn, J., Plomin, R., & Nettles, M. (1985). Consistency of mothers' behavior towards infant siblings. *Developmental Psychology, 21,* 1188–1195.

Durkin, K. (1985). Television and sex-role acquisition, Part 1: Content. *British Journal of Social Psychology, 24,* 101–113.

Elasmar, M., Hasegawa, K., & Brain, M. (1999). The portrayal of women in U.S. prime time television. *Journal of Broadcasting and Electronic Media, 43,* 20–34.

Elkind, D. (1995). The family in the postmodern world. *National Forum, 75,* 24–28.

Elliot, J. (1984). The daytime television drama portrayal of older adults. *Gerontologist, 24,* 628–633.

Faludi, S. (1999). *Stiffed: The betrayal of the American man.* New York: William Morrow and Company, Inc.

Feshbach, N., Dillman, A., & Jordan, T. (1979). Portrait of a female on television. Some possible effects on children. In C. B. Kopp (Ed.), *Becoming female: Perspectives on development* (pp. 363–385). New York: Plenum.

Fields, S. (1994, October 11). Ozzie and Harriet did provide morals in our complex world. *Houston Post,* p. A-17.

Filene, P. G. (1976). *Him/her/self: Sex roles in modern America.* New York: Harcourt Brace Jovanovich.

Fisher, C. (1974). Marital and familial roles on television: An exploratory sociological analysis. (Doctoral dissertation, Iowa State University, 1974). *Dissertation Abstracts International, 35,* 599A.

Fiske, S. T. (1980). Attention and weight in person perception: The impact of negative and extreme behavior. *Journal of Personality and Social Psychology, 38,* 889–908.

Fitch, M., Huston, A. C., & Wright, J. C. (1993). From television forms to genre schemata: Children's perceptions of television reality. In G. L. Berry & J. K. Asamen (Eds.), *Children and television: Images in a changing sociocultural world* (pp. 38–52). Newbury Park, CA: Sage.

Fitzgerald, F. (1987). *Cities on a hill.* New York: Simon & Schuster.

Fitzpatrick, M. A. (1987). Marital interaction. In C. R. Berger & S. H. Chaffee (Eds.), *Handbook of communication science* (pp. 564–618). Newbury Park, CA: Sage.

Fitzpatrick, M. A., & Badzinski, D. M. (1985). All in the family: Interpersonal communication in kin relationships. In M. L Knapp & G. R. Miller (Eds.), *Handbook of interpersonal communication* (pp. 687–736). Beverly Hills, CA: Sage.

Fitzpatrick, M. A. & Badzinski, D. M. (1994). All in the family: Interpersonal communication in kin relationships. In M. L Knapp & G. R. Miller (Eds.), *Handbook of interpersonal communication* (pp. 726–771). Beverly Hills, CA: Sage.

Frazer, J. M., & Frazer, T. C. (1992). *Father Knows Best* and *The Cosby Show:* Nostalgia and the sitcom tradition. *Journal of Popular Culture, 27,* 163–172.

Friedan, B. (1963). *The feminine mystique.* New York: Norton & Co.

Friedman, D. (1995, May 22). Working women: Findings from a sweeping new study. *U.S. News & World Report,* p. 55.

Friend, T. (1993, March). Sitcoms seriously. *Esquire,* p. 119.

Fuller, L. K. (1992). *The Cosby Show: Audiences, impact, and implications.* Westport, CT: Greenwood Press.

Fuller, T. (1990, August). *Television vs. the real world: A content analysis of family configuration.* Paper presented at the annual convention of the Texas Association of Broadcast Educators, Dallas, TX.

Gans, H. J. (1967). *The Levittowners: Ways of life and politics in a new suburban community.* New York: Vintage Books.

Gans, H. J. (1968). *The uses of television and their educational implications.* New York: The Center for Urban Education.

Gallup, G. H. (1936). *The Gallup poll: Public opinion* (Vol. 1, Survey #45). New York: Random House.

Gallup, G. H. (1992, September). Survey GO 322014**. *The Gallup Poll Monthly,* p. 4.

Gates, A. (2000, April 9). Men on TV: Dumb as posts and proud of it. *The New York Times,* pp. 1, 35.

Gerbner, G., Gross, L., Signorielli, N., & Morgan, M. (1980). Aging with television: Images on television drama and conceptions of social reality. *Journal of Communication, 30,* 37–47.

Gilder, G. (1992). *Life after television.* New York: Norton & Co.

Glenn, N. D. (1991). The recent trend in marital success in the United States. *Journal of Marriage and the Family, 53,* 261–270.

Glenn, N. D., & Weaver, C. N. (1988). The changing relationship of marital status to reported happiness. *Journal of Marriage and the Family, 50,* 317–324.

Glennon, L., & Butsch, R. (1982). The family as portrayed on television 1946–1978. In D. Pearl, L. Bouthilet, & J. Lazar (Eds.), *Television and behavior: Ten years of scientific progress and implications for the eighties: Vol. 2: Technical reviews.* (DHHS Publication No. ADM 82-1196; pp. 264–271). Washington, DC: U.S. Government Printing Office.

Goedkoop, R. J. (1983). Elements of genre in television situation comedy. *Feedback, 25,* 3–5.

Goffman, E. (1974). *Frame analysis.* New York: Harper & Row.

Gordon, I. (1998). *Comic strips and consumer culture 1890–1945.* Washington, DC: Smithsonian Institution Press.

Gorer, G. (1964). *The American people: A study in national character.* New York: W. W. Norton Co., Inc.

Greenberg, B. S. (1982). Television and role socialization: An overview. In D. Pearl, L. Bouthilet, & J. Lazar (Eds.), *Television and behavior: Ten years of scientific progress and implications for the eighties* (DHHS Publication No. ADM 82-1196, Vol. 2, pp. 179–190). Washington, DC: U.S. Government Printing Office.

Greenberg, B. S., Abelman, R., & Neuendorf, K. (1981). Sex on soap operas: Afternoon delight. *Journal of Communication, 31,* 83–89.

Greenberg, B. S., & Atkin, C. K. (1978, August). *Learning about minorities from television.* Paper presented at the annual conference of the Association for Education in Journalism, Seattle, WA.

Greenberg, B. S., & Brand, J. E. (1994). Minorities and the mass media: 1970s to 1990s. In J. Bryant & D. Zillman (Eds.), *Media effects: Advances in theory and research* (pp. 273–314). Norwood, NJ: Ablex.

Greenberg, B. S., Brown, J. D., & Buerkel-Rothfuss, N. L. (1993). *Media, sex, and the adolescent.* Cresskill, NJ: Hampton Press.

Greenberg, B. S., & Busselle, R. W. (1996). Soap operas and sexual activity: A decade later. *Journal of Communication, 46,* 153–160.

Greenberg, B. S., & Collette, L. (1997). The changing faces on TV: A demographic analysis of network television's new seasons, 1966–1992. *Journal of Broadcasting & Electronic Media, 41,* 1–13.

Greenberg, B. S., Hines, N., Buerkel-Rothfuss, N. L., & Atkin, C. K. (1980). Family role structures and interactions on commercial television. In B. S. Greenberg (Ed.), *Life on television: Content analyses of U. S. TV drama* (pp. 149–160). Norwood, NJ: Ablex.

Greenberg, B. S., Korzenny, F., & Atkin, C. K. (1979). The portrayal of the aging: Trends on commercial television. *Research on Aging, 1,* 319–334.

Greenberg, B. S., Linsangan, R., Soderman, A., Heeter, C., Lin, C., & Stanley, C. (1987). *Adolescents and their exposure to television and movie sex* (Report No. 4 to the Office of Adolescent Pregnancy Programs, U.S. Department of Health and Human Services). East Lansing: Michigan State University Press.

Greenberg, B. S., & Neuendorf, K. (1980). Black family interactions on television. In B. S. Greenberg (Ed.), *Life on television: Content analyses of U. S. TV drama* (pp. 173–181). Norwood, NJ: Ablex.

Gunter, G. (1998). Ethnicity and involvement in violence on television: Nature and context of on-screen portrayals. *Journal of Black Studies, 28,* 683–703.

Haefner, M. J., & Comstock, J. (1990). Compliance gaining on prime time family programs. *Southern Communication Journal, 55,* 402–420.

Hamilton, D. L., & Huffman, L. F. (1971). Generality of impression-formation processes for evaluative and non-evaluative judgments. *Journal of Personality and Social Psychology, 20,* 200–207.

Hamilton, D. L., & Zanna, M. P. (1972). Differential weighting of favorable and unfavorable attributes in impression formation. *Journal of Experimental Research in Personality, 6,* 204–212.

Hanlon, H., Farnsworth, J., & Murray, J. (1997). Aging in American comic strips: 1972–1992. *Ageing and Society, 17,* 293–304.

Haralovich, M. B. (1989). Sitcoms and suburbs: Positioning the 1950s homemaker. *Quarterly Review of Film & Video, 11,* 61–83.

Harrington, C. L., & Bielby, D. D. (1991). The mythology of modern love: Representations of romance in the 1980s. *Journal of Popular Culture, 24,* 129–144.

Harris, A. J., & Feinberg, J. F. (1977). Television and aging. *Gerontologist, 17,* 464–468.

Harrison, E. (2000, August 27). Black comedy. *The Houston Chronicle,* Zest, pp. 8–9, 27.

Harvey, R. C. (1990). *The encyclopedia of American comics: From 1897 to the present* (pp. 37–38). New York: Facts on File.

Hawkins, R. P., & Daly, J. (1988). Cognition and communication. In R. P. Hawkins, J. M. Wiemann, & S. Pingree (Eds.), *Advancing communication science: Merging mass and interpersonal processes* (pp. 191–223). Newbury Park, CA: Sage.

Hartmann, S. M. (1982). *The home front and beyond: American women in the 1940s.* Boston, MA: Twayne.

Heintz, K. E. (1992). Children's favorite television families: A descriptive analysis of role interactions. *Journal of Broadcasting and Electronic Media, 36,* 443–451.

Heintz-Knowles, K. E. (1995). *The reflection on the screen: Television's image of children* (Report). Oakland, CA: Children Now.

Heintz-Knowles, K. E. (2001). Balancing acts: Work–family issues on prime-time TV. In J. Bryant & J. A. Bryant (Eds.), *Television and the American family* (2nd ed., pp. 177–206). Mahwah, NJ: Lawrence Erlbaum Associates.

Heintz-Knowles, K. E., & Chen, P. (2000). *Fall colors.* Study commissioned by Children Now, Oakland, CA.

Heintz-Knowles, K. E., Chen, P., Miller, P., & Haufler, A. (2000). *Fall colors II.* Study commissioned by Children Now, Oakland, CA.

Heintz-Knowles, K. E., Parker, M. A., Miller, P., Glaubke, C., Thai-Binh, S., & Sorah Reyes, T. (2001). *Fall colors III.* Study commissioned by Children Now, Oakland, CA.

Hess, B. B. (1974). Stereotypes of the aged. *Journal of Communication, 24,* 76–85.

Hoffman, A. (1994, February 4–6). Reality check: Roseanne vs. Donna. *USA Weekend,* p. 24.

Honey, M. (1984). *Creating Rosie the riviter: Class, gender, and propaganda during World War II.* Amherst: University of Massachusetts Press.

Honeycutt, J. M., Wellman, L. B., & Larson, M. S. (1997). Beneath family role portrayals: An additional measure of communication influence using time series analyses of turn at talk on a popular television program. *Journal of Broadcasting and Electronic Media, 41,* 40–57.

Hunt, M. M. (1955, April). Decline and fall of the American father. *Cosmopolitan,* pp. 20–24.

Jensen, E. (1995, March 27). It's 8 p.m. Your kids are watching sex on tv. *The Wall Street Journal,* pp. B1, B5.

Johnsson-Smaragdi, U. (1983). *TV use and social interaction in adolescence: A longitudinal study.* Stockholm: Almquist & Wiskell.

Jones, G. (1992). *Honey, I'm home! Sitcoms: Selling the American dream.* New York: Grove Weidenfeld.

Kantrowitz, B., & Wingert, P. (May 28, 2001). Unmarried with children. *Newsweek,* pp. 46–52, 54.

Katzman, N. (1972). Television soap operas: What's been going on, anyway? *Public Opinion Quarterly, 36,* 200–212.

Kelley, H. (1979). *Personal relationships: Their structures and processes.* Hillsdale, NJ: Lawrence Erlbaum Associates.

Kelley, H., & Thibaut, J. (1979). *Interpersonal relations: A theory of interdependence.* New York: Wiley.

Key, E. (1909). *The century of the child.* New York: Putnam.

Kibler, M. A. (1999). *Rank ladies: Gender and cultural hierarchy in American vaudeville.* Chapel Hill: University of North Carolina Press.

Kinsey, A. C. (1953). *Sexual behavior in the human female.* Philadelphia, PA: Saunders.

Knapp, M. L., & Vangelisti, A. L. (1992). *Interpersonal communication and human Relationships* (2nd ed.). Boston, MA: Allyn and Bacon.

Kotelchuck, M. (1976). The infant's relationship to the father: Experimental evidence. In M. E. Lamb (Ed.), *The role of the father in child development* (pp. 329–344). New York: Wiley.

Kozol, W. (1994). *Life's America.* Philadelphia: Temple University Press.

Kubey, R. (1990). Television and family harmony among children, adolescents, and adults: Results from the experience sampling method. In J. Bryant (Ed.), *Television and the American family* (pp. 73–88). Hillsdale, NJ: Lawrence Erlbaum Associates.

Kubey, R., & Csikszentmihalyi, M. (1990). *Television and the quality of life: How viewing shapes everyday experience.* Hillsdale, NJ: Lawrence Erlbaum Associates.

Lamb, M. E. (1977). The development of mother–infant and father–infant attachments in the second year of life. *Developmental Psychology, 13,* 637–646.

Larson, M. S. (1991). Sibling interactions in 1950s versus 1980s sitcoms: A comparison. *Journalism Quarterly, 68,* 381–388.

Larson, M. S. (1993). Family communication on prime time television. *Journal of Broadcasting and Electronic Media, 37,* 345–357.

Larson, M. S. (2001). Sibling interaction in situation comedies over the years. In J. Bryant & J. A. Bryant (Eds.), *Television and the American family* (2nd ed., pp. 163–176). Hillsdale, NJ: Lawrence Erlbaum Associates.

Lee, J. (1995). Subversive sitcoms: Roseanne as inspiration for feminist resistance. In G. Dines & J. M. Humez (Eds.), *Gender, race, and class in media* (pp. 469–475). Beverly Hills, CA: Sage.

Leibman, N. C. (1995). *Living room lectures: The fifties family in film and television.* Austin: University of Texas Press.

Lemish, D. (1986). Viewers in diapers. In T. Lindlof (Ed.), *Natural audiences: Qualitative research in media uses and effects* (pp. 33–57). Norwood, NJ: Ablex.

Lemon, J. (1977). Women and Blacks on prime-time television. *Journal of Communication, 27,* 70–79.

Leupnitz, D. A. (1988). *The family interpreted: Psychoanalysis, feminism, and family therapy.* New York: Basic Books.

Lewis, J. (1991). *The ideological octopus: An exploration of television and its audience.* New York: Routledge.

Lichter, S. R., Lichter, L. S., Rothman, S., & Amundson, D. (1988). TV and the family: The parents prevail. *Public Opinion, 10,* 19, 51–54.

Liebes, T., & Katz, E. (1990). *The export of meaning: Cross-cultural readings of* Dallas. New York: Oxford University Press.

Lindlof, T. R., Shatzer, M. J., & Wilkinson, D. (1989). Accommodation of video and television in the American family. In J. Lull (Ed.), *World families watch television* (pp. 158–192). Newbury Park, CA: Sage.

Linz, D. G., & Donnerstein, E. (1989). The effects of violent messages in the mass media. In J. J. Bradac (Ed.), *Message effects in communication science* (pp. 263- 293). Newbury Park, CA: Sage.

Livingstone, S. M. (1990). Interpreting a television narrative: How different viewers see a story. *Journal of Communication, 40,* 72–85.

Livingstone, S., & Liebes, T. (1995). Where have all the mothers gone? Soap opera's replaying of the Oedipal story. *Critical Studies in Mass Communication, 12,* 155–175.

Long, E. (1985). *The American dream and the popular novel.* Boston, MA: Routledge & Kegan.

Lull, J. (1980). The social uses of television. *Human Communication Research, 6,* 197–209.

Lynd, R. S., & Lynd, H. M. (1937). *Middletown in transition: A study of cultural conflicts.* New York: Harvest Books.

Lynd, R. S., & Lynd, H. M. (1956). *Middletown: A study in modern American culture.* New York: Harvest Books.

Maccoby, E. E. (1951). Television: Its impact on schoolchildren. *Public Opinion Quarterly, 15,* 421–444.

Mackey, W. D., & Hess, D. J. (1982). Attention structure and stereotypy of gender on Television: An empirical monograph. *Genetic Psychology Monographs, 106,* 199–215.

Manes, A. L., & Melnyk, P. (1974). Televised models of female achievement. *Journal of Applied Social Psychology, 4,* 365–374.

Marc, D. (1989). *Comic visions: Television comedy and American culture.* Boston: Unwin Hyman.

Marks, J. (1996, April 22). The American uncivil wars. *U.S. News & World Report,* pp. 66–72.

Marshall, C. L., & Wallenstein, E. (1973). Beyond Marcus Welby, cable TV for the health of the elderly. *Geriatrics, 28,* 182–186.

Mastro, D. E., & Greenberg, B. S. (2000). The portrayal of minorities on prime time television. *Journal of Broadcasting & Electronic Media, 44,* 690–703.

May, E. T. (1988). *Homeward bound: American families in the Cold War era.* New York: Basic Books.

May, E. T. (1995). *Barren in the promised land: Childless Americans and the pursuit of happiness.* New York: Basic Books.

Mayerle, J. (1991). Roseanne—How did you get inside my house? A case study of a hit blue-collar situation comedy. *Journal of Popular Culture, 24,* 71–88.

McCrohan, D. (1987). *Archie & Edith, Mike & Gloria: The tumultuous history of* All in the Family. New York: Workman Publishing.

McLuhan, M. (1951). *The mechanical bride: Folklore of industrial man.* New York: Vanguard Press.

McNeil, A. (1984). *Total television: A comprehensive guide to programming from 1948 to the present.* New York: Viking Penguin.

McNeil, J. (1975). Feminism, femininity, and the television series: A content analysis. *Journal of Broadcasting, 19,* 259–269.

Meadowcroft, J. J., & Fitzpatrick, M. A. (1988). Theories of family communication: Toward a merger of intersubjectivity and mutual influence processes. In R. P. Hawkins, J. M. Wiemann, & S. Pingree (Eds.), *Advancing communication science: Merging mass and interpersonal processes* (pp. 253–275). Newbury Park, CA: Sage.

Medrich, E. A., Roizen, J., Rubin, V., & Buckley, S. (1982). *The serious business of growing up.* Berkeley: University of California Press.

Mellancamp, P. (1986). Situation comedy, feminism, and Freud. In T. Modleski (Ed.), *Studies in entertainment.* Bloomington, IN: Indiana University Press.

Mellman, M., Lazarus, E., & Rivlin, A. (1990). Family time, family values. In D. Blankenhorn, S. Bayme, & J. B. Elshtain (Eds.), *Rebuilding the nest: A new commitment to the American family* (pp. 54–66). Milwaukee, WI: Family Service America.

Merritt, B., & Stroman, C. A. (1993). Black family imagery and interactions on television. *Journal of Black Studies, 23,* 492–499.

Messaris, T. (1983). Family conversations about television. *Journal of Family Issues, 4,* 293–308.

Miller, M. M., & Reeves, B. (1976). Dramatic TV content and children's sex-role stereotypes. *Journal of Broadcasting, 20,* 35–50.

Mintz, S., & Kellogg, S. (1988). *Domestic revolutions: A social history of American family life.* New York: The Free Press.

Mitz, R. (1980). *The great TV sitcom book.* New York: Richard Marek Publishers.

Moore, M. L. (1992). The family as portrayed on prime-time television, 1947–1990: Structure and characteristics. *Sex Roles, 26,* 41–60.

Morley, D. (1986). *Family television: Cultural power and domestic leisure.* London: Comedia.

Morley, D., & Silverstone, R. (1990). Domestic communication—technologies and meanings. *Media, culture, and society, 12,* 31–55.

National Family Opinion, Inc. (1994, March). American families today: How they feel about personal issues (Study commissioned by Kraft Cheese). *Good Housekeeping, 218,* 80–84.

Neuendorf, K., & Abelman, R. (1987). An interaction analysis of religious television programming. *Review of Religious Research, 29,* 175–198.

Newcomb, H. (1974). *TV: The most popular art.* New York: Anchor Press.

Newman, K. S. (1988). *Falling from grace: The experience of downward mobility in the American middle-class.* New York: Free Press.

Northcott, H. (1975). Too young, too old—Age in the world of television. *Gerontologist, 15,* 184–186.

Olson, B. M., & Douglas, W. (1997). The family in television: Evaluation of gender roles in situation comedy. *Sex Roles, 5/6,* 409–427.

O'Sullivan, J. (1990). *The great American comic strip: One hundred years of cartoon art.* Boston: Bulfinch Press.

Overbeck, J. (1995, March 4). Ten to watch together. *TV Guide, 43,* 35.

Parke, R. D., & Tinsley, B. J. (1987). Family interaction in infancy. In J. D. Osofsky (Ed.), *Handbook of infant development* (pp. 579–641). New York: Wiley.

Perry, G., & Aldridge, A. (1971). *The Penguin book of comics.* London: Penguin Books.

Perse, E. M., Pavitt, C., & Burggraf, C. S. (1990). Implicit theories of marriage and evaluations of marriage on television. *Human Communication Research, 16,* 387–408.

Petersen, M. (1973). The visibility and image of old people on television. *Journalism Quarterly, 50,* 569–573.

Pingree, S., & Thompson, M. E. (1990). The family in daytime serials. In J. Bryant (Ed.), *Television and the American family* (pp. 113–127). Hillsdale, NJ: Lawrence Erlbaum Associates.

Poindexter, P. M., & Stroman, C. A. (1981). Blacks and television: A review of the research literature. *Journal of Broadcasting, 25,* 103–122.

Popenoe, D. (1988). *Disturbing the nest: Family change and decline in modern societies.* New York: Aldine de Gruyter.

Popenoe, D. (1993a). Scholars should worry about the disintegration of the family. *Chronicle of Higher Education, 39,* p. A48.

Popenoe, D. (1993b). American family in decline, 1960–1990: A review and appraisal. *Journal of Marriage and the Family, 55,* 527–542.

Popenoe, D. (1995). The American family crisis. *National Forum, 75,* 15–19.

Popenoe, D. (1996). *Life without father.* New York: The Free Press.

The Population Council (1995, June 12). A global weakening of the ties that bind. *U.S. News & World Report,* p. 10.

Press, A., & Strathman, T. (1994). Work, family, and social class in television images of women: Prime-time television and the construction of postfeminism. *Women and Language, 16,* 7–15.

Py-Lieberman, B. (February, 2002). Any bonds today? *Smithsonian, 32,* 65–66.

Quayle, D. (May 28, 2001). Why I think I'm still right. *Newsweek,* p. 52.

Rainer, P. (1995, May 21). Hollywood hankers for family. *Los Angeles Times,* pp. 24, 28–29.

Ramsdell, M. L. (1973). The trauma of TV's troubled soap families. *The Family Coordinator, 22,* 299–304.

Rapping, E. (1992, April). A family affair. *The Progressive,* pp. 36–38.

Rapping, E. (1994, July). In praise of Roseanne. *The Progressive,* pp. 36–38.

Reep, D. C., & Dambrot, F. H. (1989). Effects of frequent television viewing on stereotypes: "Drip, drip" or "drench"? *Journalism Quarterly, 66,* 542–550, 556.

Reid, L. N., & Frazer, C. (1980a). Children's use of television commercials to initiate Social interaction in family viewing situations. *Journal of Broadcasting, 24,* 149–157.

Reid, L. N., & Frazer, C. (1980b). Television at play. *Journal of Communication, 30,* 66–73.

Richards, L. (1911). From *Good Housekeeping.* Quoted in E. T. May (1995) *Barren in the promised land: Childless Americans and the pursuit of happiness* (p. 83). New York: Basic Books.

Robinson, E. J., & White, D. M. (1963). Who reads the funnies—and why? In D. M. White & R. H. Abel (Eds.), *The funnies: An American idiom* (pp. 179–189). New York: The Free Press.

Robinson, J. (1972). Television's impact on everyday life: Some cross-national evidence. In E. Rubenstein, G. Comstock, & J. Murray (Eds.), *Television and social behavior* (Vol. 4, pp. 410–431). Washington, DC: U.S. Government Printing Office.

Robinson, J., Andreyenkov, V., & Patruchev, V. (1989). *The rhythm of everyday life: How Soviet and American citizens use time.* Boulder, CO: Westview Press.

Robinson, J., & Skill, T. (2001). Five decades of family on television: From the 1950s through the 1990s. In J. Bryant & J. A. Bryant (Eds.), *Television and the American family* (2nd ed., pp. 139–162). Mahwah, NJ: Lawrence Erlbaum Associates.

Robinson, J., Skill, T., Nussbaum, J., & Moreland, K. (1985). Parents, peers, and television characters: The use of comparison others as criteria for evaluating marital satisfaction. In E. C. Lange (Ed.), *Using the media to promote knowledge and skills in family dynamics* (pp. 11–15). Dayton, OH: Center for Religious Telecommunications.

Rothschild, N., & Morgan, M. (1987). Cohesion and control: Adolescents' relationships with parents as mediators of television. *Journal of Early Adolescence, 7,* 299–314.

Rowles, G. D. (1994). Evolving images of place in aging and "aging in place." In D. Shenk & W. A. Achenbaum (Eds.), *Changing perceptions of aging and the aged* (pp. 115–125). New York: Springer.

Samuelson, R. (1996, April 8). Why men need family values. *Newsweek,* p. 43.

Schramm, W. L., Lyle, J., & Parker, E. B. (1961). *Television in the lives of our children.* Stanford, CA: Stanford University Press.

Sears, R. R., Maccoby, E. E., & Levin, H. (1957). *Patterns of child rearing.* Evanston, IL: Peterson.

Seggar, J. F. (1975). Imagery of women in television drama: 1974. *Journal of Broadcasting, 19,* 273–282.

Select Committee on Children, Youth, and Families of the U. S. House of Representatives. (1987). U. S. children and their families: Current conditions and recent trends (SuDoc No. Y1.1/8:100-259). Washington, DC: U.S. Government Printing Office.

Shaner, J. (1982). Parental empathy and family role interactions as portrayed on commercial television. (Doctoral dissertation, The University of North Carolina, Greensboro). *Dissertation Abstracts International, 42,* 3473A.

Sheehy, G. (1976). *Passages.* New York: Bantam.

Sheff, D. (1988, May 5). Portrait of a generation. *Rolling Stone,* p. 62.

Shorter, E. (1975). *The making of the modern family.* New York: Basic Books.

Signorielli, N. (1982). Marital status in television drama: A case of reduced options. *Journal of Broadcasting, 26,* 585–597.

Signorielli, N. (1989). Television and conceptions about sex roles: Maintaining conventionality and the status quo. *Sex Roles, 21,* 341–360.

Signorielli, N., & Gerbner, G. (1978). The image of the elderly in prime-time television drama. *Generations, 3,* 10–11.

Silver, M. (1995, October 30). Geared for girls. *U.S. News & World Report,* p. 22.

Singer, J. L., & Singer, D. G. (1983). Psychologists look at television: Cognitive, developmental, personality, and social policy implications. *American Psychologist, 38,* 826–834.

Singer, J. L., & Singer, D. G. (1986). Television-viewing and family communication style as predictors of children's emotional behavior. *Journal of Children in Contemporary Society, 17,* 75–91.

Singer, J. L., Singer, D. G., Desmond, R., Hirsch, B., & Nicol, A. (1988). Family mediation and children's cognition, aggression, and comprehension of television: A longitudinal study. *Journal of Applied Developmental Psychology, 9,* 329–347.

Skill, T., & Robinson, J. D. (1994). Four decades of families on television: A demographic profile, 1950–1989. *Journal of Broadcasting and Electronic Media, 38,* 449–464.

Skill, T., Robinson, J. D., & Wallace, S. (1987). Family life on prime-time television: *Journalism Quarterly, 64,* 360–367, 398.

Skill, T., & Wallace, S. (1990). Family interactions on prime-time television: A descriptive analysis of assertive power interactions. *Journal of Broadcasting and Electronic Media, 34,* 243–262.

Skill, T., Wallace, S., & Cassata, M. (1990). Families on prime-time television: Patterns of conflict escalation and resolution across intact, nonintact, and mixed-family settings. In J. Bryant (Ed.), *Television and the American family* (pp. 129–163). Hillsdale, NJ: Lawrence Erlbaum Associates.

Skolnick, A. (1991). *Embattled paradise: The American family in an age of uncertainty.* New York: Basic Books.

Smith, V. J. (1983). *Programming for radio and television, revised edition.* Washington, DC: University of America Press.

Spigel, L. (1992). *Make room for TV: Television and the family ideal in postwar America.* Chicago: University of Chicago Press.

Stacey, J. (1995). The family values fable. *National Forum, 75,* 20–23.

Staples, S. (1984). *Male–female comedy teams in American vaudeville 1865–1932.* Ann Arbor, MI: University of Michigan Press.

Stavitsky, A. G. (2000). Theory-into-practice: By the numbers: The use of ratings data in academic research. *Journal of Broadcasting and Electronic Media, 44,* 535–539.

Steiner, G. A. (1963). *The people look at television: A study of audience attitudes.* New York: Knopf.

Stroman, C. A., Merritt, B. D., & Metabane, P. W. (1989–1990). Twenty years after Kerner: The portrayal of African Americans on prime-time television. *The Howard Journal of Communication, 2,* 44–56.

Sweeper, G. W. (1984). The image of the Black family and the White family in American Prime-time television programming 1970 to 1980 (Doctoral dissertation, The University of North Carolina, Greensboro). *Dissertation Abstracts International, 42,* 3473A.

Taylor, E. (1989). *Prime-time families: Television culture in postwar America.* Berkeley: University of California Press.

Thibaut, J., & Kelley, H. (1959). *The social psychology of groups.* New York: Wiley.

Thomas, S., & Callahan, B. P. (1982). Allocating happiness: TV families and social class. *Journal of Communication, 33,* 184–190.

Terman, L. M., & Miles, C. C. (1936). Sex and personality; studies in masculinity and *femininity.* New York: McGraw-Hill.

Timmer, S. G., Eccles, J., & O'Brien, K. (1985). How children use time. In F. T. Juster & F. P. Stafford (Eds.), *Time, goods, and well-being.* Ann Arbor, MI: University of Michigan Press.

Tokar, N. (Director). (1958, July 16). *Leave it to Beaver* [Television Broadcast]. New York: CBS Broadcasting Network.

Turow, J. (1974). Advising and ordering: Daytime, prime time. *Journal of Communication, 24,* 138–141.

Uhlenberg, P. (1989). Death and the family. In A. S. Skolnick & J. H. Skolnick (Eds.), *Family in transition: Rethinking marriage, sexuality, child rearing, and family organization* (pp. 87–96). Glenview, IL: Scott, Foresman and Co..

U.S. Bureau of the Census. (1960). *Historical statistics of the United States: Colonial times to 1957.* Washington, DC: U.S. Government Printing Office.

U.S. Bureau of the Census. (1998, March). *Current Population Reports, Series P20-514, Marital Status and Living Arrangements* (Update). Washington, DC: U.S. Government Printing Office.

U.S. Bureau of the Census. (1999, January). [Online]. http://www.census.gov/population/socdemo/ms-la/tabch-1.txt.

U.S. Commission on Civil Rights. (1977). *Window dressing on the set: Women and minorities on television.* Washington, DC: U.S. Government Printing Office.

Vande Berg, L. R., & Streckfuss, D. (1992). Prime-time television's portrayal of women and the world of work: A demographic profile. *Journal of Broadcasting and Electronic Media, 36,* 195–208.

Walsh, T. J. (1995). The male daze: Men lost in the vast wasteland. *Feedback, 36,* 16–20.

Walters, J. K., & Stone, V. A. (1971). Television and family communication. *Journal of Broadcasting, 15,* 409–414.

Waters, H. F. (1978, May 15). Saving the family. *Newsweek,* pp. 63–70.

Waters, H. F. (1993, August 30). Fractured family ties. *Newsweek,* pp. 50–52.

Waugh, C. (1947). *The comics.* Jackson, MS: University of Mississippi Press.

Weigel, R. H., & Loomis, J. W. (1981). Televised models of female achievement revisited: Some progress. *Journal of Applied Social Psychology, 11,* 58–63.

Weingarten, K. (1991). The discourses of intimacy: Adding a social constructionist and feminist view. *Family Process, 30,* 285–306.

Weiss, A. J., & Wilson, B. J. (1990). Emotional portrayals in family television series that are popular among children. *Journal of Broadcasting and Electronic Media, 40,* 1–29.

Westbrook, R. (1990). I want a girl, just like the girl that married Harry James: American women and the problem of political obligation in World War II. *American Quarterly, 42,* 587–614.

Whitman, D., Ito, T. M., & Kost, A. (1996, March 4). A bad case of the blues. *U.S. News & World Report,* pp. 54–56, 59–60, 62.

Williams, A., & Coupland, N. (1998). The socio-political framing of aging and communication research. *Journal of Applied Communication Research, 26,* 139–154.

Wober, J. M., & Gunter, B. (1987). *Television and social control.* Aldershot: Gower.

Wright, J. C., St. Peters, M., & Huston, A. C. (1990). Family television use and its relation to children's cognitive skills and social behavior. In J. Bryant (Ed.), *Television and the American family* (pp. 227–251). Hillsdale, NJ: Lawrence Erlbaum Associates.

Yankelovich Partners Inc. (1995, June 12). Unpopular culture. *Time,* p. 26.

Yogman, M. W. (1981). Games mothers and fathers play with their infants. *Infant Mental Health Journal, 2,* 241–248.

Young, C. (1945–1980). *Blondie* (Special collections). East Lansing: Michigan State University Press.

Young, D., & Marschall, R. (1981). *Blondie and Dagwood's America.* New York: Harper & Row.

Zillmann, D., & Bryant, J. (1988). Effects of prolonged consumption of pornography on family reality. *Journal of Broadcasting, 26,* 813–829.

Zoglin, R. (1990, April 16). Home is where the venom is. *Time,* pp. 85–86.

Author Index

Subject Index